Injun Joe's Ghost

Injun Joe's Ghost

The Indian Mixed-Blood in American Writing

Harry J. Brown

University of Missouri Press
Columbia and London

Library of Congress Cataloging-in-Publication Data

Brown, Harry J. (Harry John), 1972–
    Injun Joe's ghost : the Indian mixed-blood in American writing /
    Harry J. Brown.
        p.   cm.
    Includes bibliographical references and index.
    ISBN 0-8262-1530-0 (alk. paper)
    1. American fiction—History and criticism.   2. Indians in literature.
3. Racially mixed people in literature.   4. Group identity in literature.
5. Ethnicity in literature.   6. Race in literature.   I. Title.
    PS374.I49B76   2004   2004003676

♾™ This paper meets the requirements of the
American National Standard for Permanence of Paper
for Printed Library Materials, Z39.48, 1984.

Designer: Kristie Lee
Typesetter: Phoenix Type, Inc.
Printer and binder: Thomson-Shore, Inc.
Typeface: ITC Galliard

For Neva and Kelly

Contents

3   From Biological to Cultural Hybridity in *Cogewea*, *Sundown*, and Twentieth-Century Magazine Fiction

Epilogue: Contemporary Reflections on Mixed Descent

Acknowledgments

I thank Pete Beidler, Ed Gallagher, John Pettegrew, Clair Willcox, Julie Schroeder, Barbara Cohen, and, especially, Dawn Keetley, for their invaluable help in the development of this project.

Injun Joe's Ghost

Introduction

It would ha'nt the place where he died.

—Mark Twain, *The Adventures of Tom Sawyer*

Sunday Morning, 18—

From his flapping, repurchased *Heath Anthology,* the casual student of nineteenth-century American literature can learn nothing about the life or work of William Apess after the publication of his politically influential *Indian Nullification* in 1835. The textbook reads simply, "sometime after 1836, Apess disappeared from public view and the details of his later life are unknown."[1] It is left to us to imagine the rest.

In the spirit of those romance writers of the early republic who reconceived the patchwork history of the colonies as the grand narrative of a fledgling empire, imagine for a moment another less grand but hitherto unwritten fiction, a hypothetical footnote in the secret history of the United States, a story of a man who went to church in rural Massachusetts sometime after 1836.

Shabbily dressed, a public nuisance, and a drunk, according to some of his neighbors, this man sits at the back of the congregation. An observer seated nearby would not guess that this man, so uncanny in aspect, had quite recently spoken loudly and eloquently in front of large crowds in Boston and had effected statewide legislation. The observer might rather recall him from a hazy night at the tavern some weeks ago, when the man boasted of his royal ancestry—as if the savage chieftain Metacomet, dubbed King Philip by the Pilgrims, were really royalty.

1. A. LaVonne Brown Ruoff, "William Apess (Pequot)," 1:1398.

1

The lads in the tavern gibed him; if the observer must admit, the man looks more like a Negro than a Pequot.

The observer could not know that this shabby man, when he was not yet twenty-five, had himself been a preacher to anyone who would listen, a minister in search of a congregation, as he bounded from one Methodist denomination to another, frequently offending his ecclesiastical superiors. Despite his charisma and his extraordinarily strong voice, he was unpopular with the faithful. Unlike the common run of New England churchmen, he would more often point to the incongruity between their faith and their action than praise their steadfastness.

The preacher now in the pulpit, young and well regarded by all, turns to 1 Corinthians 7:14. Had he known this was a sore and familiar spot with the man seated at the back of the congregation, he might have turned elsewhere: "For the unbelieving husband is sanctified by the wife, and the unbelieving wife is sanctified by the husband: else were your children unclean; but now are they holy." Even with the success of the Removal Bill, it seems that talk of amalgamation will never cease: "If there be any good in the union of Christian and Indian," the young preacher graciously instructs, "it may be that the wife is sanctified by her husband and that her sons and daughters made children of God, else were they unclean." For his more literate listeners, the preacher's allusion recalls a proposition now fashionable among the nation's politicians and writers. Savages, they suggest, may be civilized more effectively through marriage than through war. Indeed, the children of such unions may through future generations be made white, cleansed by the mingling of blood rather than the shedding. Although many in his congregation are not averse to this idea, the young preacher speaks subtly and cautiously; the Commonwealth still prohibits these intermarriages.

The shabby man rises from his seat at the back of the congregation, visibly piqued though not without his sense, and retorts with Malachi 3:14: "Wherefore? Because the Lord hath been witness between thee and the wife of thy youth, against whom thou hast dealt *treacherously:* yet *is* she thy companion, and the wife of thy covenant!"

Accustomed to the good manners and assenting nods of his listeners, the young preacher is dumbfounded by this rude interjection. William Apess—is that the brute's name?—glares at the pulpit. He does not expect a spirited exegetical volley from his flushed, unequal opponent, but he demands recognition with the vehemence of one weary of being ignored. A torturous silence fills the country meetinghouse as this rude man does not, as everyone expects, sit down; does not withdraw his challenge; does not politely exit.

Only recently have scholars discovered from a terse, long-forgotten obituary that William Apess died in New York City on April 10, 1839, succumbing to "apoplexy." While he had championed unprecedented legislation in 1834, successfully lobbying with the Commonwealth of Massachusetts for the autonomy of the Mashpee, a tribe of mixed-bloods settled near Barnstable, he had sunk to obscurity and alcoholism soon afterward. Barry O'Connell, editor of Apess's writings, calls the Pequot's final silence "eerie" and offers only vague speculation about his decline after 1835: "he may have turned to rum, in bitterness or for consolation."[2] In his autobiography, *A Son of the Forest* (1829), Apess, then at the beginning of his short public career, casually remarked on his travels through Utica and Albany: "The people in this part of the country, seeing I was an Indian, took but little notice of me."[3] Perhaps Apess's final bitterness arose from this growing sense of invisibility, acutely felt by Native American writers who even today, like the half-real, half-imaginary man at the back of the congregation, demand recognition.

The Invisible Indian

The invisibility felt by William Apess in 1829 originates in Europe's earliest encounter with the Indian. In February 1493, while anchored off the Azores and awaiting more propitious winds to begin the last leg of his triumphant return journey to the Spanish court, Christopher

---

2. Barry O'Connell, introduction to *On Our Own Ground: The Complete Writings of William Apess, a Pequot*, xxxvii. O'Connell also entertains more intriguing theories of Apess's demise, including Elemire Zolla's argument that he was murdered by shadowy adversaries of Indian reform, though such scenarios seem to O'Connell "unlikely."

3. William Apess, *On Our Own Ground: The Complete Writings of William Apess, a Pequot*, 36. Further references to *A Son of the Forest* and Apess's essays will be derived from this edition.

Columbus composed a letter announcing his arrival and recounting the initial weeks of exploration in the Indies. He describes a paradisiacal natural harbor on the Cuban coast, explaining, "I sent two men inland to discover whether there was a king or any great cities. They traveled for three days, finding only a large number of small villages and great numbers of people, but nothing more substantial."[4] The admiral's remark, though understandable from a trade emissary for whom great numbers of people are less fortuitous than resources of gold or spices, nonetheless represents the first recorded evidence of a European's inability or unwillingness to "see" the Indian.

This failure of recognition characterizes white representations of Indians throughout five centuries of colonization, demonstrating in a myriad of forms the Indian's inscrutability to the white observer. It motivates Thomas Jefferson's excavation of an Indian barrow, which uncovers not buried people, but rather an impossible jumble of bones, broken bits of "a thousand skeletons," the deepest indistinguishable from the stones that cover them. It characterizes the savages in the popular frontier stories of the nineteenth and twentieth centuries, with their stereotypically stoic expressions, opaque eyes, and unintelligible animal grunts. Considering the nearly eighty films she surveys in *West of Everything*, Jane Tompkins explains that the Indians she expected to see "did not appear," or functioned only as "props, bits of local color, textural effects." As people, she observes, "they had no existence. Quite often they filled the role of villains, predictably, driving the engine of the plot.... But there were no Indian characters, no individuals with a personal history and a point of view.... Images of Indians sprang to mind.... But no people.... Indians are repressed in Westerns—there but not there." Armando José Prats identifies the nonrepresentation of Indians in the Hollywood Western as the central problem of his study, *Invisible Natives*, claiming that Indian invisibility forms a crucial component in America's "Myth of Conquest": "The conqueror must produce an Other whose destruction is not only assured but justified. The Indian's absence is inevitable, foregone. Even so, the Vanishing American must return... not only to be violently made absent again, but to vindicate... the 'his-

---

4. Christopher Columbus, "Letter of Columbus to Various Persons Describing the Results of His First Voyage and Written on the Return Journey," 116.

tory' that transmutes might into right. . . . The Indian Western . . . deploys its strategies and methodologies, its historical claims and cultural assumptions, in order to transform its figure of the Indian into the many forms that leave only the Indian's trace."[5]

Perhaps more surprisingly, academic discourse has itself manifested the same blindness that Tompkins and Prats find in popular culture. Perry Miller's classic discussion of the "the massive narrative of movement of European culture into the vacant wilderness of America" seemingly does not acknowledge that people existed in this world prior to the European advance. Conscious of resistance to the Indian presence in her own book, Tompkins remarks finally that she cried when she realized that "after Indians had been decimated by disease, removal, and conquest, and after they had been degraded and caricatured in Western movies," she too had ignored them.[6] While few match Tompkins's confessional tenor, other scholars have indeed come to sense this chronic unawareness in their professional discourse, which tends to replicate images of the vanishing Indian even as it labors to interpret and subvert them. Lucy Maddox writes in *Removals:*

> Critical discourse . . . is still essentially replicating nineteenth-century criticism when it comes to the subject of Indians. Either the Indian presence is ignored, or the Indians are remythologized by the critic. I would even assert that contemporary criticism is still showing signs of the same resistance to speaking about Indians that many nineteenth-century critics expressed—a resistance based (I believe) on the sense that Indians cannot be moved from the margins to the center of sophisticated intellectual discourse; for the critic to attempt to do so is to run the risk of relegating her own discourse to the margins. . . . The most important point I have to make . . . is that most of us who teach and write about American literature still do not believe that it is necessary, or even important, to know much about American Indians or about the history and politics of Indian affairs in order to do our teaching and writing confidently and authoritatively.[7]

5. Thomas Jefferson, *Notes on the State of Virginia*, 99 (further citations will be made parenthetically with the abbreviation *NV*); Jane Tompkins, *West of Everything: The Inner Life of Westerns*, 8–9; Armando José Prats, *Invisible Natives: Myth and Identity in the American Western*, 2, 4.

6. Perry Miller, *Errand into the Wilderness*, vii; Tompkins, *West of Everything*, 10.

7. Lucy Maddox, *Removals: Nineteenth-Century American Literature and the Politics of Indian Affairs*, 174, 177.

From the royal court of Spain to a Virginia barrow to Hollywood and the academy, a system of reduction renders the Indian spectral or insubstantial, simultaneously present and absent, there and not there. Five centuries after Columbus dismissed the people of the New World as insubstantial, almost two centuries after the hypothetical William Apess demanded recognition at the back of the church, *we* are still trying to decipher *them*.

Although a number of scholars in the last decade, such as Cheryl Walker, Priscilla Wald, and Susan Scheckel, have addressed this critical blindness and discussed at length the relation of the vanishing Indian to national consciousness, one figure has yet remained spectral, lingering in our cultural unconscious even as he has played a central role in our literature and history: the Indian-white mixed-blood. In 1824, when Lydia Maria Child introduced him to American readers in her novel *Hobomok*, reviewers found her bold gesture "revolting" and judged miscegenation a subject unfit for American literature, just as the Massachusetts legislature judged it anathema to New England society. In 1969, however, N. Scott Momaday, himself a mixed-Kiowa, won the Pulitzer Prize for his novel *House Made of Dawn* (1968), the story of a mixed-blood army veteran unable to find his place among either Indians or whites. Werner Sollors, in *Beyond Ethnicity*, remarks on the hybrid character of the nation, which Momaday's prize seemed to herald: "It is well worth it to interpret America not narrowly... but more broadly as ethnic diversity."[8]

Somehow the half-breed, a figure once too horrendous for public discourse, has come to signify America itself, completing a striking but rarely noted transformation in the American racial consciousness. In *Colonial Desire*, Robert Young explains this change more clearly, suggesting that hybridity in recent decades has taken a cultural rather than a physiological meaning. This semiotic shift, Young explains, "raises questions about the ways in which contemporary thinking has broken absolutely with the racialized formulations of the past."[9] In my own study I articulate some of these questions as they concern the Indian

8. Werner Sollors, *Beyond Ethnicity: Consent and Descent in American Culture*, 8.
9. Robert J. C. Young, *Colonial Desire: Hybridity in Theory, Culture, and Race*, 16.

mixed-blood: What does it mean to be *mixed-blood,* and how has our understanding of this term changed over the last two centuries? What processes have shaped American thinking on racial blending? Why has the figure of the mixed-blood, once thought too offensive for polite literature, become the dominant representative of contemporary Indian consciousness?

In this book I will address these questions within the interrelated contexts of anthropology, U.S. Indian policy, and American fiction, mapping the evolution of hybridity from a biological category to a cultural category, a transformation integral to our understanding of the processes that once mandated the mixed-blood's invisibility and that have recently effected his ascendance as the central figure in contemporary Native American writing. More obviously, the half-breed has remained spectral because the racialist doctrines underlying nationalist fiction mandate his invisibility, but also, more subtly, because scholars have tended to interpret these texts dialectically, as negotiations between self and other, colonizer and colonized, or white and Indian, unwittingly excluding in-between figures like the mixed-blood who confound this binary picture of race and culture. My primary difficulty in this book, then, is not the obvious and extensively documented scientific racism in American writing on Indian-white blending but rather the ways in which this racism has unconsciously influenced contemporary critical discourse.

Hybridity, Alternation, and Simultaneity

In 1978, during a wave of critical interest among historical and literary scholars in Native America, James Axtell called for further investigation of "points of intercultural contact, perhaps through the study of people who traveled back and forth across the cultural frontier, such as 'half-breeds.'" In 1984, Annette Kolodny also observed a "studied literary silence on the subject of Indian-white miscegenation," both in American literature and in critical analysis. Since then, even with the recent proliferation of scholarship assessing the significance of the Indian in national culture, the mixed-blood remains forgotten. William Scheick's *The Half-Blood* has provided an indispensable survey of nineteenth-century texts representing the mixed-blood, but Scheick's short book is necessarily limited in its critical depth, cursorily contrasting fictional half-bloods on the basis of the regional identification of their various authors.[10]

A more extensive investigation of the mixed-blood in American writing inevitably converges with two significant postcolonial issues: hybridity, the condition of mediating two competing racial, cultural, or discursive realities; and authenticity, the potential of the hybrid subject for self-representation as he or she is circumscribed by the dominant discourse. Hybridity poses a major conundrum to postcolonial literary theory: Since hybrid voices often assimilate elements of both the dominant discourse and the suppressed discourse, do such voices represent more accurately the speech of the subaltern or the circumscription of that speech by dominant forms? As Gayatri Spivak more concisely asks, "Can the subaltern speak?" In *Native American Identities,* Scott Vickers poses this same question in terms more specific to Native Americans: "If Indian history since 1492 has been 'written' (authored) by white authority, then how can it attain or retain authentic identities in the present . . . [when] the [white] author of history also assumes the power of author of identity and the arbiter of authenticity[?]"[11]

Scholars conventionally respond to this fundamental question in two ways. Spivak herself, inviting controversy, argues that the subaltern cannot speak, since the dominant discourse inevitably translates such speech into its own terms. Critics of Native American literature such as Charles Larson, Arnold Krupat, and Karl Kroeber similarly claim that all Native writing is necessarily inauthentic, since any textualization of an origi-

---

10. James Axtell, "The Ethnohistory of Early America: A Review Essay," 141; Annette Kolodny, *The Land before Her: Fantasy and Experience of the American Frontiers, 1630–1860,* 70; William J. Scheick, *The Half-Blood: A Cultural Symbol in Nineteenth-Century American Fiction.* Scheick's work divides a large selection of nineteenth-century fiction into regional categories, which determine competing ideas of the mixed-blood. Scheick more broadly describes two sorts of half-bloods: the "twilight hybrid," a suspicious creature lurking on the shadowy frontier between white and Indian, civilization and wilderness, light and darkness; and the "symbolic American prototype," the embodiment of a hopeful racial alliance definitive of American identity. A dense one hundred pages, *The Half-Blood* deserves credit as the first serious exploration of the mixed-blood as a particular cultural symbol.

11. Gayatri Chakravorty Spivak, "Can the Subaltern Speak?" Scott B. Vickers, *Native American Identities: From Stereotype to Archetype in Art and Literature,* 9.

nally oral culture represents the translation of Native speech into the terms of Western discourse. On the other hand, Homi Bhabha argues that the subaltern is indeed always speaking, if not directly, at least obliquely in the ways it fractures the dominant discourse that can never fully contain it. In the constant "vacillation" between the dominant "pedagogical" discourse and the subversive "performative" discourse, Bhabha describes the nation as a "contested cultural territory... *internally* marked by cultural difference and the heterogeneous histories of contending peoples, antagonistic authorities, and tense cultural locations," where "the subject of cultural discourse... is split in the discursive ambivalence that emerges in the contestation of narrative authority between the pedagogical and the performative."[12] Hybridity emerges for Bhabha as the ambivalence between the pedagogical and performative, a process of alternation and exchange between two separate and competing discourses. Scholars such as Cheryl Walker, Gerald Vizenor, and Louis Owens adopt Bhabha's more fluid model of hybridity in their emphasis on the potential for Indian counternarratives, even through the processes of translation and cultural negotiation, to disturb the racial and national boundaries so strenuously enforced by the dominant discourse.

In spite of their differences, Spivak's view of relatively stable hegemony and Bhabha's view of hegemony in flux are similarly dialectical, sharing the assumptions of the fundamental oppositions between the self and the other, the dominant and the subversive, the pedagogical and the performative. Because most current discussions of the Indian and the nation rest on either of these dialectical models, they have traditionally recognized, in Bhabha's terms, only two "contending peoples, antagonistic authorities, and tense cultural locations": the white and the Indian. Even Bhabha's description of hybridity as a state of "vacillation" between two contending discourses imagines this in-between-ness as a fleeting condition that must quickly alternate in either direction to restore the equilibrium of productive conflict. Neither view recognizes the potential for a third discursive dimension in which the subject is not alternately, not ambivalently, but simultaneously and per-

12. Homi K. Bhabha, "DissemiNation: Time, Narrative, and the Margins of the Modern Nation," in *Nation and Narration*, 297, 299.

manently self and other, dominant and subversive, white and Indian: a synthetic rather than a dialectical understanding of hybridity. The prolific appearance in the American literary tradition of mixed-bloods, those who are neither and yet simultaneously white and Indian, and the incongruous lack of scholarship on the subject attest to the limitation of our theoretical vocabulary, the necessity for exploration of this third discursive dimension, the expansion of the binary analytical tools that cannot yet account for it.

In March 1885, Louis Riel, the militant leader of a Canadian mixed-Ojibwe clan, declared the independence of a nation of mixed-bloods in the Northwest Territories, an action that recalled William Apess's campaign for Mashpee autonomy fifty years earlier. Riel resented the term "half-breed," since it suggested "half-people," and demanded, "Why should we concern ourselves about what degree of mixture we possess of European or Indian blood? If we have ever so little of either gratitude or filial love, should we not be proud to say, *We are Métis?*"[13] The Canadian army crushed Riel's provisional government, later known as the Northwest Rebellion, in May of the same year. Riel himself was tried and hung as a traitor in July. While his defense lawyer pleaded insanity, Riel opposed the plea, asserting his soundness of mind and using his trial as a platform to argue for the rights of mixed-bloods. Riel founded this new nation, a "strange empire" in the words of Joseph Kinsey Howard, and coined this new term—*Métis*—because the old words and countries did not fit his life as he saw it. Today we similarly search for a way to describe our heterogeneous history and national identity in terms other than the strictly dialectical or the halfway.

Lucy Maddox wonders "whether a single version of American history is possible or whether there must always be at least two [Indian and white] American histories," whether we are able to approach a "bicultural" understanding of the past or whether competing discourses must destroy each other when brought into contact. Susan Scheckel also asks "why nineteenth-century representations [of the Indian] mark a cultural problem that no single text or logic seems capable of containing."

13. Gerald Vizenor, *Earthdivers: Tribal Narratives of Mixed Descent*, x. For a more extensive discussion of Riel and the Northwest Métis, see Joseph Kinsey Howard, *Strange Empire: A Narrative of the Northwest*.

Cheryl Walker finally proposes, "the only way to avoid being captured by the reductivism of hegemony is by preserving the oxymoron: that is, the contradiction implied by two incompatible discourses within which it becomes clear there are gaps and fissures one cannot dismiss."[14] But even these gestures toward a new discursive mode imply an inescapable twoness, while Riel's Métis exist independently of the Indian-white dialectic, occupying a space between races only fearfully imagined in nineteenth-century culture and only faintly sensed in current criticism.

Like Riel's staking out a mixed-blood nation independent of both the reservation and the white government, I seek in this book to redefine Indian-white hybridity beyond the dialectic, as simultaneity rather than alternation, as a synthesis of racial, cultural, and discursive conditions that traditional racialist thought and current literary criticism both perceive as mutually exclusive. A great leap forward occurs early in the twentieth century, when anthropologists and writers redefined the Indian as a cultural rather than a biological entity, and consequently expanded the definition of hybridity, previously understood as a measurable combination of blood and bone, to encompass the blending of more immeasurable qualities like language, belief, and education. This crucial realization that race represents something more than heredity, that an individual is somehow more than his component chromosomes—the movement in American thinking from positivism to pluralism—enables American literature, as it may enable literary scholarship, to conceive of hybridity not as a condition of exclusion and vacillation but of synthesis and simultaneity.

In order to introduce the discussion that will carry us toward these important changes in racial thought, this introduction considers two texts representing distinct visions of racial mixing in America. Mark Twain's *The Adventures of Tom Sawyer* (1876) most famously illustrates the old cultural fears of racial blending, while Susanna Rowson's *Reuben and Rachel; or, Tales of Old Times* (1798) hints at racial synthesis in its imagination of a new American type embodying both the Native and the European.

14. Maddox, *Removals*, 3–4; Susan Scheckel, *The Insistence of the Indian: Race and Nationalism in Nineteenth-Century American Culture*, 7; Cheryl Walker, *Indian Nation: Native American Literature and Nineteenth-Century Nationalisms*, xv.

The Murderin' Half-Breed in *Tom Sawyer*

Prats's description of films that conjure the Indian for the purpose of making him disappear recalls mythmakers of the early republic such as Lydia Maria Child, Catharine Maria Sedgwick, and James Fenimore Cooper, who, unable to contain the prospect of racial blending, consistently evaded the subject in their novels, tentatively raising the possibility of Indian-white intermarriage as a haunting alternative to removal or genocide only to dismiss it as a distasteful impossibility. But the premise of Prats's argument, "Otherness is absence and absence otherness," bears a significant flaw: the other is not completely absent. As Prats himself asks, "To what extent does Otherness persist in a civilized America if the violent encounter with the Indian really is, as the Western tells us, the crucible in which the American character comes to be wrought?" Tompkins also senses a persistence of otherness in her description of Indians in popular Westerns who were "there but not there," ghostly figures, as Kathleen Brogan similarly describes them in *Cultural Haunting*, whose disappearance precedes national emergence. Brogan, however, sees these Native ghosts as something more than metaphysical residue. For Brogan, as for scholars such as Gerald Vizenor, Native spectrality can itself be a form of active resistance, a "performativity": "Spirits of the dead...bear witness to the destruction of traditional native cultures and the subsequent cultural invisibility of Native Americans.... Ghosts [in their returning from the dead], however, can also represent continuity with the past.... The retrieval of lost traditions in much contemporary Native American literature is signaled by the appearance of spirits." Brogan and Alan Velie reveal a connection between Native ethnicity and ghostly motifs in recent American literature, suggesting that the ghost provides an apt metaphor for the Indian's quality of being there but not there.[15]

The mixed-blood, perhaps more than the generic Indian in Tompkins's, Brogan's and Velie's analyses, similarly embodies both the American nation and the Indian tribes who must vanish in its wake; he is

15. Prats, *Invisible Natives*, 5, 14; Tomkins, *West of Everything*, 8–9; Kathleen Brogan, *Cultural Haunting: Ghosts and Ethnicity in Recent American Literature*, 31; Alan Velie, "Magical Realism and Ethnicity: The Fantastic in the Fiction of Louise Erdrich."

simultaneously there but not there and represents the best answer to Prats's question about the extent to which otherness persists in America following the removal of the Indian. As William Scheick explains, the mixed-blood "could not be treated evasively because, whereas the full-blood Indian could be restricted to America's prehistory or history, could be safely confined in the past, the mixed-blood Indian belonged very much to the present and quite possibly to the future of America."[16] If the vanishing Indian represents the ghost of the nation's troubled past, the mixed-blood, for early American writers, represents the ghost of America's uncertain future.

One of the most frightful and notorious of these hybrid specters appears at the center of the quintessentially American tale, *Tom Sawyer:* "that murderin' half-breed," Injun Joe. In Twain's novel, Injun Joe is the disturbingly real villain who invades the imaginary adventures of the boy pirates, Tom Sawyer and Huckleberry Finn. He terrifies the boys both in their sleep and in their waking, pursuing them in the subterranean gloom of McDougal's Cave and in the subconscious darkness of their nightmares. Tom and Huck first spy Injun Joe engaged in grave robbing, one of his regular occupations. As they covertly watch Joe and his cohorts, whom they first perceive as spirits of the dead, from their hiding place in the graveyard elms, the scene transforms from merely dastardly to monstrous. Joe stabs to death the young physician for whom he has just disinterred the body, claiming revenge for an old wrong. As the young man lies dying, Joe hisses: "Five years ago you drove me away from your father's kitchen one night, when I come to ask you for something to eat, and you said I warn't there for any good; and when I swore I'd get even with you if it took a hundred years, your father had me jailed for a vagrant. Did you think I'd forget? The Injun blood ain't in me for nothing. . . . *That* score is settled—damn you."[17] Joe then frames his partner Muff Potter, drunk and unconscious during the fight, but he is foiled and forced to run off when Tom, overcoming his mortal fears of Injun Joe and the revenge he might unleash, reveals before a court what he had witnessed in the graveyard.

The villainous half-breed is uncomplicated by Twain's standards,

16. Scheick, *Half-Blood*, 2.
17. Mark Twain, *The Adventures of Tom Sawyer*, 92–93.

unconflicted by mixed motives, unsympathetic in his brute language, unredeemable in his inhuman vengeance for petty wrongs. He grows directly from the dime-novel tradition that flourished alongside more respectable literature like *Tom Sawyer*, in which half-breed outlaws, made vile by the taint in their blood, likewise wreak havoc upon the world, avenging their own birth to a hostile world. This double-edged hatred, pointed with equal force toward the half-breed himself and his enemies, inevitably leads in the dime novel and in *Tom Sawyer* to spectacular self-destruction. While Joe might preserve himself by fleeing south, beyond the grasp of St. Petersburg lawmen, he courts danger by lingering near the town in McDougal's cave, plotting both to claim a cache of robber's gold and to assail Widow Douglas, whose late husband, once justice of the peace, had him horsewhipped for vagrancy, as Joe himself bitterly recalls, "like a nigger!—with all the town looking on!" He seeks not to kill her—too merciful—but to torture, disfigure, and shame her. Joe explains to another henchman, "When you want to get revenge on a woman you don't kill her—bosh! You go for her looks. You slit her nostrils—you notch her ears like a sow!... I'll tie her to the bed. If she bleeds to death, is that my fault? I'll not cry, if she does." His plan for revenge on the widow further aligns him with the unregenerate half-breed villains rife in the dime novel.[18] Sadism, not misguided justice, drives his revenge, and his hellish fantasies cause only his own torturous and well-deserved demise.

After Huck foils Joe's attack on the widow, the novel reaches its climax when Tom and his sweetheart, Becky Thatcher, exhausted and nearly starving, escape the labyrinthine passages of McDougal's Cave, leaving Injun Joe trapped inside the barred entrance. They have not found the gold they sought, but they are grateful to escape with their lives, especially when they discover that Joe has met the fate they might have shared. When Judge Thatcher and a posse of townsmen unlock the cavern door, even Tom pities his nemesis: "Injun Joe lay stretched upon the ground, dead, with his face close to the crack of the door, as

18. Ibid., 254–55. As Twain's readers likely knew, Injun Joe's proposed punishment for the Widow Douglas alludes to the actual practice among Plains Indians of mutilating the nose or ears of an adulterous woman. Sensational accounts of such customs permeated the popular consciousness in the forms of travelers' reports and mass-market fiction, discussed in more detail in Chapter 2.

if his longing eyes had been fixed, to the latest moment, upon the light and cheer of the free world outside." A quick investigation reveals that Joe, unable to pry or scratch his way out or to satisfy his hunger on the wax candles that littered the cave, died a slow and horrifying death, desperately lapping water droplets from a stalagmite he had fashioned to catch moisture from above. But in death Joe's threat is even more pervasive; in his absence his presence is more persistent. When Tom, at the conclusion of the novel, leads Huck through a secret passage to the long-sought treasure, the boys hesitate to grab the prize, still fearful that Joe might appear. Huck warns Tom, "Yes—leave it. Injun Joe's ghost is round about there, certain. . . . I know the ways of ghosts, and so do you."[19] Such is the power of the mixed-blood in our cultural consciousness to haunt us in death, to remain simultaneously dead and alive, there and not there, and to deny, as Walker's oxymoron, the Indian-white dialectic on which American identity rests. In the nationalist fiction of the nineteenth and twentieth centuries, Injun Joe and his kin became a troublesome presence that could neither share in the shining destiny of the whites nor be erased with the Indians.

An indefinite but intriguing sign of Injun Joe's haunting presence in visions of America's future appears in Twain's unfinished novel *Huck Finn and Tom Sawyer among the Indians* (circa 1884). Twain's partial manuscript follows the mischievous duo beyond the conclusion of *The Adventures of Huckleberry Finn* (1885), when Huck famously resolves to light out for the Territory. As they venture along the Oregon Trail toward the West and toward the future, they meet a white woman among a band of wandering Indians. The intriguing narrative does not tell who she is, how she came there, or why she remains, for it abruptly discontinues, left by Twain for another time that never came. While we cannot know the reason that Twain abandoned his novel at this point, it is nonetheless suggestive that the narrative breaks just as the specter of miscegenation appears, just as Twain met the decision to portray a white woman as a captive or a consort. As Injun Joe, the offspring of this unnatural rape, haunts the dreams of Tom Sawyer, he might have haunted Twain himself, who perhaps hesitated to reimagine in this new novel the rebirth of his ugliest creation. Like the vanishing Indians in

19. Ibid., 288, 296.

earlier historical romances, Injun Joe is better left dead and gone, a sacrificial figure whose miserable tomb becomes Huck and Tom's treasure house, and whose death becomes, like the vanishing Indians of earlier romance, a cause for both communal celebration and a deeper, secret fear; for Americans know the ways of ghosts. Some writers, however, did not reject this possibility of racial blending as an aberration, nor did they put down their pens when they imagined a white and an Indian meeting in intimacy. Instead of myths of racial separation, some created myths of American emergence based on a genealogy of Europeans and Natives who join and give birth not to monsters but to a vigorously hybrid nation.

Racial Amity in *Reuben and Rachel*

William Scheick views the American exploration of hybrid identity as a peculiarly nineteenth-century phenomenon connected with the troubles of expansion and Indian conflict, but the Native American renaissance of the last thirty years has demonstrated a continuing interest in the problem. As Hertha Dawn Wong claims, "so much of twentieth-century Native American experience ... *is* this experience of multiple marginality."[20] This renewed interest in mixed identity springs, like the more familiar image of the half-breed villain, from earlier tales. Rowson's *Reuben and Rachel* provides a useful beginning for the exploration of an alternative American genealogy based on racial intermarriage that culminates in the current work of critics such as Wong and novelists such as Momaday, Leslie Silko, Louise Erdrich, and Sherman Alexie.

Rowson's work, addressed to an adolescent female audience, combines swashbuckling adventure with gothic romance, waiting to introduce the titular twin heroes until the beginning of the second volume. The first volume describes the previous nine generations of Reuben and Rachel's ancestors, both Indian and white, among whom Rowson eminently counts an Incan princess, William Penn, Francis Drake, and Christopher Columbus himself. Through Reuben and Rachel, emblems

---

20. Hertha Dawn Wong, *Sending My Heart Back across the Years: Tradition and Innovation in Native American Autobiography*, v.

of the new American self, Rowson traces national history to the Edenic union of Don Ferdinando, stepson of Columbus, and Orrabella, daughter of the king of Peru. Genealogy, intermingled racial threads, and the patterns, ironies, and revelations that surface when individual identity is telescoped into the distant past and merged with ancestral identity fascinated Rowson, as today they fascinate Louise Erdrich. Like Cally Roy, the central figure in Erdrich's *The Antelope Wife* (1998), who descends directly from an American cavalryman and the Ojibwe woman he slaughters during a raid, Reuben and Rachel claim ancestors from both the Old World and the New World. They represent both the colonizing nations and the colonized people, embodying the covenant, as Rowson understood it, which must be forged between America's contending races, as well as the condition of simultaneity yet unarticulated in postcolonial analysis.

Rowson's imagined American genealogy recalls the idea voiced by our hypothetical young preacher that Indians may be cleansed through intermarriage with whites, and that superior white blood would eventually absorb the Native taint and, with proper acculturation, finally eradicate any trace of our Indian forebears. Thomas Jefferson was among the first to consider seriously proscriptive miscegenation as a formula for national development in the era leading to the passage of the Indian Removal Act (1830). In 1826, the *North American Review,* though it censured novels that represented miscegenation, granted that intermarriage might solve the Indian problem, since superior white blood would inevitably cleanse the Indian blood. As our hypothetical preacher intoned from 1 Corinthians, "the unbelieving wife is sanctified by the husband: else were your children unclean." As Removal became imminent, however, the United States' national idea became dependant on a dialectical model, on separation rather than blending.[21] The policy that would provide the living space for the growing American nation divided the continent in half, banishing Indians beyond the Mississippi and opening

21. Throughout this book I will use the capitalized terms "Removal," "Allotment," "Reorganization," and "Termination" to refer respectively to the Indian Removal Act, the General Allotment Act, the Indian Reorganization Act, and the Termination Act. I will use uncapitalized terms to refer to general practices not specifically connected to these laws.

the promised lands of the East to white settlement. To violate this fixed geographic and racial boundary would threaten American posterity.

Reuben and Rachel, however, offers no promise that red blood will be made white, nor does it adopt this separatist view. Rowson's vision of the marriage between Ferdinando and Orrabella and the birth of their daughter, Isabella, does not exemplify Bhabha's arrangement of tense alternation but rather a stable alliance, modeled on that of John Rolfe and Pocahontas, formed to ensure the simultaneous coexistence and mutual success of both peoples, who would, in time, become one people, a hybrid model of indigenous American vigor. Rowson writes, "Columbus looked at the union as a mean of insuring wealth and power to his posterity, and Orrozombo [the Incan king] imagined, by resigning his daughter to this young stranger [Ferdinando], he secured himself a powerful friend and ally in Columbus." Rowson portrays the marriage not as the seizure of power but as a sharing of power. Isabella, though raised on a vast Spanish estate, instructs her mixed-blood daughter, Columbia, that she is heir to possessions in both Spain and Peru, and that she should value one as well as the other. William Dudley, a seventeenth-century descendant of the original union between Ferdinando and Orrabella and the grandfather of the twins, renews this racial covenant by marrying Oberea, the princess of a Massachusetts tribe, and by "harbouring a fond hope that by this union with the family of a sachem, he might promote the interests of his countrymen in general, and be the cement to bind them in bonds of lasting amity."[22] William's countrymen are significantly both whites and Indians, for whom he has equal sympathy. A white man raised among the Indians, he does not, like the assimilated captives of later frontier stories, recognize one group or the other as his enemy. As William and Otoogano, his Indian father-in-law, ally in a war against the English, the mixed-race Americans find their identity not in opposition to an Indian other but to a European other. Rowson's Americans are not strictly identified as Anglo-Saxons, as they would be in the historical romances of the 1820s, but rather are vigorous, blended, and joined against Europe, the adver-

22. Mrs. [Susanna] Rowson, *Reuben and Rachel; or, Tales of Early Times,* 24, 158.

sary, as Rowson imagines, that naturally befits the romance of American emergence.

Yet within a generation, this national myth of racial amity is usurped by the myth of racial warfare popularized by Cooper and personified by figures like Injun Joe. Even within the second volume of Rowson's novel, signs of change appear. Reuben and Rachel, grandchildren of the alliance between William and Oberea, are "lively" and "brown" in their childhood, beaming with a hybrid "health" and "cheerfulness" that set them apart from the degenerate, self-hating half-breeds of later Westerns. They are not the wilting heirs of degenerate nobility, "neither strikingly beautiful, or remarkably brilliant," just democratically and "naturally good." Later in the novel, however, Reuben (as would Mary Conant's half-breed son in *Hobomok*) disavows his Indian roots, choosing as his mate Jessy Oliver, an aristocratic English girl, over Eumea, a "darkish" half-breed "squaw." Rowson's brief characterization of Eumea reflects the biological determinism of much nineteenth-century racial thought. Eumea's white blood renders her more receptive to "culture and education" than her Mohawk kin, while her Indian blood predisposes her to the "violent affliction" of impetuosity, the unthinking fits of temper that would mark later fictional mixed-bloods as unregenerate outlaws and leads Eumea herself to suicide.[23]

Scheick offers little explanation for this "gap between the image of the half-blood as a symbol for a new American identity in the first volume and Reuben's repudiation of his Indian side in the second volume" beyond his suggestion that Rowson's hodge-podge novel manifests innumerable inconsistencies and "other narrative defects."[24] This diagnosis of "inconsistency," we will see, is repeatedly rendered by scholars confronted by *A Narrative of the Life of Mrs. Mary Jemison, A Son of the Forest, Joaquín Murieta, Cogewea, Sundown,* and *House Made of Dawn,* texts that do not submit to interpretive singularity. The division within Rowson's novel testifies more immediately to the division taking place within American culture as a whole at the turn of the nineteenth century, when the new republic adopted the Indian as its foil rather than

23. Ibid., 174, 295, 354.
24. Scheick, *Half-Blood*, 43.

its partner and rejected racial blending as a model for development. My investigation begins at this significant juncture, following the turns and, ultimately, the reversals of this fiction into the twentieth century. After a century of expansion and forced assimilation had made once-fixed racial and geographic frontiers indistinct, Rowson's model of a national mixture, originally perceived as inimical to myths of racial purity and progress, is revived, and the mixed-blood, once indistinct himself, demands, like the man at the back of the church, our recognition.

Methods and Overview

Because America's national idea mandates the separation of races and perpetuates the dual myth of the decline of the Indian and the ascendance of the Anglo-Saxon, popular nationalist literature such as that produced by Twain and Cooper registers Indian-white hybridity in images of degeneracy, atavism, madness, violence, or criminality: the antithesis to the biological and historical teleology of Manifest Destiny. An alternative tradition, inaugurated by Rowson, contests these images of the outcast half-breed by envisioning hybrid vigor as a model for the new, culturally heterogeneous nation. This book traces these traditions in narratives of racial mixing, exploring the process of alternation between them that Bhabha describes, and, finally, their convergence in the twentieth century. It examines the reasons for the ascendance of Cooper's model over Rowson's and, in spite of the insistence on racial separation in nationalist narratives, the continued persistence of Rowson's claim that America itself is a nation of half-breeds. While this method risks reestablishing the dialectical categories of the pedagogical white voice and performative Indian voice and might inevitably remain bound to them, it also seeks the hidden space between them where the mixed-blood lurks, synthesizing his experience into the discursive equivalent of Louis Riel's independent Métis nation.

My discussion will focus primarily but not solely on popular fiction. As Benedict Anderson suggests in his analysis of the relationship between national consciousness and print capitalism in *Imagined Communities,* the broad dissemination of mass fiction such as the historical romance and the dime Western "laid the bases for national consciousness" by establishing a "fixity" in language and by enabling readers to recognize

in their new cultural uniformity a shared "antiquity."[25] Popular historical fiction thus represents one of the most useful tools for gauging the
trends and transitions in the national self-concept.

I will, however, consider some fiction that met only a limited reader-
ship and texts more properly called autobiographies, ethnographies, or
essays. These exceptional documents not only provide a necessary context in which we can more effectively interpret popular fiction, but, by
contrast, provide insight into the ideological functions of genre conventions and the literary marketplace. An entire tradition of writers
from William Apess, James Seaver, John Rollin Ridge, and Helen Hunt
Jackson to Mourning Dove, John Joseph Matthews, N. Scott Momaday,
and Sherman Alexie consciously manipulate the formal conventions of
mass fiction and the expectations of common readers to reshape thinking about race that has itself been ingrained by popular writing. These
manipulations, which often result in entanglements of fiction with personal history, tribal history, and national history; with ethnography, anthropology, and public policy; and with Native oral tradition and tribal
spirituality, embody the discursive synthesis I hope to illuminate in this
book. To include, then, as-told-to autobiographies like Seaver's *A Narrative of the Life of Mrs. Mary Jemison* (1824) that depend on readers'
knowledge of popular captivity stories, or obscure romance novels like
Mourning Dove's *Cogewea* (1927) that model themselves on Native
myth, inevitably sacrifices some methodological consistency for a greater
understanding of the vacillation and synthesis between the historical
and the fictional, the pedagogical and the performative, the Indian and
the white.

The chronological parameters of the book most generally span
Thomas Jefferson's meditation on amalgamation in 1787 to Louise
Erdrich's publication of *The Antelope Wife* in 1998, but the majority of
my discussion concerns the long and eventful century between 1824,
when *Hobomok* appeared, and 1934, when John Joseph Mathews published his autobiographical novel, *Sundown*. During these years, the
federal government enacted three significant pieces of legislation: the
Indian Removal Act (1830), the General Allotment Act (1887), and the

25. Benedict Anderson, *Imagined Communities: Reflections on the Origin and
Spread of Nationalism*, 44.

Indian Reorganization Act (1934). Each of these laws sought to address mounting uncertainty, often directly caused by the mixed-blood himself, about the political relationship between the nation and the Indian and generated widespread debate about racial blending. I use these policies as historical touchstones in each of my three main chapters to mark the major transitions in the ways American culture and policy approached hybridity.

My understanding of Indian hybridity owes a debt to the scholarship of Leonard Cassuto, who has written on black-white miscegenation and the mulatto. Cassuto's *The Inhuman Race* describes the "racial grotesque" in narratives of black-white blending as evidence of the American cultural tendency to "try to imagine other people as nonhuman," to represent oppressed human beings as "beasts" in order to rationalize oppressive systems such as slavery. The grotesque, Cassuto argues, appears when these attempts fail—when the human subverts representations of the nonhuman—and then result in the image of a race "betwixt and between" animal and man, more human than a beast and yet more beastly than a human. Cassuto further argues that apparitions of the mulatto grotesque signal "disruptions" or "intrusions" upon the "desired order of the world," an "anomalousness . . . hard to apprehend because it doesn't fit neatly into any category."[26]

Although Cassuto does not consider the Indian-white mixed-blood as a manifestation of the racial grotesque, he presents the mulatto as a comparable example of an anomaly who bridges the categories between the white self and the black other, and who consequently disturbs the imagined order of the world as conceived by nineteenth-century American literature. My own discussion considers in detail the half-breed grotesques as they were conceived by contemporary anthropological thought and holds that the mixed-blood similarly threatens the dialectic that forms America's national idea and the binary terms that postcolonial theory has adopted to deconstruct that idea. The Indian mixed-blood and Cassuto's mulatto likewise find themselves "sentenced to a grotesque space . . . between the categories of human and beast," a "monster . . . outside the categories that classify the natural world."[27]

26. Leonard Cassuto, *The Inhuman Race: The Racial Grotesque in American Literature and Culture*, xiii, 8.
27. Ibid., 34.

In spite of the relevance of Cassuto's book to my own, I have chosen not to engage the problem of the mulatto here. The Indian has become entwined with our national idea in a way that the African slave has not; or at least the Indian poses a unique set of problems. As scholars such as Richard Slotkin have shown, his disappearance necessarily precedes national emergence, and so in narratives of emergence he assumes a primacy unaccorded to the African American or the mulatto. When he fails to disappear, as he does in the lingering image of mixed-blood in antebellum writing, he undermines the most fundamental assumptions that allow the idea of America to exist. While nineteenth-century science regarded Natives and blacks as similarly less-evolved castes, the law, especially before 1863, regarded them much differently. While blacks *were* potentially property that might be possessed, Indians *occupied* property that might be possessed, and in vast quantity. Indian legislation and treaties, as well as the problem of Indian-white blending that made the execution of these laws and treaties more difficult, were therefore bound to land claims and geography in ways that the issue of black-white blending was not. In the twentieth century, mixed-blood writers incorporate Native languages into their texts as a particularly modern expression of hybrid consciousness. These writers, we will see, represent themselves in ways that contemporary African American writers, whose own precolonial tribal languages have been almost entirely eradicated, cannot. Because the Indian mixed-blood stands in this unique position relative to American history and culture, I have chosen to treat him as a distinct problem, though I welcome readers to compare my conclusions with their own ideas on other varieties of hybridity.

Chapter 1 examines Child's *Hobomok: A Tale of Early Times,* Cooper's *The Last of the Mohicans* (1826), and Catharine Maria Sedgwick's *Hope Leslie; or, Early Times in the Massachusetts* (1827). As these nationalist romances confront, in the words of one of Cooper's heroines, the "horrid alternative" of Indian-white miscegenation, they transform from the historical to the gothic, manifesting hybridity as the physical and psychological degeneracy that the French racial theorist Count Buffon describes in his argument for the "diminishing fertility" of hybrid pairs. Much as they confound current theoretical oppositions, mixed or miscegenated figures in these novels deny the foundational categories of the national

identity most notably instituted by the radically divisive Indian Removal
Act: white and Indian, civilization and nature, future and past. Consequently, nationalist fiction, when it admits their presence at all, represents these cursed figures as irrational, perverse, or doomed. The chapter
also considers James E. Seaver's *A Narrative of the Life of Mrs. Mary
Jemison* (1824) and William Apess's *A Son of the Forest* (1829), as well
as Apess's treatises "An Indian's Looking-Glass for the White Man"
(1833) and *Indian Nullification* (1834), texts that resist this widely disseminated myth of hybrid degeneration, remove miscegenation and hybridity from a gothic context, and assert the natural law that encourages rather than forbids racial blending.

Chapter 2 assesses representations of the mixed-blood in a selection
of dime Westerns within the context of the emerging discourse on criminal anthropology, a refinement of Buffon's earlier theory that held that
the races derived from separate hereditary origins and therefore could
not successfully blend. The chapter also considers the popular anxiety
attending the imminent passage of the General Allotment Act, a sweeping revision of federal Indian policy that conditionally invited Indians
to join the United States as property-holding, legally entitled citizens.
The mixed-blood—the inevitable product of the new policy that encouraged more intimate economic and social relations between Indians
and whites—initially emerges in popular frontier stories such as Walt
Whitman's anonymously published *The Half-Breed* (1846) as a degenerate half-devil, a grotesque manifestation of the cultural fear of racial
crossing inherited from earlier historical romance. In later dime novels
such as Ann Stephens's *Malaeska* (1839, revised 1860), Joseph Badger's
Redlaw, the Half-Breed; or, the Tangled Trail (1870), Mayne Reid's
The White Squaw (1876), and Edward Ellis's *The Half-Blood; or, the
Panther of the Plains* (1882), the atavistic mixed-blood evolves into a
more definitive symbol of outlawry, an element of criminal instability in
a historical moment when the institution of law becomes paramount to
a nation conceived in reason and yet, with Allotment, anxiously anticipating the integration of an element the best scientists deemed savage
and irrational. A competing tradition of frontier stories, represented
here by John Rollin Ridge's *The Life and Adventures of Joaquín Murieta,
the Celebrated California Bandit* (1854) and Helen Hunt Jackson's
Ramona (1884), views racial blending as the natural course of demo-

cratic civilization. In their sympathetic representations of racially crossed and outlaw figures, these novels demonstrate that outlawry derives not from ill-conceived interracial couplings but rather from ill-conceived laws. By defining outlawry in political rather than biological terms, these novels prepare for the emergence of the modern understanding of race in the twentieth century.

Chapter 3 examines representations of the mixed-blood in the era, disastrous for reservations, between Allotment and the Indian Reorganization Act. As Allotment encouraged assimilation through interaction between newly propertied Indians and their more "civilized" white and mixed-blood neighbors, the formerly anomalous mixed-blood assumed a new prominence and necessitated a redefinition of racial boundaries. Anthropologist Franz Boas proposed that racial difference consists not in heredity but in language and cultural practice, marking the fundamental revision in the anthropological view of the Indian that inspired Reorganization, a policy that restored tribal control of reservation land and sought to nurture Native cultural independence. The most widely read magazines of the era, including the *Saturday Evening Post,* reflect these changing political and scientific views of the mixed-blood as nostalgia for the older, more familiar image of the Indian, but also as a more modern consciousness of hybridity defined independently of pure Indianness or pure whiteness. These more progressive ideas about racial mixing fostered the emergence of contemporary Native American literature in Mourning Dove's *Cogewea* and John Joseph Mathews's *Sundown,* two novels that revise hybridity in cultural terms and, in their formal and linguistic variations, exemplify the discursive simultaneity that eludes current scholarly analysis. These revolutionary fictions anticipate the Native literary renaissance of the later twentieth century in which hybridity assumes its significance as a consequence of the trauma of forced assimilation but also, simultaneously, as the capacity for survival, resistance, and renewal.

While the epilogue briefly considers this most recent Native writing, about which an ocean of criticism has accumulated during the last three decades, I cite it only briefly as the flowering of what seems to me the much longer and much less discussed process of development that has shaped American thinking about Indian hybridity from the emergence of a self-consciously nationalist literature in the early nineteenth century to the modernist revaluation of this literature in the early twentieth century. Susanna Rowson's forgotten mythology of a racially blended nation once again resonates in Momaday's *House Made of Dawn*, Leslie Silko's *Ceremony* (1977), James Welch's *The Death of Jim Loney* (1979), and more recently with Sherman Alexie's *Indian Killer* (1996) and Erdrich's *The Antelope Wife*. Like *Reuben and Rachel*, Erdrich's novel imagines a secret history in which the grandson of a U.S. cavalryman marries an Ojibwe woman, a union that gives birth to the confusing but vibrant blend of races that characterizes the contemporary urban landscape. In all of these novels, mixed-blood characters, while bearing the burden of the history and mythology discussed in the previous chapters, embody the synthesis of past and future, tradition and progress, and the commingled genealogies, languages, and histories contained within themselves. As Gerald Vizenor writes, these "recast culture heroes . . . dive into unknown urban places now, into the racial darkness in the cities, to create a new consciousness of coexistence." This new consciousness of coexistence, which I describe here as discursive simultaneity, was unthinkable in early national culture, but now grows from the realization that the words "mixed-blood" and "hybridity" have become detached from biology, and that "blood mixture," as Vizenor concludes, "is not a measurement of consciousness, culture, or human experiences."[28]

I do not offer a comprehensive survey of the vast catalog of American writing representing the mixed-blood, and many readers will note significant examples that I do not consider here. Instead I present more detailed discussion of a selection of texts that most lucidly represent the crystallizations and transitions in the process I have described. My hope, then, is not to settle discussion of this complex and yet ongoing process but rather to initiate it, to invite readers to explore other stories and other writers that have likewise remained at the edge of our discourse, and to test for themselves the divination of Susanna Rowson, of N. Scott Momaday, and of the man there and not there at back of the congregation: that within the depth of the American self lurks the shadow of the mixed-blood, Injun Joe's ghost.

---

28. Vizenor, *Earthdivers*, ix.

Miscegenation and Degeneracy in Antebellum Historical Romance

But enough has been said on this subject, which I should not have mentioned at all, but that it has been rung in my ears by almost every white lecturer I ever had the misfortune to meet.

—**William Apess,** *Indian Nullification* (1834)

Magua's Horrid Alternative

One might easily imagine the lascivious Magua, his knife point teasing brave Cora's breast, grinning awfully as he proposes the exchange. If she would willingly share his wigwam, he would spare her sister's life. Duncan and Alice, helpless and quivering, await slow and excruciating deaths. Our heroine faces a terrifying choice. She asks her sister, "Is life to be purchased by such a sacrifice? Will you, Alice, receive it at my hands, at such a price?" and Alice cries, "Cora! Cora! you jest with our misery! Name not the horrid alternative again; the thought itself is worse than a thousand deaths!" Fortunately, Duncan breaks his bonds and Hawk-eye rushes to their rescue before the Hurons' burning splinters can mar Alice's virginal complexion. Another narrow but nonetheless expected escape spares the Munro sisters—and readers—the consequences of Cora's choice and makes either sacrifice unnecessary.[1]

This brief episode from *The Last of the Mohicans*, overshadowed perhaps by more sensational scenes at Glenn's Falls and Fort William Henry,

This chapter was published in different form as "The Horrid Alternative: Miscegenation and Madness in the Frontier Romance," *Journal of American and Comparative Cultures* 24, no. 3 (2002): 137–51, and is reprinted with permission.
1. James Fenimore Cooper, *The Last of the Mohicans*, 109. Further citations will be made parenthetically with the abbreviation *LM*.

represents a critical moment both in Cooper's novel and in the culture's evolving view of Indian-white miscegenation. Faced with only two possibilities—death by torture or the thousand-times-more-horrid alternative of marriage to an Indian—Cora, the dark sister, surrenders her decision to the stainless Alice, who would unhesitatingly give her own life to spare her sister the nightmare of becoming Magua's woman. Though the Huron appears treacherous and demonic in contrast to the noble and messianic Uncas, the scene casts a pall over the developing romance between Cora and the young Mohican. Alice, representative of America's uncompromising white future, refuses to imagine a union with the Indian and in doing so dramatizes what Annette Kolodny calls "America's studied literary silence on the subject of white-red intermarriage."[2] As Alice stops her sister before she can again utter the terrible thought, the scene betrays the fear motivating Removal, that a marriage between white and Indian held consequences much worse than death. Antebellum romance thus preempts racial mixing as a possibility for the young nation's future. As Cora's suggestion of her union with Magua elicits Alice's plea, "Name not the horrid alternative," these novels tentatively raise the possibility of miscegenation only to deny its viability, dispelling Susanna Rowson's vision, expressed a generation earlier, that America's races might meet in amity rather than violence.

But why should it be so? Scholars generally conclude that miscegenation represents a fundamental contradiction to the national ideology of racial separatism and that the historical romance, intent upon the creation of a national literature, registers this contradiction as a tense silence. Kolodny claims that such extreme forms of cultural exchange as Indian-white intermarriage and the adoption of white children by Indian tribes are "always disturbing to . . . white society" because they call "into deepest question the Europeans' claim to a superior cultural organization." Richard Slotkin cites the natural repugnance between the races, a widely held scientific doctrine in the eighteenth and nineteenth centuries. An Indian-white union, he argues, would have been inimical to Cooper's purpose since his many readers would associate "racial mongrelization" with national degeneracy. More recent readings of *Hobomok*

2. Kolodny, *Land before Her,* 70.

and *Hope Leslie,* which view miscegenation in these novels as a subversive alliance against white patriarchal authority, admit, as Carolyn Karcher does, that these romances "never resolve . . . the tensions between questioning and reinforcing America's dominant creed."[3]

But, hearing only murmurs or silence, perhaps we have not been listening closely enough; beneath the superficial silence, perhaps on a lower frequency, these texts resound in frantic cacophony. They have so far seemed silent to us because our current critical vocabulary, bound to the same dialectical categories as the historical romance itself, limits the ways we can talk about hybridity in these novels. When Child's *Hobomok,* Cooper's *The Last of the Mohicans,* and Sedgwick's *Hope Leslie* confront the specter of miscegenation, we can no longer read them as historical romance with the insisted demarcation between Indian and white. We hear more if we attune ourselves more closely to the moments when these historical novels transform into gothic fantasies, as did Mark Twain's comedy when Tom Sawyer fled the murderous half-breed in the subterranean labyrinth of McDougal's Cave. Unlike historical romance, gothic fantasy, where day blends with night, death blends with life, and heroism blends with madness, offers a more appropriate vocabulary to describe and interpret the ghostly, twilight half-breed in nineteenth-century fiction and his simultaneous embodiment of the opposing ideals imagined by the romance. Listening more closely to these odd, gothic moments, we find that racial blending is manifested not as silence but more sharply as madness, degeneracy, and horror. We find a convergence of science and sensationalism, as the theory of the diminishing fertility of racially mixed pairs manifests itself in these novels as insanity or living death, the degenerative principle reflected as a curse summoned by the unnatural mingling of white and Indian blood. In his synthesis of the antithetical categories of the sociobiological order invoked both by these romances and the Indian Removal Act, the half-breed most frequently appears as science imagined such threats: irrational, perverse, or doomed.

This chapter also considers texts that resist this widely disseminated myth of degeneration: Seaver's *A Narrative of the Life of Mrs. Mary*

3. Ibid., 68; Richard Slotkin, "Introduction to the 1831 Edition," xiv–xvii; Carolyn L. Karcher, introduction to *Hope Leslie; or, Early Times in the Massachusetts,* xxxiii.

Jemison, published in the same year as *Hobomok* and equal to *The Last of the Mohicans* in popularity; and William Apess's *A Son of the Forest,* "An Indian's Looking-Glass for the White Man," and *Indian Nullification.* Seaver's and Apess's texts, like the hybrid documents later produced by Ridge and Mourning Dove, exploit the conventions of mass fiction and the expectations of readers, raising romantic ideas of degeneracy only to detach them from their familiar, nationalized, contexts. Because they are, in Bhabha's terms, simultaneously pedagogical and performative, they seem to critics sometimes to accept and sometimes to subvert nineteenth-century racialism, sometimes inauthentically Native and sometimes authentically so. Like *Reuben and Rachel, Joaquín Murieta,* and *Cogewea,* these texts seem rhetorically inconsistent to some critics because these critics are yet unable to recognize that texts, like people, may simultaneously embody two opposing ideals. This chapter gestures to a recognition of this simultaneity in antebellum culture.

National Literature and the Vanishing Indian

A lecture delivered in 1882 remains a hallmark of contemporary discussions of nationalism: Ernst Renan's "What Is a Nation?" Renan observes that culturally, linguistically, and racially diverse groups of people might be unified by a national idea based on "a heroic past, great men, glory." He claims that "to have common glories in the past and to have a common will in the present; to have performed great deeds together, to wish to perform still more—these are the essential conditions for being a people.... These are the kinds of things that can be understood in spite of differences of race and language." But, Renan argues, a nation's heroic past is more frequently an idea that is imagined than a reality that is remembered. When the imagined past conflicts with the remembered past, "forgetting," or willful "historical error," becomes a "crucial factor in the creation of a nation, which is why progress in historical studies often constitutes a danger for [the principle of] nationality." More recently, Benedict Anderson echoes Renan's association of national consciousness with forgetting: "all profound changes in consciousness, by their very nature, bring with them characteristic amnesias. Out of such oblivions, in specific historical circumstances, spring narratives."[4] Within these narratives, in Bhabha's analysis, the subaltern voice fractures the dominant myth, and performative discourses exist in continual exchange with the pedagogical discourse, forming the contested ground that is home to the hybrid subject.

Anderson more specifically explains that the nineteenth-century United States, where images of the half-breed emerge in mass culture, was particularly susceptible to such amnesias and discursive exchanges, witnessing "a half-fortuitous, but explosive, interaction between a system of production and productive relations (capitalism), a technology of communications (print), and the fatality of human linguistic diversity." Generated by new print technologies, historical romances and dime novels saturated an increasingly literate market, nurturing a national amnesia that scholars have called the vanishing Indian. Robert Berkhofer summarizes the strategy of these novels, which romantically represent the Indian as "rapidly passing away before the onslaught of civilization," arousing not only pity for the "dying race" of noble savages but also nostalgia for an imagined national past. Richard Slotkin similarly explains that "Cooper had used the genre to create a literary basis for the nascent nationalism" of middle-class audiences, recovering "some crisis period from the nation's past and show[ing] in the resolution a definitive step toward realizing the destined and glorious present." In order that the new might grow, the story goes, the old must pass away. The Indian's setting sun is followed by the white man's dawn, when the heroic Indian character mounts a rocky prominence, extends his arm to western forests, and delivers the farewell oration of his dying race. Child's Narragansett chief Hobomok "paused on a neighboring hill, looked toward his wigwam till his strained vision could hardly discern the object, with a bursting heart again murmured his farewell and blessing, and forever passed away from New England." Cooper's Chingachgook laments, "I am a 'blazed pine in a clearing of the pale-faces.' My race has gone from the shores of the salt lake and from the hills of the Delawares. . . . I am alone" (*LM*, 349). And Sedgwick's Indian heroine Magawisca pleads before a Puritan court, "Take my own word, I am

---

4. Ernst Renan, "What Is a Nation?" 19, 11; Anderson, *Imagined Communities*, 204.

your enemy; the sun-beam and the shadow cannot mingle. The white man cometh—the Indian vanisheth."[5]

In addition to its regular appearance in historical romance, the lyrical Indian elegy ornaments the widely read poetry of Philip Freneau, William Cullen Bryant, and Henry Wadsworth Longfellow, and the well-worn pages of any schoolchild's McGuffey reader. Asher Durand, in his painting *The Last of the Mohicans,* frames the scene pictorially with a great oak tree rising heavenward, mountains fading into a distant horizon, and a lone Indian warrior uplifting both arms to the setting sun, which suffuses all of nature in its orange glow. This myth, at once evoking the tragic demise of one race and the triumphal ascendance of another, imagined in the past the same western exile that Removal soon enacted in its banishment of the tribes to the far wilderness beyond the Mississippi. As exercises in historical error, the works of Child, Cooper, and Sedgwick rewrite the history of Puritan New England and of the French and Indian War and provide the mythological foundation necessary to rationalize the Trail of Tears. In their prefaces and prophetic narrative interludes, they reveal their self-consciousness both as *American* writers and as creators of a myth that would give their work a global significance. Even before her readers watch Hobomok pass away from New England forever, Child foreshadows that the Indian's loving sacrifice makes possible the growth of the nascent American empire, for "the tender slip which he protected, has since become a mighty tree, and the nations of the earth seek refuge beneath its branches" (*H,* 150). The "proud and populous emporium of six flourishing states" for which Hobomok prepares a future becomes "the embryo of political powers, which were so soon to be developed before the gaze of anxious and astonished Europe" (*H,* 100). Sedgwick, casting her own narrative gaze over the steeples of the first small churches built on Massachusetts Bay, churches that Magawisca indirectly works to preserve, avers in these symbols of the colony "prophecies of its future greatness" (*HL,* 133).

5. Anderson, *Imagined Communities,* 42–43; Robert F. Berkhofer Jr., *The White Man's Indian: Images of the American Indian from Columbus to the Present,* 88; Slotkin, introduction, xiii; Lydia Maria Child, *Hobomok and Other Writings on Indians,* 141 (further citations will be made parenthetically with the abbreviation *H*); Catherine Maria Sedgwick, *Hope Leslie; or, Early Times in the Massachusetts,* 309 (further citations will be made parenthetically with the abbreviation *HL*).

In their invention of this national idea, novelists worked in close cooperation with critics, most notably those of Boston's *North American Review*, who explicitly challenged young American writers to create a new American literature distinct from European forms. The nineteen-year-old Child, after reading John Gorham Palfrey's review of James Wallis Eastburn and Robert Sands's Indian epic poem, *Yamoyden*, was inspired to write *Hobomok*, her first novel. Bruce Mills explains that the review was one of many by Palfrey and fellow *Review* critics William Tudor, John Knapp, and William Howard Gardiner that exhorted "utilization of the untamed landscape, New England's Puritan heritage, and Indian customs."[6] Writers who met the standards established by the *Review* were repaid with exposure, acclaim, and lasting reputation, founding an American canon in which aesthetic value merged with nationalist ideology.

The story of the vanishing Indian might have furnished us with an ideal national mythology—tragic, bloody, beautiful, historical, and yet beyond history—but for a few who would not vanish gracefully, the spectral, present-absent figures who complicate Armando José Prats's definition of *otherness* as "absence." Not white, not Indian, but both and neither, the degenerate half-breed lingers in the gothic-historical romance in ghostly form after his noble father has passed away from America's peaceful vales. His brief and tense appearance, followed by his quick erasure, might be viewed as an example of the alternation Bhabha describes, but, as we will see, our uncertain but persistent sense of his presence even before he appears and after he disappears lends the quality of simultaneity of being, rather than alternation—like Injun Joe's ghost in McDougal's cave, both there and not there. To fully understand the gothic undertones this ghostly presence produces in the historical romance, we must first examine the association between hybridity and degeneracy conceived in antebellum racial theory.

Jefferson, Buffon, and the Marriage of Races

Racial theorists throughout the eighteenth and nineteenth centuries stood divided between the theory of monogenesis, the idea that the

---

6. Bruce Mills, *Cultural Reformations: Lydia Maria Child and the Literature of Reform*, 15.

peoples of the earth derived from a single hereditary origin and were therefore a single species, and the theory of polygenesis, the idea that the races derived from distinct hereditary origins and thus represented distinct species. Buffon was among the first to establish amalgamation, or the interbreeding of distinct races, as the most widely accepted test to settle the matter, determining that the infertility he claimed to find between mixed individuals proved that the individuals differed not just in race but, more fundamentally, in species.[7] By the middle nineteenth century, the Scottish racial theorist Robert Knox concluded the question in *The Races of Men* (1850): "I have heard persons assert, a few years ago, men of education too, and of observation, that the amalgamation of races into a third or new product, partaking of the qualities of the two primitive ones from which they were sprung, was not only possible, but that it was the best mode for improving the breed. The whole of this theory has turned out to be false.... Nature produces no mules; no [healthy] hybrids, neither in man nor animals." While the growing and vigorous mixed-race populations of the Western Hemisphere seemed to determine empirically that human beings were derived from one species comprising many races, proponents of polygenesis continued to argue that although unions between different species may produce fertile offspring, their fertility and vigor faded through successive generations. Knox continues, "when they [hybrids] accidentally appear they soon cease to be, for they are either non-productive, or one or other of the pure breeds speedily predominates, and the weaker disappears." Polygenist reasoning promised one of two results concerning Indian-white interbreeding: it would either elevate the Indian or degrade the white; both scenarios would end with the complete absorption of one race by the other. Knox, in fact, supported the hope of those like Jefferson who saw intermarriage as a possible alternative to removal,

7. See Young, *Colonial Desire*, 6–19, for a more extensive account of the monogenesis-polygenesis debate. Before outlining its competing theories, Young usefully defines its key terms. Prior to the 1860s, he explains, *amalgamation* denoted the fertile fusion of two distinct races. In the middle nineteenth century, *miscegenation* became the more widely used term. In this book, I will more frequently use *miscegenation*, though I will sometimes use *amalgamation* to refer specifically to antebellum racial thought. See also George W. Stocking Jr., *Victorian Anthropology*, chapter 2, for a detailed discussion of pre-Darwinian debates concerning the origins of humanity.

finally predicting that American experiments in amalgamation would destroy the Indians, the weaker race "from whom nothing could be expected; a race whose vital energies were wound up; expiring: hastening onwards also to ultimate extinction." He did not, however, fully dispel the much more terrifying possibility, citing the *mestizo* population of Latin America, who more closely resemble the primitive Indians than the Celtic Spanish with whom they mixed.[8]

This hypothesis of diminishing fertility, of the potential degradation or disappearance of the Anglo-American people if they mixed with the indigenous American population, not only fueled the proliferation of images of hybrid degeneracy in antebellum fiction but also resonates in contemporary critical discourse. As Knox asserts that the blending of two races must inevitably result in the extinction of one of them, post-colonial theory alternately views the hybrid subject as one who is entirely assimilated by the dominant culture, or one who vacillates between performative and a pedagogical roles. Neither of these views recognizes that the hybrid subject may simultaneously embody both races, both roles; critical theory, like nature, "produces no mules; no hybrids."

Because Jefferson sometimes imagined and sometimes publicly declared the destiny of the United States as a marriage of its various races, the idea of diminishing fertility of interracial unions was particularly troubling for him. While Jefferson's idea of intermixing begins with the Indians' adoption of white agriculture and white family structures, as the General Allotment Act would also enjoin in 1887, he finally invites them to "mix with us by marriage" and prophesies in an 1809 address to a group of Algonquian tribes, "your blood will run in our veins and will spread with us over this great island."[9] But although he describes the future nation as a marriage of its various peoples, seemingly as Rowson had in *Reuben and Rachel,* Jefferson, mindful of the problem of diminishing fertility, remains uncertain of what fruit this union would bear.

An inconspicuous textual variant reveals Jefferson's ambivalence. In one of the least controversial queries in *Notes on the State of Virginia,* Jefferson compares the colony's census results of 1607 with those of

8. Robert Knox, *The Races of Men,* 64–65, 65–66, 67.
9. Thomas Jefferson, *The Writings of Thomas Jefferson,* 8:227.

1669 and notes that the Indian tribes native to Virginia were in the space of six decades "reduced to one third of their former numbers," attributing this precipitous decline to "Spirituous liquors, the small-pox, war, and an abridgement of territory." Jefferson concludes that these sundry ravages "had committed terrible havock among them, which the infecundity of their women, was not likely to make good" (*NV,* 96).

The passage was one that Jefferson revised during the time between the original composition of *Notes* in 1781 and the publication of its final form in 1787. In 1781, Jefferson submitted the manuscript to his friend and fellow Councillor of the American Philosophical Society, Charles Thomson, an adopted member of the Delaware, who was regarded as an expert in Indian affairs. Thomson returned the manuscript to Jefferson with short commentaries addressing Jefferson's discussion of Indians throughout *Notes.*[10] The bulk of these commentaries, valued enough by Jefferson to be included by him as the first appendix of his first published edition, focuses specifically on the doctrine of diminishing fertility advanced by Buffon. As part of his more general theory of the degeneracy of all New World species of flora and fauna compared to those of Europe, Buffon, as Jefferson cites him, argues that Indians commonly have "small organs of generation . . . love their parents and children but little . . . look upon their wives only as servants for all work" and produce "only few children" as a result of their diminished sexual capacity and "indifference to the other sex." This "fundamental defect" in the Indians, Buffon concludes, "weakens their nature, prevents its development, and . . . destroy[s] the very germs of life" (*NV,* 58–59).

Challenging Buffon's claims, Thomson attributes Indians' perceived sexual indifference to culture rather than biology. The warlike culture of the Indians, he explains, demands emotional distance in the men and "great subjection" in the women, consequently misinterpreted by Europeans as frigidity. Thomson writes to Jefferson:

> [Buffon] says their organs of generation are smaller and weaker than those of Europeans. Is this a fact? I believe not; at least it is an obser-

10. In his notes to Jefferson's *Notes on the State of Virginia,* William Peden provides information about Jefferson's correspondence with Charles Thomson and his subsequent manuscript revision of *Notes* (*NV,* 281, 296), but he does not suggest a connection between these revisions and the amalgamation debate or the marriage metaphor in Jefferson's letter to the Indians.

vation I never heard before. [Buffon writes] "They have no ardour for their female." It is true, they do not indulge in those excesses, nor discover that fondness which is customary in Europe; this is not owing to a defect in nature, but in manners. If a young man were to discover a fondness for women before he has been to war, he would become the contempt of the men, and the scorn and ridicule of the women.... The seeming frigidity of the men, therefore, is the effect of manners, and not a defect of nature. [The women] being brought up in great subjection, custom and manners reconcile them to modes of acting, which, judged of by Europeans, would be deemed inconsistent with the rules of female decorum and propriety. (*NV,* 200–201)

Apparently influenced by Thomson's remarks, Jefferson, at some point, rewrites the phrase, "Spirituous liquors, the small-pox, war, and an abridgement of territory had committed terrible havock among them, which the *infecundity of their women* was not likely to make good," as "Spirituous liquors, the small-pox, war, and an abridgement of territory had committed terrible havock among them, which *generation, under the obstacles opposed to it among them,* was not likely to make good" (*NV,* 96, 281; emphasis added). The rhetorical distinction between the phrases "generation, under the obstacles..." and "infecundity of their women" seems slight, but in the context of the debate over diminishing fertility, Jefferson's revision is significant. While the term "infecundity" connotes a natural defectiveness in Indians' procreative capacity and consequently underscores Buffon's argument for the diminishing fertility of mixed and hybrid pairs, "generation, under obstacles" suggests that environmental difficulties are to blame for the Indian decline and is more consistent with Jefferson's position that Indian degeneracy is due not to a difference of nature, but of circumstance.

This small revision holds great significance for Indian policy throughout the nineteenth century, as it became crystallized in Removal and Allotment. If Indians were naturally degenerate, as Buffon argued, any possibility of biological assimilation was necessarily doomed; such was the implication of Removal. If, on the other hand, the decline in the Native population could be explained by adverse environmental conditions, Indians might be revived through assimilation to white society or through marriage to white mates; such was the implication of Allotment. More importantly, mixed-blood offspring, nurtured with proper care, would not inherit any natural deficiencies from their Indian parent.

Jefferson's vision of a marriage of races in America therefore rests on the argument that circumstance and not nature determines fertility, a fundamental point that informs the writings of John Rollin Ridge, Helen Hunt Jackson, and Franz Boas, all of whom opposed arguments for the biologically determined degeneracy or criminality of the half-breed in the later nineteenth century.

Immediately following Buffon's discussion, Jefferson observes that "Indian women, when married to white traders, who feed them and their children plentifully and regularly, who exempt them from excessive drudgery, who keep them stationary and unexposed to accident, produce and raise as many children as the white women" (NV, 61). Jefferson makes the observation to demonstrate that Indian wives' fertility is a consequence of the material improvements of their daily existence and reinforces Thomson's argument that Indian defectiveness is due not to biology but to environment. Under these improved conditions, Jefferson shows, miscegenation is abundantly fertile, and he can rationalize his proposed racial marriage. Jefferson's own science and personal observation tell him that, as the union of a white and an Indian would produce healthy offspring, so would the union of the white race and the Indian race produce a healthy nation, mixed and yet one people.

But while Jefferson's dream seems progressive in its apparent evocation of a racial middle ground that the historical romance could not imagine, and while he appeals to lived experience and empirical observation to dispel cultural myths, as Franz Boas would in his dismantling of nineteenth-century anthropology, Jefferson's concept of racial mixture is relatively conservative. He does not imagine this marriage of races as a marriage of equals. Whites clearly assume the masculine role, as Indians, in their surrender of name and property, are feminized. Jefferson implies that Indians' mixture with whites will revitalize the race that circumstance has made degenerate, but only with the condition that Indians fully adopt white social practices and surrender their name and property to whites as a wife surrenders them to her husband. The alternative, he flatly concludes, is their "total disappearance from the face of the earth."[11]

11. Jefferson, *Writings*, 8:226–27.

As he concludes his discussion of the "Aborigines" in *Notes on the State of Virginia*, Jefferson moves from this speculation about the fertility of mixed marriages to a brief inquiry about Indian origins. More than a century, we will see, before American anthropologists such as Franz Boas and Henry Weatherbee Henshaw proposed the "test of language" as the surest means to discover the geographical origins of the Indians, Jefferson argues, "A knowledge of [the Indians'] languages would be the most certain evidence of their derivation which could be produced. . . . It is to be lamented then . . . that we have suffered so many of the Indian tribes to extinguish, without our having previously collected and deposited in the records of literature, the general rudiments at least of the languages they spoke" (*NV,* 101). Jefferson appears prescient in his anticipation of later anthropologists' focus on language families, but his understanding of the way language can be used to study the Indians differed significantly from that of Boas and Henshaw. Jefferson regarded language as a form of data that could reveal much, for instance, about migration routes, but he did not imagine that language should replace biology as the privileged criterion for ethnic identification. For researchers of the later nineteenth century, on the other hand, language revealed not only where the Indians came from or how long they had been here, but also who they were. For Jefferson, race remained in the blood and the bone, and linguistic assimilation could not substitute for miscegenation.

Even in his most progressive moments, Jefferson remains decided on the idea of one people, one emergent race, perhaps stirred with the Indian, as Knox would later suggest, but finally white. National culture could not imagine hybridity as a condition of simultaneity but rather conceived it as a combination in which the Indian element was dissolved and the white element, perhaps, corrupted. In spite of Jefferson's hopeful views of miscegenation both as biological experiment and national metaphor, the interracial unions dramatized in the historical romance written by his intellectual heirs are not only infertile, but degenerative, both physically and mentally, to the white women who would surrender themselves to such a fate. In its starkest terms, polygenesis likens miscegenation to bestiality, a union between two distinct species and a horrible affront to nature. The romances of Child, Cooper, and Sedgwick represent this affront as the gradual mental decline of vibrant heroines following their sexual contact with Indians. Like the interracial couplings theorized by Buffon, those in the historical romance rarely conceive offspring, and those half-breeds that somehow issue from the ill-advised matches emerge, especially in later frontier stories, as spectacularly diminished creatures, monstrous, fanged goblins, seemingly born of the pagan congress of a maiden and a forest satyr. As a transgression against the laws of nature, racial mixing in antebellum romance is punished by disease and madness, reflecting a dark logic when the historical romance momentarily appropriates the images of degeneracy more common in gothic fantasy. But even as nationalist mythology evokes darkness, fear, and the unnatural to urge the separation of races, the gothic, twilight atmosphere in which characters wander uncertainly between life and death, sanity and madness, waking and sleeping, also offers just the right light for glimpsing the hybrid figures who themselves embody this indeterminate state.

Gothic Degeneracy and *Edgar Huntly*

In *Love and Death in the American Novel*, Leslie Fiedler sketches the conventions of the European gothic novel that took unique shape in antebellum America, illuminating the vocabulary the historical romances use to describe miscegenation. The gothic novel in both its European and American forms, Fiedler explains, cultivates the "power of darkness," breaking with the sunnier tradition of sentimental romance in its fundamental "substitution of terror for love as a central theme." The gothic story centers not on the innocent heroine but on the persecuting villain, who often appears in the guise of the heroine's protector or confidante: "The villain-hero is, indeed, an invention of the gothic form, while his temptation and suffering, the beauty and terror of his bondage to evil, are among its major themes." The villain-hero's "bondage to evil" derives from some hidden degeneracy, a "secret sin" finally revealed, as in the British novels of Ann Radcliffe and Monk Lewis, as incest, the "breach of the primal taboo."[12]

12. Leslie A. Fiedler, *Love and Death in the American Novel*, 120, 114–15.

For Fiedler, this repudiation of the sentimental tradition arises in Europe from specific historical conditions. The French Revolution ignited fierce antiaristocratic, anti-Catholic feelings and a deep suspicion of Europe's feudal past. The villain-heroes spawned in the European gothic novel are most frequently degenerate clerics or noblemen who draw their prey into the decayed ruin of their abbey, castle, or dungeon. Fiedler cites the Marquis de Sade, who himself calls the gothic novel, which many of his contemporaries regarded as a particularly shocking form of pornography, as "the inevitable fruit of the revolutionary shocks felt by all of Europe," a nightmare born of the mind of "man in this Iron Age." For both Fiedler and the Marquis, the gothic sensibility is most basically motivated by the perception of social degeneracy in a moment of historical transition or calamity.[13]

In the early American republic, another postrevolutionary society in the shock not of class warfare but rather of racial warfare, this sensibility also thrived, but in the trust of American novelists such as Charles Brockden Brown, the nightmare assumed different proportions. Without a history of feudal oppression, the American gothic novel had to conceive new villains and new evils. Fiedler describes this "change of myth": "In the American gothic . . . the heathen, unredeemed wilderness and not the decaying monuments of a dying class, nature and not society, becomes the symbol for evil. Similarly not the aristocrat but the Indian, not the dandified courtier but the savage colored man is postulated as the embodiment of villainy."[14] As Child, Cooper, and Sedgwick adapt Walter Scott to an American milieu, Brown adapts Radcliffe. In his preface to *Edgar Huntly; or, Memoirs of a Sleep-Walker* (1799), he writes:

America has opened new views to the naturalist and politician. . . . The sources of amusement to the fancy and instruction to the heart, that are peculiar to ourselves, are equally numerous and inexhaustible. It is the purpose of this work to profit by some of these sources; to exhibit a series of adventures, growing out of the condition of our country. . . . One merit the writer may at least claim; that of calling forth

13. Ibid., 122–23.
14. Ibid., 149.

the passions and engaging the sympathy of the reader. . . . Puerile superstition and exploded manners; Gothic castles and chimeras, are the
materials usually employed for this end. The incidents of Indian hostility, and the perils of the western wilderness, are far more suitable;
and, for a native of America to overlook these, would admit of no
apology.[15]

By substituting bestial Indians for European "Gothic chimeras," Brown
appropriates gothic writing for the profit of conceiving a national literature, specifically casting the Indian, as Radcliffe casts the aristocrat, as
the emblem of a dark past that the troubled present must attempt to
forget.

Fiedler, however, ends his discussion of antebellum gothic writing
with Brown, Hawthorne, and Poe, briefly noting its connection to the
historical romance in its "concern with the past," but distinguishing in
Cooper's writing a significantly different stance toward the past, "something clean and heroic, immune to darkness and the demonic," a conservative nostalgia for the "settled bourgeois life" rather than a radical
repudiation.[16] Fiedler's analysis of the "power of darkness" does not
extend to the historical romance, though these novels are not entirely
immune to darkness and the demonic, which seizes the cleaner, more
heroic imagination of the past at the moments it conjures the specter of
miscegenation. And while Fiedler views the Indian as the replacement
for the villainous aristocrat of the European gothic tradition, he does
not posit a substitute sin for the aristocrat's incest. In my reading of
Hobomok, The Last of the Mohicans, and Hope Leslie, miscegenation replaces incest as the "primal taboo" in antebellum nationalist fiction, and
the breach of this taboo is punished in the historical romance exactly as
Madeline Usher's suggested incest is punished in "The Fall of the House
of Usher": the physical and psychological degeneration of the formerly
vital white woman to a state of catalepsy, or deathlike insensibility.

While miscegenation threatens degeneracy in the individual mind
and body in these women, it likewise threatens the corruption of the
social and national body, as Jefferson's ambivalence toward the marriage
of races attests. Just as the gothic novel in revolutionary Europe repre-

15. Charles Brockden Brown, *Edgar Huntly; or, Memoirs of a Sleep-Walker*, 3.
Further citations will be made parenthetically with the abbreviation *EH*.
16. Fiedler, *Love and Death*, 150, 153.

sented the lascivious clergy and the incestuous nobility as sick vestiges of the old order that stood in direct opposition to the new, the historical romance envisions miscegenation and its hybrid issue as remnants of an older, darker, more barbaric America, when Indian warriors toted captive maidens into the pagan wild never to return them or to return them only years later, speaking heathen gibberish, wearing animal skins, or—horror of horrors—coddling a half-Indian nursling. Conjuring these anxieties in the decade culminating with Removal, the gothic-historical romance exposes the Trail of Tears as a direct political result of the nation's fear of its own past, a history, now willfully forgotten, when Indians and whites lived in more intimate proximity.

In *Gothic America*, Teresa Goddu claims that American gothic writing performs the difficult task of reconciling national identity with its own inherent contradictions.[17] A nation "intermixed," in Jefferson's words, and yet radically divided by Removal presents one of the most vexing contradictions of antebellum culture. At once potentially degenerative and potentially invigorating, the blending of white and Indian blood first preoccupies the generation of writers before Cooper's, who appropriated gothic motifs to address this secret sin, this most troubling contradiction.

In Brown's *Edgar Huntly*, the sleepwalking Edgar becomes a savage, losing his reason as he falls to sleep and wanders half-naked and unconscious into an underground chasm in the rocky, wilderness region of Norwalk. In the sepulchral depth, Edgar wanders blind and delirious "in a wakeful dream" (*EH*, 154), eventually driven by hunger to the extremity of savagery, when he kills a lurking panther with his Indian tomahawk and greedily devours its raw flesh. Edgar recounts this episode to his beloved Mary Waldegrave "with loathing and horror," reflecting on it "as on some hideous dream . . . some freak of insanity" (*EH*, 160).

Following Edgar's devouring of the panther, we learn that his peculiar mental disturbance, somnambulism, was induced by the childhood trauma of witnessing his parents massacred during an Indian raid. While this memory ostensibly provides Edgar with justification for the five savage Indian killings that he is about to commit, it also makes the connection between madness and Indianness that would inform anthropo-

---

17. Teresa A. Goddu, *Gothic America: Narrative, History, and Nation*, 10.

logical thought throughout the nineteenth century. In his attempt to explain the uncharacteristic violence and cunning he displays during his single-handed counterattack on the Indian raiding party, Edgar writes to Mary: "Think not that I relate these things with exultation or tranquility. All my education and the habits of my life tended to unfit me for a contest and a scene like this. But I was not governed by the soul which usually regulates my conduct. I had imbibed from the unparalleled events which had lately happened a spirit vengeful, unrelenting, and ferocious" (*EH*, 184). Although Brown's novel seemingly evades the abhorrent issue of miscegenation, Edgar himself becomes a psychological half-breed, white and rational in his waking hours, savage and frenzied in his sleepwalking hours. The novel graphically reinforces this doubling after the climax of the fighting, when an exhausted Edgar faints and awakens prostrate on the body of one of the Indians he has just killed. The blood from the deep gash in Edgar's own cheek mingles with that oozing from the Indian's chest wound. Brown represents the horror of the mixing of white and Indian blood not through an act of sex, as Child would venture to do, but, like Cooper, through combat. In Edgar's nighttime metamorphosis into a savage, in his laying down with the Indian and mixing his blood with that of his enemy, Brown explored the issue of miscegenation and degeneracy symbolically, before the culture, notwithstanding *Reuben and Rachel*, permitted writers to do so more explicitly. Even in the next generation, when the historical romance brought the problem to the forefront of American fiction, critics censured it as a pornographic stunt, as European critics had greeted the portrayal of incest in Lewis's *The Monk* (1796).[18] Like Jefferson, Brown imagines hybridity more as an alternation between two conflicting identities than a synthesis of identities. As nationalist discourse vacillates between the pedagogical and the performative, Edgar vacillates between his savage and rational selves, alternately becoming Indian or white according to his circadian rhythm of sleeping and waking, and never reconciling a stable balance.

In the generation before Cooper's, national culture, even in the experimental fictions of Brown and Rowson, seems yet unready to accept

18. See Fiedler, *Love and Death*, 116–17, for a brief discussion of the popular and critical reception of *The Monk*.

the implications of a marriage of race, of the vanishing Indian who yet lingered in the form of his mixed-blood children, both there but not there. Yet as we find in fiction throughout the nineteenth and twentieth centuries, this ghostly figure would not be fully erased from our national story. We find his shadow in *Reuben and Rachel,* in Jefferson's inconspicuous revision of *Notes on the State of Virginia,* and in the conclusion of *Edgar Huntly,* where the conflicted hero remains unable to completely subdue his savage self, uneasily bearing the "phrenzy" that lies dormant within him, always threatening to fracture his civilized facade.

The Last of the Mohicans

In the generation that followed Rowson, Jefferson, and Brown, the specter indeed awakens to fracture the historical romance. Brown's association of savagery and "phrenzy," or temporary insanity, establishes a pattern adopted by Cooper, Sedgwick, and Child where miscegenated white women, like Edgar, lose their reason and come to behave like Indians, not brandishing tomahawks or killing panthers but rather speaking their language, wearing their clothes, or bearing their children. The type of insanity recurring in romantic heroines who are stained with Indian intimacy resembles both Edgar's somnambulism and the catalepsy symptomatic in Poe's women, taking its shape both from the European gothic tradition and the racialist discourse of hybrid degeneracy. According to this view, mixed-race unions, as naturally abhorrent as incestuous ones, produced successively inferior and ultimately infertile generations of offspring, and characters that represent such unions in the historical romance are sapped of their vitality and awareness. As the European gothic novel sought to bury the memory of feudal culture, the gothic-historical romance, anticipating Removal as Europe anticipated revolution, sought to bury America's heterogeneous past by reminding readers of the degenerative consequences that racial mixing would bring and remained unable to conceive of the synthesis of the future and the past, the white and the Indian. In their attempt to forge a national mythology, Child, Cooper, and Sedgwick consciously modeled their romances on those of Walter Scott, but as these novels approach miscegenation, their conventions turn, perhaps unconsciously, to those of the somnambulistic nightmare conceived by Brown, transforming from novels of love to novels of terror, from narratives of national ascendance to narratives of national decay.

The Last of the Mohicans seems to retreat from Jefferson's and Rowson's experiments of integrating the mixed-blood into national culture toward more violent nightmares of racial blending such as Brown's. The racial division in Cooper's writing has received ample attention from scholars. Cooper identifies his hero as "a man without a cross," careful to show that while Hawk-eye dresses as an Indian and possesses unsurpassed skill in hunting, tracking, and shooting, his blood is not stained by mixture. The master frontiersman tells his Indian companion, Chingachgook, "I am not a prejudiced man, nor one who vaunts himself on his natural privileges, though the worst enemy I have on earth, and he is an Iroquois, daren't deny that I am genuine white" (*LM*, 31). Chingachgook likewise affirms his pure bloodline, in that his nobler Mohican blood has not blended with that of the inferior Iroquois. He tells Hawk-eye, "my tribe is the grandfather of nations, but I am an unmixed man. The blood of chiefs is in my veins, where it must stay for ever.... I am on a hill-top, and must go down into the valley; and when Uncas follows in my footsteps, there will no longer be any blood of the Sagamores, for my boy is the last of the Mohicans" (*LM*, 33). Richard Slotkin explains that Cooper's insistence on racial separatism arises from a theory familiar in the early republic that envisioned all races as subject to a cycle of growth, miscegenation, and subsequent degeneracy, a pattern that determines the outcomes of wars and the fates of empires. Slotkin notes Cooper's peculiar "Aryanization of the Mohicans," a myth that envisions the Mohicans as the grandfather race, diminished in power and feminized by intermarriages with other tribes, and supposes that Cooper borrows this idea from Joseph Heckewelder, whose *History, Manners, and Customs of the Indian Nations* (1819) posited an original race of Indians, a "first people." From European racial theory Cooper borrows the parallel notion of a proto-European race, as Slotkin says, "morally and genetically purer than their technologically more advanced descendants ... diminished in number or quality by intermarriage or the vicissitudes of war and disease." According to Slotkin, Cooper's aim is "to unite the fragmentary history of the Indians into a single story of origin, rise to grandeur, intermarriage, decline, and fall ... prefiguring the cycle of civilizational rise and fall that was a major concept of contemporary historiography."[19] As Cooper more explicitly identifies mongrelization as the catalyst of decline, hybridity becomes more explicitly identified with degeneracy in *The Last of the Mohicans* than it does in Child's or Sedgwick's novels.

Less immediately obvious than Cooper's insistence on racial separation and almost wholly ignored by scholars is the gothic language with which he articulates these theories of racial degeneracy. Although contemporary scholarship does not regard *The Last of the Mohicans* as part of the transatlantic gothic tradition, early reviewers found clear continuity between Cooper and his gothic predecessors. W. H. Gardiner notes Cooper's affinity with established gothic writers, praising him for "the same sort of magical authority over the spirit of romance, which belongs in common to Scott, Radcliffe, Walpole, and our countryman Brown." Four months earlier, in the March 1826 *New York Review and Atheneum*, an anonymous reviewer similarly praises *The Last of the Mohicans* for its invocation of gothic phantasms:

> We are carried onward, as through vision of a long and feverish dream. . . . We are borne through strange and fearful, and even agonizing scenes of doubt, surprise, danger, and sudden deliverance; while, like some persecuting daemon of slumber, the fiendlike image of a revengeful spirit scowls everywhere, and haunts the powerless fancy. . . . And, as in the changes of an uneasy dream, the monarch Reason sometimes lifts up its head, and suggests that it all is an illusion, a wholesome council which the soul assents to, but is yet dragged away by the irresistible power, which hurries it into new fantastic perplexities.[20]

These reviewers' assessments of Cooper's novel indicate that some historical romances were tinged by recognizably gothic images. Closer attention to these images reveals their connection to the fears of racial blending widespread in the decade before Removal, of the curses brought by past sins, and of the catastrophes future transgressions would bring. Unlike Child, who more flagrantly teased the national imagination with her portrayal of intimacy between a white woman and an

19. Slotkin, introduction, xxiii. For a more extensive discussion of this theory of "degenerationism" in the context of the European intellectual tradition, see Stocking, *Victorian Anthropology*, chapter 1.

20. Reviews reprinted in George Dekker and John P. McWilliams, eds., *Fenimore Cooper: The Critical Heritage*, 105–6, 90.

Indian man, Cooper, though he raises the specter, compulsively dispels it with threats of apocalyptic violence.

We find within Cooper's work a narrative pattern that juxtaposes fitful meditations on racial mixing with images of grotesque violence, a revision of the same unreason that characterizes Edgar Huntly's frenzied descent into barbarism. These striking convulsions in the novel's meandering plot are linked directly to revelations about Cora's mixed African descent or her potential union with Uncas. In the hours preceding the attack at Glenn's Falls, in impenetrably dark caverns reminiscent of Brown's Norwalk, the doomed romance between Cora and Uncas begins to flower. Lavishing attention on Cora, Uncas's "dark eye lingered on her rich, speaking, countenance," but just as Cooper suggests the possibility of a union, he reminds the reader that "nature has made an impenetrable barrier," both in the roaring cataract that bars their escape and in the blood now rising within them (*LM,* 56, 60). Although the narrative momentarily alternates toward the possibility of miscegenation, Cooper quickly mends the fracture by affirming the naturally determined difference between the two. As his desire for the white man's daughter simmers in the darkness of the cave, the noble Uncas momentarily transforms into a dark-eyed, threatening presence vaguely kin to the rapacious Magua. Like the conflicted villain-hero of gothic romance who struggles against his own evil nature, Uncas's desire strains his nobility and wisdom. Meanwhile, the Huron enemies gather for attack, and Cooper renders the ensuing skirmish in bloody detail. After watching the first Mingo slip from a rock and fall shrieking into the abyss below the cataract, Hawk-eye and Uncas quickly shoot two more. The frontiersman draws his knife and grapples with another attacker, driving his "sharp weapon through his naked bosom to the heart," as Uncas nearly severs the hand of another Indian who is about to kill Heyward (*LM,* 71). Finally, Hawk-eye shoots and wounds the remaining attacker, who dangles from a tree in prolonged agony before plunging to his death.

Later, Colonel Munro's revelation of his affair with a slave and Cora's mixed parentage, the moment that marks the beginning of a decline in Cora, carries the plot toward the even more grisly episode of the Fort William Henry massacre. In the bloodiest scene of a bloody novel, maddened Hurons slaughter the defenseless evacuees of the fort. At the climax of the massacre, the Indians fall upon the corpses of women and children to inflict "furious blows long after their victims were beyond the power of their resentment" and "drink freely, exultingly, hellishly" of the blood flowing from the white bodies (*LM,* 176). Cooper depicts this Indian blood feast with more gleeful abandon than we find in Brown's posed image of Edgar Huntly lying with a slain Indian, wound pressed to wound, but both novels imagine the mingling of Indian and white blood as phantasmagoria. The massacre, immediately juxtaposed to Munro's shocking revelation, represents the clearest example of the convulsive reaction the specter of miscegenation prompts in Cooper's romance, ultimately signifying expiation for Munro's sin against nature, which condemns not only the people at the fort under Munro's care, but also Munro's own daughter, who cries to the benevolent chief Tamenund, "the curse of my ancestors has fallen heavily on their child!" (*LM,* 305).

Like Poe's women and, we will see, Mary Conant in *Hobomok* and Faith Leslie in *Hope Leslie,* Cora undergoes a physical and psychological decline under the burden of this curse. Her warm and wild robustness, her "rich, speaking, countenance," fades to a "death-like paleness" (*LM,* 56, 305). Her courage is transfused to her sister, who grows stronger and more resolved as Cora is drawn toward her inevitable death. Although Munro commits his sin with an African slave, the curse Cora must now bear manifests itself as Magua, the Huron who would take her to his wigwam. Having captured Heyward and the sisters following the massacre, Magua offers Cora the "horrid alternative" of becoming his wife or dying a torturous death with Alice and Heyward. Cora leaves the choice to Alice, who at first shrinks in fear but then responds with "deep, unconquerable disapprobation . . . 'No, no, no; better that we die, as we have lived, together!'" (*LM,* 110). Magua's ultimatum, repeated later in the novel as Magua holds Cora over the fatal precipice, represents a significant transition in the novel, as the dark sister, until now the more decisive and self-sufficient, reverses roles with the usually wilting Alice. Cora's deathlike state, her apparent resignation to her fate in the second part of the novel, resembles the imbecilic stupor we will witness in Mary Conant, as she surrenders herself to Hobomok, and in Faith Leslie, as she elopes with the Indian Oneco, a pattern associating miscegenation with the physical and psychological degeneration of vital white women.

Cooper ultimately emphasizes the folly of racial blending in the shared elegy of Cora and Uncas at the conclusion of the novel. The Indian mourners regret that the romance between the two had not ended differently and ask, "Why should not such a predilection [between and Indian man and a white woman] be encouraged! That she was of a blood purer and richer than the rest of her nation, any eye might have seen" (*LM*, 343). When in the course of this lamentation the mourners promise a union between Uncas and Cora in the "blessed hunting ground of the Lenape" or in the "Heaven of the pale-faces," Hawk-eye "shook his head, like one who knew the error of their simple creed," denying miscegenation in life and in death (*LM*, 344). Munro bids the scout to have hope for a "time . . . when we may assemble . . . without the distinction of sex, rank, or colour" around the throne of "the Being we all worship, under different names," but Hawk-eye refuses to perpetuate the happy illusion: "To tell them this . . . would be to tell them that the snows come not in the winter" (*LM*, 347). This grim conclusion shrinks not only from Child's introduction of a mixed-blood love child in *Hobomok* but even from Jefferson's more abstract metaphor of America as a marriage of races. Munro's hope for an egalitarian, amalgamated future, which echoes Jefferson's promise to the fading Algonquians, now appears the delusion of a deeply aggrieved father, quickly dispelled by the pragmatic philosopher-warrior Hawk-eye, who represents the voice of the future and the argument for Removal. As polygenist and positivist anthropologists throughout the nineteenth century would proclaim biologically determined differences between the Indian and white races, Hawk-eye emphasizes that separation is writ in nature, and that the Indian race must wilt before the Anglo-Saxon advance as surely as Cora fades before Alice and summer passes to winter.

Hope Leslie

Catharine Maria Sedgwick was inspired to publish *Hope Leslie* in 1827 partly by the success of *The Last of the Mohicans* and partly by the story of her own ancestor, Eunice Williams, captured by Indians as a child in

1704. Williams was adopted and raised by her captors, bore two children with her Indian husband, and, even after returning with them to live among her white family in Massachusetts, continued to wear Indian clothing and slept in an Indian lodge within sight of puzzled townsfolk. As Cooper repudiates the nation's history of interracial intimacy with the same shock that the gothic novel purged Europe's feudal past, Sedgwick similarly revises her family history by portraying the marriage between Faith Leslie and the Indian prince Oneco as infertile.

Although Sedgwick's novel follows *Hobomok* and *The Last of the Mohicans* chronologically, it stands somewhere between them ideologically. While *Hope Leslie* does not include a mixed-blood character in its pageant of national ascendance, it seems at least to entertain the possibility of the alternative, hybrid genealogy imagined by Rowson. In addition to the successful romance between Hope Leslie and Everell Fletcher, Sedgwick considers two other permutations in the pairing of Everell with the Indian maiden Magawisca and of Faith with Oneco. But in its ultimate portrayal of these interracial romances as degenerate or simply unwise, Sedgwick's fiction remains compatible with polygenism and Cooper's prophecies of Indian extinction. Following her intimacy with an Indian man, Faith Leslie, like Cora before Magua, falls into a weakened and insensate condition, the wage of incest in the gothic novel and of miscegenation in gothic-historical romance. And like the impossible romance of Cora and Uncas, the potential attraction between Everell and Magawisca falters before the lovers' better judgment and, for insurance, is snuffed by spectacular violence before it can grow and bear bad fruit.

The courtship of Faith and Oneco, the first of the two Indian-white romances Sedgwick portrays, emphasizes certain deficiencies in both characters. As a child, Faith is "petted . . . wayward and bashful" (*HL*, 29), repelled rather than warmed by the caresses of her adoptive father. Oneco is similarly childlike, "giving not one thought to the past, and not one care to the future" (*HL*, 34), and seemingly unworthy of his high birth. Already fated to be together in the imagination of the reader, Faith and Oneco appear from the beginning as ignoble and unnaturally stunted compared to their respective sisters, Hope and Magawisca. In a letter to her husband, Martha Fletcher writes of her misgivings about Faith's character: "a spoiled child is she, and it seemeth a pity that the name of Faith was given to her, since her shrinking timid character doth not promise in any manner, to resemble that most potent of the Christian graces" (*HL*, 34). The novel immediately connects her "shrinking timid character" to her affection for Oneco, who "hath always some charm to lure her waywardness" (*HL*, 34). Oneco also lacks the confidence of his father, Mononotto, who favors Magawisca and considers his son "volatile" and "unimpressive," with a "character [that] was unfit for his purpose" (*HL*, 203).

Faith's eventual marriage to Oneco leads to further psychological degeneration. On Digby's Island, Hope attempts to convince her sister to return to her white family. She is stunned when Faith resists and fails even to remember the English language or her bond to her sister. When Hope observes Faith's closeness with Oneco, "her heart died within her; a sickening feeling came over her, an unthought of revolting of nature" (*HL*, 237). She searches her sister's dull features for traces of remembrance but finds that Faith remains "passive . . . rather abashed and confounded" (*HL*, 238). Faith's only reply, "No speak Yengees," strengthens Hope's desperate and clumsy efforts to reclaim her from Oneco. She replaces Faith's Indian mantle with her own silk cloak, only to learn that "she does not like the English dress" (*HL*, 239). She reminds Faith of their shared childhood and their mother, but Magawisca, who translates for the sisters, tells Hope that these memories for Faith are "faint and distant, like the vanishing vapour on the far-off mountain" (*HL*, 239). Hope entreats Faith with diamond rings, but these baubles purchase "child-like delight" rather than the filial devotion Hope seeks. As Hope, "her cheek glowing with impassioned feeling," finally surrenders her sister to Oneco as she would surrender her to death, Faith appears inert, "pale and spiritless," her face barely "redeemed from absolute vacancy by an expression of gentleness and modesty" (*HL*, 240). In vivid contrast to her sister's robustness, Faith's degenerate, dull state results from her marriage to Oneco. Later, when Faith is temporarily rescued from her Indian husband, Hope has already resigned herself to the loss of her sister and finds nothing to excite affection for Faith, who has finally become dead to her, "spiritless, woe-begone—a soulless body—repelled, with sullen indifference, [by] all Hope's efforts to win her love" (*HL*, 359). The scene recalls the fading of Cora's vitality and forms part of the pattern in nationalist literature where interracial romances drain women of sense, reason, will, and life. Borrowing from both polygenist theory and gothic imagery of sin and social decay, miscegenation in the historical romance, while it cannot be ignored, produces a fracture in America's narrative of emergence, ambivalent moments of vacillation between madness and reason, death and life, Indian and white.

Women in the historical romance rise to maturity and heroism when they recognize and abide by this dialectical law of separation, when cowering Alice becomes unconquerable in the face of the horrid alternative, and when Magawisca throws herself on the executioner's block to save Everell. Sedgwick's initial description of Magawisca locates the "peculiar beauty of the young savage" in her "European" features and aristocratic bearing:

> [She] was tall for her years. . . . Her form was slender, flexible and graceful; and there was a freedom and loftiness in her movement which, though tempered with modesty, expressed a consciousness of high birth. Her face, although marked by the peculiarities of her race, was beautiful even to an European eye. . . . Her hair, contrary to the fashion of the Massachusetts Indians, was parted on her forehead. . . . The mantle and her straight short petticoat or kilt of the same rare and costly material, had been obtained, probably, from the English traders. . . . Stockings were an unknown luxury, but leggins, similar to those worn by the ladies of Queen Elizabeth's court, were no bad substitute. . . . The apparel of this daughter of a chieftain . . . harmonized well with the noble demeanor. (*HL,* 23)

This blend of nubility and nobility, characteristic of native girls since English audiences were first allured by stories of Pocahontas, is, however, stripped from Magawisca at the moment that her love for Everell is fully revealed. When her arm is severed in a sacrifice that would spare Everell's life, he "threw his arms around her and pressed her to his heart," not as the unspoken love she had been until now but rather "as he would a sister," firmly and briefly, before he leaves her for dead and without pause rushes to the freedom she has gained for him (*HL,* 97). Everell later realizes that his affection for Magawisca was impetuous if not unnatural. When Digby tells his young master that he had once imagined him "mated" with the "tawny Indian," Everell confesses, "Yes, Digby, I might have loved her," but only "before she had done the heroic deed, to which I owe my life" and only if he had "forgotten that nature had put barriers between us" (*HL*, 224). Digby suggests that "things would have naturally taken another course," that Everell's love for Hope would have naturally eclipsed his feeling for Magawisca, and that, with Hope replacing the Indian girl, "all is as it should be; as your mother—blessed be her memory—would have wished, and your father, and all the world" (*HL*, 224).

Everell and Magawisca, in their recognition of these natural barriers, represent a contrast to Faith and Oneco, who, contrary to the better senses of both white and Indian societies, indulge their unnatural desire. Everell's rejection of Magawisca and his subsequent paring with Hope replicates the second volume of *Reuben and Rachel*, where Reuben leaves the half-breed Eumea for a well-bred English girl. As Rowson seems to compromise the Edenic match between Indian and white that she portrays in her first volume, Sedgwick likewise suggests that a marriage of races would bear no fruit. Everell and Magawisca grow into positions of power and responsibility within their respective communities, while Faith and Oneco become inconsequential, both in the plot of the romance and in the project of building the future republic.

In these opposing romances then, *Hope Leslie* offers alternating narratives: in Fiedler's terms, a story of love and a story of terror, one of nostalgia and one of repudiation, two narratives irreversibly severed when the Indian axe severs the arm of Magawisca, who is instantly transformed from the white man's potential lover to another vanishing Indian. This ideological doubleness causes scholars to find inconsistency in Sedgwick's novel, as William Scheick likewise finds discrepancies between the first and second volumes of *Reuben and Rachel*. Carolyn Karcher, for example, believes that "Sedgwick deserves credit for exploring an alternative most other novelists had shunned" but concludes that "the possibility that Faith and Oneco incarnate, [Sedgwick] intimates, is barren for America's future." Maria Karafilis finds Sedgwick's novel "both subversive of and complicit in conquest," a text that "disrupts the notion of a homogeneous nation yet seeks to consolidate a national literature." Douglas Ford detects a similar "dissatisfaction" in the novel "with the existing discourse available for the representation of Native

Americans, as well as a difficulty of creating a place outside it."[21] Each of these readers apprehends a mixed message in the novel but may only describe this discursive middle ground dialectically, as a contradiction between two opposing discourses and never as a synthesis.

The historical romance itself presents a problematic contradiction in its attempt to reconcile national myths of equality, democracy, and cooperation, with principles of racial separation and exclusion, a dilemma inherited from Jefferson and his address to the Algonquians. To those Indians who were promised a fruitful partnership with their white neighbors yet faced imminent dispossession, Jefferson must have seemed a Great Father who embraced his children with one arm and cast them away with the other. The novels of Jefferson's heirs register this uncertainty about the marriage of races in images of gothic duality: sinister abductors in the guise of lovers; witty, willful heroines seized by cataleptic madness; marriages that cannot be consummated. Like Jefferson, Sedgwick asserts in her preface that "the difference of character among the various races of the earth, arises mainly from difference of condition" (*HL,* 4), setting herself in direct opposition to the polygenist idea of natural repugnance and the subsequent generations of positivist anthropologists who would assume a biological basis for racial difference. Yet the derangement and pallor we see in Faith clearly represents the imagined degenerative consequences that intermarriage would have for the burgeoning empire, an "embryonic power," in Sedgwick's words, still threatened from within by the dark races and the unstable, antithetical forces they embody. *Hope Leslie* seems capable of accepting miscegenation on an intellectual level and in this sense represents, as Karcher says, a counterpoint to *The Last of the Mohicans.* But the novel shrinks from miscegenation on an experiential level as Hope shrinks from the sight of Faith with Oneco. While Sedgwick sees nothing wrong with marrying an Indian, she probably would not want her sister marrying one, and she surely would not marry one herself.

Although American fiction would not fully reconcile these contradictions until the twentieth century, with the reversal of the scientific

21. Karcher, introduction to *Hope Leslie,* xxii, xxiii; Maria Karafilis, "Catherine Maria Sedgwick's *Hope Leslie:* The Crisis between Ethical Political Action and U.S. Literary Nationalism in the New Republic," 342; Douglas Ford, "Inscribing the 'Impartial Observer' in Sedgwick's *Hope Leslie,*" 90.

understanding of tribal culture as unevolved and the advent of the modern understanding of the Indian as a cultural rather than a biological entity, Lydia Maria Child, Sedgwick's contemporary, ventured closer to an understanding of hybridity as simultaneity than any of her contemporaries.

Hobomok

The first three quarters of *Hobomok* appear, as some critics have argued, to be a spirited attack on male tyranny in the form of a secret, subversive alliance between Mary Conant and the Indian Hobomok against Puritan authorities. The novel, however, takes a different turn following the presumed death of Mary's true love, Englishman Charles Brown, when Child's brash heroine sinks quickly into a "bewilderment of despair that almost amounted to insanity," a "derangement of...[her] faculties." She retreats to the cemetery, both to weep at her mother's grave and to lay her head down on the "cold sod, in hopes it would cool the burning agony of her brain." In this death of reason, this "chaos in Mary's mind...which was rapidly darkening into misery," Hobomok seems to carry Mary into the underworld. Through her grief and, as she later believes, through "the effect of witchcraft on his [Hobomok's] part," Mary becomes "insensible...broken and confused," and finally wilts before the Indian: "I will be your wife, Hobomok" (*H*, 120–21).

Child offers in this scene an American version of the European gothic paradigm, where the innocent maiden succumbs to the dark machinations of a hero, who in her moment of crisis becomes a villain and abductor. Child does not demonize the noble Hobomok as Brown demonizes the hulking savages of *Edgar Huntly* and Cooper demonizes Magua, but she suggests that the Indian lover takes advantage of Mary "in the desolation of the moment" (*H*, 121). Mary's dreamlike insensibility during her three-year marriage to Hobomok casts the Indian as incubus, preying on a woman who, in her "stupefied state," is unable to resist (*H*, 135). Although Karcher and other critics find in Mary's flirtation with paganism a repudiation of Puritan patriarchy, her moonlit elopement with Hobomok offers no evidence of female empowerment. In fact, Mary is "melancholy...half-bewildered" (*H*, 123, 124) and drained of the irrepressible will that has characterized her throughout the novel. The scene resembles an abduction rather than an elopement, as the Indian, suddenly stripped of his previous nobility as Mary is of her will, assumes the aspect of a "dark chieftain . . . exulting in his prize" (*H*, 123). No longer is Hobomok "identified with the English" as he formerly was (*H*, 31). At the moment of this supreme transgression against his white allies, the primal taboo in nationalist romance, the "contrast of their countenances," becomes quite apparent, the "dark chieftain" wearing an "expression of gladness," his "prize" mute, "wretched," as "pale and motionless as a being from another world" (*H*, 123).

The scene uniquely blends Indian captivity narrative with a gothic abduction scene, and the destination of Mary's boat ride is not only despoilment but a kind of death. Child emphasizes that Mary's union with Hobomok is not an empowering act of will but rather the tragic consequence of the collapse of her will. Even as she elopes with the Indian, her few conscious words summon the spirit of her late true love, Charles, to forgive her before she slips into "mournful and incoherent" soliloquies on the forest path toward the Indian village (*H*, 123). Hobomok observes in Mary's condition the same "dreadful ruins of mind" (*H*, 123), presumably caused by drink, among the women of his own tribe, and both he and his mother fear that she is insane. Yet these fears only prompt Hobomok to hurry the marriage ceremony in the more pressing apprehension that Mary would return to her senses and "shrink from the strange nuptials" (*H*, 124). In the ensuing ceremony, performed quickly and in the "Indian form," Mary remains "listless and unmoved, apparently unconscious of any change in her situation," yet she does not fail to remember Charles, presumed gone, in her vow to Hobomok—"I love him [Hobomok] better than anyone living"—and undermine her vows to the Indian by covertly affirming her greater and more natural bond to her white lover, whom she thinks dead (*H*, 125).

The authoritarian Puritan fathers Mary has battled throughout the novel regain credibility in their opposition to Mary's marriage to the Indian. Bigoted and blind in every other instance, Mary's father justly assesses Mary's motivation for running away with Hobomok. In his pleading letters to her, he accepts that she was "bereaved of reason . . . not . . . in her right mind," and "in a moment of derangement" when she fled with Hobomok (*H*, 133, 136). For weeks, Mary continues in this semiconscious state: "She would lie through the livelong day, unless she was requested to rise; and once risen, nothing could induce her to change her posture" (*H*, 135). As she slowly awakens to a sense of her situation, her mistake becomes bitterly obvious. Though she grows in her affection for her Indian husband, his inferiority to the absent Charles grows clearer. Her reason revived, she becomes once again conscious of the opinions of the Puritans, who judge her "lost and degraded" (*H*, 135). She is unable to deny these charges, answering her father's letters contritely and hinting at "the deplorable state of mind which had led her to this extremity" (*H*, 136).

In spite of this gradual change of heart and the assurances from her father that her Indian marriage is unlawful and invalid, Mary feels that she is bound to Hobomok by the mournful circumstance of her newborn, half-breed son. Child's reviewers at the *North American Review* were likewise troubled by this stunning turn of the plot. In July 1824, the magazine praised *Hobomok* for its dramatic use of "American material," but concentrates more closely on Child's portrayal of miscegenation, condemning Mary's union with Hobomok and the birth of "the infant semisavage" as "not only unnatural, but revolting...to every feeling of delicacy in man or woman."[22] Child likely anticipated this reception, for she was careful to show her readers that Mary's decision to give herself to Hobomok is influenced by witchcraft and insanity. At the same time, her revelation of an Indian-white sexual relationship is revolutionary, gesturing toward an understanding of racial synthesis that escapes Jefferson and Brown and exploding this primal taboo in the literature of the early republic.[23] Mary Jemison's narrative, which appeared in the same year as *Hobomok*, as well as later frontier stories,

22. Mills, *Cultural Reformations*, 12.
23. In addition to Mary Conant's child, a few other mixed-bloods appear in the historical romance tradition, but these references were not as widely disseminated as Child's novel. For example, in Cooper's *The Wept of Wish-ton-Wish* (1829), Ruth, a white girl, is captured by Indians and quickly married to a sachem. When Puritans execute her Indian husband, Ruth herself expires in shock and dies, leaving her languishing child unattended. The infant's fate remains uncertain even in the novel's conclusion, when all the other open questions are hastily resolved. Another notable omission from my discussion here is John Neal's *Rachael Dyer* (1828), a novel set in Puritan times. George Burroughs, Neal's mixed-blood character, embodies the conflict between Old World civilization and New World nature, white reason and Indian instinct. Burroughs struggles to balance these forces within himself as Puritan society similarly weighs reason against superstition during the witch craze.

such as Stephens's *Malaeska*, Jackson's *Ramona*, and Walter Edmonds's Dygartsbush series, portray the birth of a half-Indian child as the final, irreversible severance between white society and a white woman adopted by Indians. The mixed-blood's appearance in this novel calculated to please critical tastes thus represents one of the most curious and controversial moments in early nationalist fiction.

In contrast to more foreboding readings of Cooper's novels, Child's novel seems to scholars more progressive for this consideration of a mixed-birth and of miscegenation as an alternative to race war, but such a reading seems inconsistent with the conclusion of the novel, which seems to reinforce the old fear of racial union. When Charles Brown, more representative of America's future than Hobomok in Child's view, miraculously returns to Massachusetts, he reacts sensitively but predictably to news of Mary's motherhood: "Disappointed love, a sense of degradation, perhaps something of resentment, were all mingled in a dreadful chaos of agony, within the mind of the unfortunate young man" (*H*, 139).[24] Charles's return cues Hobomok's exit and abruptly ends the alliance between the white woman and the Indian. Mary now joins her proper ally, who, despite his Anglican leanings, will shortly build his house next to that of Mary's staunchly Puritan father and take his place among the patriarchal elite. Usurped, Hobomok occupies the familiar role of the Indian nobly sacrificing his life and progeny to the rightful claims of the whites. He stoically accepts that "Mary loves him [Charles] better than she does me.... The sacrifice must be made for her.... Hobomok will go far off among some of the red men in the west. They will dig him a grave, and Mary may sing the marriage song in the wigwam of the Englishman" (*H*, 139).

This conclusion undermines Karcher's reading of miscegenation as an alliance against patriarchy, and the predatory nature of Hobomok's marriage to Mary offers another understanding of the recurrent pairing in nationalist fiction of white women with Indian men.[25] In spite of its conscious attempt to distinguish itself from the European tradition, the historical romance inevitably remains bound to the European trope

24. For a parallel scene, see Edmonds's "Dygartsbush," published more than a century later and discussed in Chapter 3.
25. The opposite pairing of an Indian woman and a white man appears more frequently in the later nineteenth and twentieth centuries, especially in stories of

of the innocent maiden pursued by the degenerate villain, especially as it evokes gothic imagery to warn against the dangerous potential of racial blending. Child's vision of the United States as a peaceful amalgamation of races is ultimately dispelled as Charles Hobomok Conant, the mixed-blood offspring of Hobomok and Mary Conant, completely assimilates to white ways. "Little Hobomok," who in his childhood is a "fearless young Indian," transforms into Charles Conant, a "distinguished graduate at Cambridge" who passes as pure white (*H*, 148, 150). By the time he departs to finish his schooling in England, his "father was seldom spoke of; and by degrees his Indian appellation was silently omitted" (*H*, 150).

Child's characters, conceived as the forebears of the nation, waver like Bhabha's narratives of national identity between two conflicting selves. Mary, like Edgar Huntly, vacillates between reason and unreason, between resistance and obedience to Puritan patriarchy, and between her Indian lover and her white lover; Charles Brown vacillates between death and life; Hobomok vacillates between noble savage and gothic abductor; and the mixed-blood Charles Conant vacillates between Indian brave and Harvard fellow. In these tense alternations, *Hobomok* seems a fractured, hybrid narrative, yet for all of its wavering it finally settles into a racial singularity and discursive stasis. After Hobomok vanishes into the trackless west, Charles Brown, Mary Conant, and Charles Conant join Puritan society to begin the work of nation-building, revealing the novel's only constant: the narrative of fragile colonies that would grow into an empire.

Even with its conviction in America's racially homogeneous destiny, Child's novel is bolder than either *The Last of the Mohicans* or *Hope Leslie*, anticipating later narratives that adopt simultaneity rather than alternation as a model of hybrid consciousness. Though the prodigal daughter has returned to the City upon a Hill and her tribal marriage

---

the American mountain man. More directly confronted by the problems of westward expansion and the assimilation of the tribes, later frontier stories return to Jefferson's idea of a conquering white man taking a submissive Indian wife as a metaphor for civilization's mastery of the wilderness. See Whitman's *The Half-Breed* and Ellis's *The Half-Blood*, discussed in Chapter 2, and Hergesheimer's "Scarlet Ibis" in Chapter 3.

has been annulled, Mary experiences through her motherhood a transformation far more drastic than that of Cora Munro and Faith Leslie,
and one that cannot be reversed. And though Hobomok has faded into
the forests, young Charles has been whitewashed at Cambridge, and
Child herself has apologized to the *North American Review* for her
transgression against good taste, a disturbing and unspoken doubt
lingers. Even in its debt to polygenist theory, its gothic conjuring of
the madness brought by miscegenation, Child's novel, in the end, fails
to assure us of any unstained progeny or, like the novels of Rowson,
Cooper, and Sedgwick, to posit a white couple to safely insure against
the potentially dangerous consequences of the miscegenation experiment. Ultimately, it is Mary's union with the Indian, not the white man,
which bears fruit, and this narrative omission of a pure white half-brother
to Charles Conant itself constitutes a subtle undermining of the prevailing theory of diminishing fertility and hybrid degeneracy. Child
concludes her novel with a word of gratitude for the vanishing Hobomok, for the "tender slip which he protected, has since become a mighty
tree" (*H*, 150), but the meaning of "tender slip" remains ambiguous.
While scholars would most likely interpret the phrase as the Puritan
colony and commonly read in this final passage a nostalgic remembrance of a heroic past or a last affirmation of Anglo-Saxon ascendance,
there is yet another possibility that this seedling is rather Mary and
Hobomok's child. If the mixed-blood is indeed the scion of which this
final passage speaks, then something of the Indian persists not only in
Charles Conant but in his children, too, and in all their descendants,
and in the family tree of all New England. This horrible implication
that Indian blood might course the proudest Brahmin veins distinguishes
Child as the first to publicly imagine the unimaginable possibility that
we are all half-breeds.

    In her reading of Child's and Sedgwick's romances, Judith Fetterly
perhaps comes closest to "preserving the oxymoron," to maintaining in
her understanding of the novels that while their overtones might be
pedagogical, a performative undertone reverberates. Fetterly suggests
that the most useful way to approach miscegenation in *Hobomok* and
Hope Leslie is to avoid the polarized views that have dominated discussions of these texts, the "hagiography directly proportional to the

misogyny informing previous treatments of these [women] writers" on one hand; and the "critique that implicates these writers . . . in a variety of nineteenth-century racist, classist, and imperialist projects" on the other. Fetterly ultimately argues that the "entanglements" and "paradoxes" that we sense within the historical romance should not be rationalized as "one or the other." This approach, she believes, "tends to produce a false sense of coherence and to rationalize too readily what are clearly incompatible stories." Rather, these texts should be recovered as evidence for "an author willing to risk engagement with the actual mess of America in the effort to realize its potential."[26] While gothic contortions within these texts reveal an uneasiness with the racial dimension of this mess, Faith's decision to remain with Oneco and Mary Conant's unfortunate mixed-blood child resist the simple solution that separation would offer, representing one nation, one body, not racially unblemished, but blended and conflicted.

A Narrative of the Life of Mrs. Mary Jemison

Whether actually personified in *Hobomok* or only anticipated in the interracial romances of *The Last of the Mohicans* and *Hope Leslie*, the mixed-blood embodies the impossible contradiction with which Jefferson wrestled a generation earlier. As the Indian represents both vitality and degeneracy in the culture of the early republic, racial mixing represents both a necessity and a threat to the emerging national idea. Throughout the nineteenth and twentieth centuries, the historical romances and adventure tales attempt to resolve the contradiction by inventing a character unique to American literature: "the white Indian." Hope Leslie, Hawk-eye, and the legendary mountain men who become vanguards of civilization in later frontier tales adopt everything noble and valuable in the Indian character but remain racially pure and immune to the mental and physical degeneration depicted in romance heroines. For a long time, white Indians remained the only critically acceptable version of the half-breed. But, as Annette Kolodny observes,

26. Judith Fetterly, "'My Sister! My Sister!': The Rhetoric of Catherine Sedgwick's *Hope Leslie*," 492, 493, 514.

"if such were the heroes that white society would publicly take to its bosom, in private that same society wondered and gossiped about the others, those who had escaped 'into the Woods' and embraced Indian life to its fullest."[27]

One of these others who privately fascinated nineteenth-century society was Mary Jemison, an Irish immigrant to western Pennsylvania who, at age fifteen, was orphaned and captured by a Seneca raiding party in 1758. After spending her long life among the Indians, Jemison became a naturalized citizen of New York State and settled on a small farm on the Genesee River, where her story became local legend. In 1823, publisher James Bemis enlisted a country doctor, James Everett Seaver, to meet with Jemison and transcribe her life story, hoping to capitalize on local interest in the "White Woman of the Genesee." When it appeared in 1824, Seaver's *A Narrative of the Life of Mrs. Mary Jemison* sold more copies than Child's *Hobomok* and Cooper's *The Pioneers*, which both appeared in the same year, and further sales rivaled those of the most popular romances, including *The Last of the Mohicans* and *Hope Leslie*. Jemison's story, though commonly classified as a captivity narrative that bears little on Child's, Cooper's, and Sedgwick's romances, directly engages their discourse of nationalism and hybrid degeneracy. Set like the historical romance during the nascent era of the United States, the *Narrative* also represents the nightmare of a white woman borne away to an Indian wigwam, but in doing so detaches this situation from the contexts of gothic abduction narrative and polygenist theory. The Indians in Jemison's story do not vanish in a rhetorical flourish like Chingachgook and Magawisca, nor are her mixed-blood children whitewashed like Little Hobomok. Rather, they live and thrive in the space between cultures that the romance cannot comprehend, the space Louis Riel would later declare the independent nation of Métis. Testing the limitations of antebellum racial theory as well as the postcolonial concept of hybridity as an unstable, vacillating dialectic, Jemison's narrative conceives a national idea that does not recognize miscegenation as degenerative and represents a woman who is not alternately but simultaneously Indian and white.

27. Kolodny, *Land before Her*, 69.

From its first printing in 1824 to the turn of the twentieth century, the *Narrative* appeared in twenty new editions in the United States and England, but its meaning and the reasons for its considerable impact in nineteenth-century culture have remained in dispute. Richard Vanderbeets, for example, reads in the legend of the "White Woman of the Genesee" the archetypal story that characterizes all captivity narratives: "that of the Hero embarked upon the...journey of initiation." For Vanderbeets, the power of the *Narrative* derives from its message of trial and triumph, its extolling of a girl who, through more than sixty years of captivity, retains her essential whiteness, remembers the Christian prayers of her youth, and still speaks with a girlish Celtic lilt. On the other hand, Susan Walsh suggests that the *Narrative* is not an archetypal story of white heroism but rather an Indian autobiography steeped more in the "preliterate Seneca traditions of life-telling" than in "Western literary paradigms and interpretive protocols" that scholars such as Vanderbeets would impose upon it.[28]

Where Vanderbeets finds a story of a white woman among Indians who imprinted her with their culture, Walsh finds the story of an Indian woman among white editors who imprinted her story with their culture. In their difference we find an example of the broader questions of authenticity at the core of all hybrid texts, not only Jemison's *Narrative,* but also Apess's *A Son of the Forest,* Ridge's *Joaquín Murieta,* Mourning Dove's *Cogewea,* Mathews's *Sundown,* and Momaday's *House Made of Dawn:* Is the subject white or Indian? Is the discourse Western or Native? Vanderbeets, whose reading suggests that any authentic historical or ethnographic information in the *Narrative* has been effaced by Western mythical archetypes, anticipates Spivak's position that the subaltern subject is inevitably circumscribed by the dominant discourse. In her appeal to Arnold Krupat's description of Native American autobiographies as sites of intersection between subversive and dominant discourses, Walsh's reading recalls Bhabha's characterization of hybridity as a tense "alternation" between competing discourses, a "site of productive conflict." She finds in Jemison's story moments of Native authenticity that fracture the surface of the romantic paradigm and

28. Richard Vanderbeets, "The Indian Captivity Narrative as Ritual," 553; Susan Walsh, " 'With Them Was My Home': Native American Autobiography and *A Narrative of the Life of Mrs. Mary Jemison,*" 51, 67.

emerge in "places where the perspectives and agendas of subject and editor are in clearest conflict."[29]

But while these scholars' conclusions differ, their interpretive strategies have something in common. Each of these theoretical stances tends to essentialize Jemison as either white or Indian, to nudge her story from its ambivalent discursive ground toward a resolution of the contradictions woven throughout the text. In place of Vanderbeets's quest archetype, Walsh substitutes traditional Seneca "self-vindication narrative." This particular debate about the provenance of the *Narrative* inevitably returns us to more fundamental questions about authenticity and reminds us of Susan Scheckel's assessment of the Indian as a "cultural problem that no single text or logic seems capable of containing." The *Narrative* challenges readers, in Cheryl Walker's terms, to "preserve the oxymoron," to simultaneously hold in mind two mutually exclusive readings and abandon the theoretical assumption that one voice must exclude or compete with the other. June Namias gestures to this inconclusive and inclusive understanding of hybrid texts, claiming that the *Narrative* stands apart from *Hobomok* and *Hope Leslie* in "Jemison's ability to achieve what nineteenth-century American culture could not: an accommodation between two cultures...an ability to adapt with integrity."[30]

Much more than the historical romance, the *Narrative* opens itself to such a reading and invites us to think about race in a modern sense since it abandons the biological determinism that provided the foundation for myths of racial separation. During the nineteenth century, scientists—polygenists and monogenists alike—considered race a matter of blood and bone. The folk tradition named Jemison the "White Woman of the Genesee," emphasizing, like Vanderbeets's "heroic" reading of the *Narrative,* her persevering whiteness: though she was adopted by Indians, gave birth to Indian children, and commonly spoke the Iroquois tongue, Mary Jemison was yet a white woman. With the twentieth-century revaluation of race as a matter of language and culture, we have come to accept what nineteenth-century culture considered an insup-

29. Walsh, "'With Them,'" 51. See also Arnold Krupat, *For Those Who Come After: A Study of Native American Autobiography,* 33.

30. Walsh, "'With Them,'" 60; Scheckel, *Insistence of the Indian,* 7; June Namias, introduction to *A Narrative of the Life of Mrs. Mary Jemison,* 12.

portable contradiction: though she was born of white parents, had white skin, and spoke snips of lilting English, Mary Jemison was yet an Indian woman. This idea underlies Walsh's conclusion that Jemison "could not have lived as a Seneca for over sixty years without living within and through Native American oral traditions and without bringing Native American perspectives . . . to bear upon the life she narrated to Seaver,"[31] as well the Iroquois claiming of Jemison, even today, as "one of their own."[32] But in the *Narrative,* Jemison appears neither essentially white nor essentially Seneca, nor even alternately white and Indian like Faith Leslie and Mary Conant. She appears, rather, one who is simultaneously Indian and white, one who accommodates both cultures.

To understand the way the *Narrative,* though steeped in the romantic tradition, revises the discourse of degeneracy and moves toward this modern understanding of race, we must consider the crucial problem of scholarship on Jemison: her collaboration with Seaver. The message of accommodation that Namias senses in the *Narrative* was perhaps lost to Seaver himself, who intended to gain a large audience not by blurring cultural and racial boundaries, but rather by appealing to the expectations of an audience conditioned by the romance and, like the romance, presenting a readable and morally unambiguous message. In his preface to the first edition, Seaver writes:

> As books of this kind are sought and read with avidity, especially by children, and are well calculated to excite their attention, inform their understanding, and improve them in the art of reading, the greatest care has been observed to render the style easy, the language comprehensive, and the description natural. Prolixity has been studiously avoided. The line of distinction between virtue and vice has been rendered distinctly visible; and chastity of expression and sentiment have received due attention. . . . No circumstance has been intentionally exaggerated by the paintings of fancy, nor by fine flashes of rhetoric.[33]

31. Walsh, " 'With Them,' " 67.

32. June Namias, *White Captives: Gender and Ethnicity on the American Frontier,* 149.

33. James E. Seaver, *A Narrative of the Life of Mrs. Mary Jemison,* 50–51. Further citations will be made parenthetically with the abbreviation *NMJ.*

Considering Seaver's explicit editorializing, Kolodny explains what has become the prevailing understanding of the *Narrative* as a strictly mediated text fractured by Jemison's own, irrepressible, authentic voice: "To insure these *improving* effects, Seaver exploited all the racial assumptions of his era. . . . At times, it simply echoes the conventions of the earlier female captivity narratives or . . . the sentimental romances . . . [or the] standard Indian war narrative. But every now and then what seems authentically to have been Jemison's story breaks out of the molds to which Seaver and his backers would consign it."[34] The inconsistencies resulting from the tension between the text's incongruous didacticism and what Namias calls the "experiential texture," those moments identified by Walsh when the "agendas of subject and editor are in clearest conflict," most clearly reveal its relationship with the historical romance and its subtexts of hybrid degeneracy and gothic horror.

We find one of these apparent disjunctions between editor and subject in the chapter recounting the eventful life of Ebenezer Allen, a frontier rascal who fought beside the British during the Revolutionary War and during peacetime gained Indian wives and land through swindle and murder. The *Narrative* recalls a particularly brutal episode when Allen, acting as a Tory scout, encounters a family of settlers, beheads the husband, dashes an infant's skull on the doorjamb, and taunts the cowering mother by casting the tiny corpse into the fireplace (*NMJ*, 116–18). Allen's wanton cruelty, which borders the psychopathic, is rooted in the romance tradition that links Indianness with madness. Bonding himself to the Iroquois to wage war against the United States, Allen, like Edgar Huntly in his unconscious savage interlude, turns frenzied and bloodthirsty. In his *Pioneer History of the Holland Purchase* (1850), Orasamus Turner summarizes the popular idea of "Indian Allen," rendered savage even in his moniker, as a "desperado" who "warred against his own race, country, and color . . . [and] vied with his savage allies in deeds of cruelty and blood-shed."[35] Allen's spectacular violence indeed resembles Edgar's frenzied butchery of his five Indian enemies and the Hurons' slaughter of the refugees at Fort William

---

34. Kolodny, *Land before Her*, 72.
35. Turner quoted in Walsh, " 'With Them,' " 60.

Henry, scenes in which Shirley Samuels finds "miscegenation made visible . . . by killing."[36] Like Brown and Cooper, the *Narrative* relates this legendary cruelty as a warning against unnatural racial crossing, as Allen's warring against his own race parallels Edgar's temporary transformation into an unreasoning savage and Magua's desire for Cora. Another voice in the *Narrative*, however, tempers the gothic romantic idea that racial crossing engenders in whites social and psychological pathology. In spite of Allen's sensational crimes—his slaughter of an innocent white family and his more heinous transgressions of "warring against his own race" and taking numerous Indian wives—he does not draw upon himself a curse or cosmic retribution as we find in the romance tradition. Jemison protects him from British authorities when he has double-crossed his former allies, emphasizes his remorse for his wartime atrocities, and generally considers him both "moderate" and "innocent" (*NMJ*, 110–14). Here, Walsh says, we find dissonance between Seaver's voice, which condemns Allen as a white savage, and Jemison's own, which almost speaks of Allen as a compatriot in opposition to American aggression. From a Seneca point of view, Walsh explains, Allen is not a desperado but rather a renegade war chief whose "wartime violence does not completely criminalize the man" and whose résumé of violent acts, like those of other Seneca warriors, establishes "his claim to expertise and authority" within the tribe.[37] More simply, while Allen's actions would horrify Seaver and his white audience, they would otherwise seem courageous to Jemison and the Seneca.

A more significant complication of polygenist-romantic discourse occurs as Jemison describes her marriage to her first husband, Sheninjee, a Delaware, and the birth of her first son, Thomas. Prior to her marriage, Jemison accompanies two of her adopted Indian sisters on a trade excursion to Fort Pitt, where Mary, observing the commerce of the white people there, becomes homesick for her former life. "It was then," she says, "that my heart bounded to be liberated from the Indians and to be restored to my friends and my country" (*NMJ*, 80). When Mary continues to express an "unspeakable anxiety to go home with them

36. Shirley Samuels, "Generation through Violence: Cooper and the Making of Americans," 103–4.
37. Walsh, "'With Them,'" 57, 61.

[whites], and share in the blessings of civilization," her sisters insist upon her marriage to Sheninjee to cement her bond to the tribe (*NMJ*, 80–81). Jemison describes her first husband as "a noble man; elegant in his appearance; generous in his conduct; courageous in war; a friend to peace, and a great lover of justice.... Yet," Jemison remains aware, "Sheninjee was an Indian" (*NMJ*, 82). At this moment, where readers of more formulaic captivity narratives and historical romances would expect Jemison to affirm the values of civilization and, like Cora contemplating marriage to Magua, lament her unspeakable fate, she says instead, "the idea of spending my days with him, at first seemed perfectly irreconcilable to my feelings: but his good nature, generosity, tenderness, and friendship towards me, soon gained my affection; and, strange as it may seem, I loved him!" (*NMJ*, 82). Their love soon produces a child, Thomas, named for Jemison's father, and over the next few years Mary's anxiety to return to the settlements diminishes. "My family was there" with the Seneca, she says, and "with them was my home" (*NMJ*, 83). To confirm her resolve, Jemison later recounts her flight with her children from John Van Sice, a Dutch trader who bargains to redeem her, and her disobedience to a Seneca chief who would profit by her ransom (*NMJ*, 92–95). In contrast to Cora Munro, who chooses death over marriage to Magua, Jemison says she would rather die than return to the whites (*NMJ*, 93). Following the death of Sheninjee, a second marriage to the Seneca Hiokatoo, and the birth of six more children, the Seneca chiefs again offer Jemison the choice to stay or to leave. She decides to "spend the rest of my days with my Indian friends, and live with my family as I had heretofore done" (*NMJ*, 120).

This scene, repeated in the Puritans' successful attempt to redeem Mary Conant from Hobomok and in Hope Leslie's unsuccessful attempt to lure Faith from Oneco, dramatizes the chronic confusion in colonial and early national culture regarding white captives' voluntary rejection of white society and embrace of tribal life. But Jemison's resolution of this frequently rehearsed conflict differs significantly from romanticized resolutions. Within the discourse of degeneracy, a white girl who chooses the wigwam becomes, like Faith Leslie, the antithesis to the heroic Alice, who chooses death for herself and her sister rather than witness the horrid alternative. The romance interprets the unimaginable scenario as a consequence of a gothic curse or a mental debilitation. The *Narrative* places Jemison in a position where she faces the same choice as these romantic heroines, and while she prefers the society of Indians, the *Narrative* does not ascribe her attachment to the Seneca as a consequence of grief, madness, or witchcraft. Jemison's voluntary and reasonable affirmation of love for her Indian husband, one never made by Mary Conant or Faith Leslie, poses a radical challenge to the assumptions of natural repugnance between the races and the diminishing fertility of interracial unions. She embraces her Indian life and children consciously, willfully, and unafflicted by the derangement of the romance heroines.

Her children, similarly unafflicted by hybrid degeneracy, grow healthy and strong. Although she buries all three of her sons as victims of violence, she persistently claims that unfortunate circumstances rather than their degenerate nature have led to her family's ruin. Having witnessed her son John kill his brothers Thomas and Jesse in drunken quarrels and John himself murdered by two of his Indian friends, she painfully reflects: "The use of ardent spirits among the Indians...will ultimately produce their extermination.... [N]ot even the love of life will restrain an Indian from sipping the poison that he knows will destroy him. The voice of nature, the rebukes of reason, the advice of his parents, the expostulation of his friends, and the numerous instances of sudden death, are all insufficient to reclaim the Indian, who has once experienced the exhilarating and inebriating effects of spirits, from seeking his grave at the bottom of his bottle!" (*NMJ*, 84, 159). Like William Apess and mixed-blood writers later in the nineteenth and twentieth centuries, Jemison attributes Indian degradation not to biological degeneracy but rather to environmental obstacles such as alcohol and poverty. While her son John seems to foreshadow popular incarnations of the criminal, self-destructive half-breed in the dime novel, Jemison in her *Narrative* does not ascribe his mischief to congenital criminality or a hereditary incapacity to adjust to civilized life, as positivist anthropologists and opponents of assimilationist policy would later in the century.

Jemison, who lived long into her tenth decade, seems to have become stronger and sharper during her life among the Seneca. Seaver observes on first meeting her that she appears younger than her years, the "crimson of youth" in her face, the "light blue" of her eyes "little faded by age, and naturally brilliant and sparkling" (*NMJ*, 55). He marvels at her quickness of step, her effortless use of the English and Seneca languages, the depth and clarity of her recollections, and the passions these recollections awaken within her (*NMJ*, 56). She is neither bereaved of reason like Mary Conant nor dumb and spiritless like Faith Leslie. Concerning her mixed-blood children, however, Jemison seems to face the same sanctions as those women trapped in romance. Early in her life with the Seneca, Jemison realizes that her children, who would be met "as enemies" or with "cold indifference" by white society, forever prevent her return to white society (*NMJ*, 120).[38] But Jemison shows a double consciousness, a sense of her simultaneous existence as white and Indian, which sets her apart from the romance heroine and manifests itself in her understanding of the difference between the way white society sees her and the way she sees herself. She knows the white community judges her, like Mary Conant, "lost and degraded," but while Mary Conant abides by their judgment and writes contrite letters to her father, Mary Jemison abides by her children and makes no apologies. Like the polygenist discourse of the historical romance, the white community represented in the *Narrative* recognizes only two states of being, Indian or white, and banishes or whitewashes the mixed-blood children who cannot be reduced to these categories. Declining her redemption and keeping her children, Jemison refuses to accept the terms the white community has handed her. Although she remains with the Seneca, she cannot, like Faith Leslie or "Indian Allen," be simply dismissed as another unfortunate evolutionary throwback, a Christian who has sunk irrevocably into barbarism and become, in effect, Indian.

In Seaver's own description of Jemison at the conclusion of the *Narrative*, a place where scholars expect editor to eclipse subject, the boundaries between Jemison's two beings become even more blurred.

38. Walsh relates an unpublished anecdote circulating among Jemison's descendants as late as 1959. Following the death of Sheninjee, the story goes, Jemison took her four-year-old son, Thomas, and attempted to rejoin the white community. The villagers, however, demanded that she "get rid of the bronze brat." Dejected, she returned to the Seneca with her son and married Hiokatoo (ibid., 56).

At the end of her life, Jemison manages several thousand acres of land as a naturalized American citizen but plants and harvests corn in the Seneca way. She learns the Indian language with a felicity that amazes even her but repeats prayers learned in childhood so that she would not forget the language of her parents, a habit that may have earned her the Seneca name, *Dehgewanus,* or Two Voices Falling. Her clothing, according to Seaver's observation, combines "Indian fashion" with "old yankee style" (*NMJ,* 56–57). Her manner of speaking her life story to Seaver over the course of three days blends the Indian affectation of "peeping from under eye-brows" with a distinctly "Irish emphasis" in her tone (*NMJ,* 55–56). Her religious belief is that which is common to Seneca and Christian, "a future state, in which the good will be happy, and the bad miserable" (*NMJ,* 58). This final picture of Jemison does not show a person who has alternated uncertainly and uneasily between two selves, as the romance portrays white captives and post-colonial theory defines hybrid consciousness, but rather a person who has settled into a comfortable and independent equilibrium, a state of cultural and discursive simultaneity. In spite of the apparent editorial appeal to romantic conventions, Jemison may not be reduced to the dialectical categories established by romance. She is neither degraded captive nor stalwart white heroine, neither vanishing Indian nor mute "squaw" wife. She is not internally rent by two warring identities like Edgar Huntly, Cora Munro, and the rabble of renegade half-breeds in later frontier tales.

The moments of incongruity between the romantic and experiential tones in the *Narrative* frequently tempt readers to try to answer the riddle: Where does Seaver's *Narrative* end and Jemison's *Narrative* begin? A century later, readers of *Cogewea* would face an almost identical problem in Mourning Dove's collaboration with Lucullus McWhorter. In both cases, though, not only is it impossible to say with certainty who contributed what to the text, but also to attempt to do so replicates the racialist romantic impulse to identify the text as one or the other, to separate the white element from the Indian element. To focus solely on the negotiation between Jemison and Seaver obscures Jemison's negotiation with herself and limits our understanding of a synthetic document, not either Native or white, either authentic or inauthentic, either subversive or co-opted, but neither and both, independent and viable beyond the discourse of opposites. Without contradiction, Jemison abhors Ebenezer Allen and yet sympathizes with him, loves the Seneca and yet longs to return to the whites, regrets the birth of her children and yet glories in their accomplishments and grieves at their dying. As a cultural half-breed who defines herself as Seneca independent of her biology, Jemison anticipates the twentieth-century departure from racial positivism and the advent of modernist meditations on cultural hybridity by John Joseph Mathews and Oliver LaFarge. Her *Narrative* emerges, then, as an important intervention in the long development of American racial thought that continues even now, assuming proportions larger than any single genre can contain. Neither the last great white captivity narrative, as Namias has it, nor, as Walsh has it, the first Native American autobiography, the *Narrative,* like Riel's Métis, embodies opposites but forms a whole that is somehow greater than the sum of its two opposing parts.

William Apess and the Children of Adam

Part red, part white, part black, reared as an Indian, bonded as a Negro, and educated as a Yankee, Apess contained multitudes in a way that even Whitman could not. He claimed to be three-quarters Pequot, a descendant of King Philip, yet this itinerant and unruly boy seems as like to Cooper's messianic Uncas as Mary Jemison is to Alice Munro. With his publication of *A Son of the Forest,* a blend of Protestant conversion narrative, autobiography, and racial manifesto, Apess, according to Arnold Krupat and Barry O'Connell, invented the Indian autobiography. For later Native writers and Apess himself, O'Connell explains, the exercise of writing one's life for a white audience "entailed being represented as in an intermediate state, a location where one was neither Native nor Euro-American but someone, at best, on the edge of either degeneracy or complete assimilation." Krupat likewise finds Apess's writing exemplary of a "hybridized" language, "the textual equivalent of the 'frontier,' as the discursive ground on which two extremely different cultures met and interacted." In *The Voice in the Margin,* Krupat discusses Apess's writing as an example of the "dialogism" that characterizes much Indian writing, a discourse that mediates between the Native writer's competing, seeming incompatible Native and Anglo voices.[39] In Krupat's view, which recalls Bhabha's definition of hybridity as a state of alternation between two competing voices, Apess searches for the seemingly nonexistent middle ground between the degenerate Magua and the assimilated Charles Conant, alternately suppressing one or the other as he attempts to speak in the language he also struggles to contest. But Apess's description of his experience as a mixed-blood suggests the inadequacy of the dialectical terms that scholars such as O'Connell and Krupat commonly apply: assimilation or degeneracy, authentic or inauthentic. Apess's autobiography, like Jemison's *Narrative,* demonstrates that the most useful way to understand ideas of hybridity in these texts involves a synthesis of contradictions without trying to fully resolve them.

Two seemingly incompatible but coexisting discourses appear even in the structure of *A Son of the Forest,* a book, in its final edition, divided into two parts: a narrative detailing Apess's youthful misadventures, spiritual struggles, and eventual ordination as a Methodist preacher, where he adopts many of the accepted conventions of traditional Protestant conversion narrative; and an appendix, nearly as long as the autobiography itself, where he contests Christian racial ideology by affirming Indians' place among God's children. Had Apess used a white amanuensis in composing *A Son of the Forest,* scholars would undoubtedly emphasize the editorial, inauthentic character of the first part. Apess, however, has no intrusive white partner like James Seaver or Lucullus McWhorter to whom we might attribute the more suspicious non-Native voice in this dialogic text. His writing thus presents a greater

39. O'Connell, introduction to *On Our Own Ground,* xli; Arnold Krupat, introduction to *Native American Autobiography: An Anthology,* 4; Arnold Krupat, *The Voice in the Margin: Native American Literature and the Canon,* 143–49. Several Indians, most notably the Mohegan Samson Occom (1768), had previously written short autobiographical accounts, but these were not published until the twentieth century. Catherine Brown's *Memoir of a Christian Indian of the Cherokee Nation* (1824), Jemison's *Narrative,* and later "as-told-to" autobiographies by Black Hawk (1833), Peter Jones (1841), and Sarah Winnemuca (1883) relied on a white amanuensis. O'Connell rejects the theory that *A Son of the Forest* was edited or ghostwritten by Lydia Maria Child or William Joseph Snelling, pointing to the text's originality, its departure from the formal structures that characterize the work of professional writers, and, more importantly, the palpable tension as Apess struggles to work with the "ideological script" he seeks also to undermine (O'Connell, introduction to *On Our Own Ground,* xliii).

difficulty than either the historical romance or Jemison's *Narrative* in that it does not easily submit to the scholarly exercise of dividing its authentic and inauthentic elements, its pedagogical and performative voices, and seems finally to represent a hybrid discourse that is not dialectic but synthetic.

Despite the ostensible differences in their ideological tenor, both sections make a concerted intervention into the debates concerning hybrid degeneracy and Indian Removal. Even in the conversion narrative, that part of Apess's autobiography that seems most constrained by the expectations of his Methodist audience, we find a synthesis of white and Native voices. Apess does not attempt to hide the events of his own dissipated youth, his disobedience of various masters, his petty crimes, or his drunkenness, and while he relates these events according to the formula of the conversion narrative, he breaks from convention to show by his own example that the degeneracy of Indians derives not from natural inferiority, but from the hostile circumstances confronting an "Indian dog" living in white society. Like Jemison, he condemns whites' introduction of alcohol to the Indians as the primary reason for their decline, attributing the "cruel and unnatural conduct" of his Indian grandparents who nearly beat him to death to "that bane of comfort and happiness . . . that curse to individuals, to families, to communities, to the nation."[40] In addition to alcohol, Apess cites the racially motivated violence of whites as another reason for Indians' apparent criminality. He leaves school not because he is unable to learn, but because he is beaten and derided by his teachers and, at the age of fifteen, runs away from his lawful master William Williams to escape severe abuse at the hands of a chambermaid (*SF*, 11–12, 22).

Like Jemison, Apess demonstrates a double consciousness, highly aware that white readers will likely perceive his early mischief as the natural peculiarity of the mixed-blood, a consequence of bad breeding. Attributing his personal sinfulness to racism, Apess's conversion narrative is simultaneously a protest document. His schoolmasters, he points out, frequently blame him for others' misdeeds because he is part Indian (*SF*, 12). As he marches toward the battles of Montreal and Lake

40. Apess, *On Our Own Ground*, 7, 47. Further citations of *A Son of the Forest* will be made parenthetically with the abbreviation *SF*.

Champlain, he is wounded by the slurs of his fellow militiamen, whom he had considered his brothers in arms (*SF,* 27). After he is discharged from military service, he believes that the government denies his pension because he is Indian and later claims that his initial request to be ordained in the Methodist congregation is rejected because he is Indian (*SF,* 31, 51). Apess's sensitivity to racism had been conditioned since his youth, when his white guardians attempted to educate him as a white. As the most revealing evidence of his divided consciousness, Apess recounts his childhood meeting with several dark-skinned women while picking berries in the forest. Filled with terror, he runs home as "his imagination had pictured out a tale of blood . . . the many stories I had heard of their [Indians'] cruelty toward the whites—how they were in the habit of killing and scalping men, women, and children." Only when Apess reflects on this encounter as an adult does he realize that "the whites did not tell me that they were in the great majority of instances the aggressors" and that if they "told me how cruel they had been to the 'poor Indian,' I should have apprehended as much harm from them" (*SF,* 10–11). While he is susceptible to sinning like any Christian, Apess modifies traditional conversion narrative by laying the blame on society in addition to himself.

Apess extrapolates his personal experience into the wider political realm. As he attributes his misdeeds more to whites who have wronged him than to his own evil nature, he likewise attributes the degeneracy of Indians as a whole on white depredations. He writes, "a most sweeping charge has been brought against the natives . . . that they are not susceptible of improvement; now, subsequent facts have proved that this assertion is false" (*SF,* 33–34). In his appendix, he affirms more definitely, "the mental qualities of the [Native] Americans are not in the least inferior to those of the Europeans. . . . We form our opinions of the Indian character from the miserable hordes that infest our frontiers" (*SF,* 61). Apess further contrasts these "miserable hordes" to Indian reservations near Montreal, comparatively isolated from white influence, where he finds "the utmost order," and he concludes that those Indians more directly influenced by white civilization are "degenerate beings, enfeebled by the vices of society, without being benefited by its arts of living. . . . No allowance is made for the difference of circumstances, and the operations of principles under which they have been educated" (*SF*, 61, 62). Apess's argument that circumstance and not nature fosters racial degeneracy—the same that Jefferson ventures in *Notes on the State of Virginia*—provides a foundation for Indian policy debates throughout the later nineteenth and twentieth centuries. Supporters of Allotment who sought to redeem the Indian through the imposition of white economic practices upon tribal society would rely on the belief, as Apess suggests here, that an improvement of condition would lead to an improvement of the race, that the Indian is certainly "susceptible of improvement," given the proper government intervention.

More immediately, Apess challenges the view, implicit in Removal, that Indian tribes suffered to remain within the borders of the United States would threaten racial purity and consequently cause the premature decline of the burgeoning empire. In his essay "An Indian's Looking-Glass for the White Man," Apess questions the logic of the Massachusetts antimiscegenation law. Since interracial marriage has come "into fashion," he suggests, and mixed-bloods can be found everywhere, why should authorities so diligently and foolishly try to decry and deny their existence? The question exemplifies the dilemma that continually dogged proponents of natural repugnance and diminishing fertility. As Robert Young expresses it in *Colonial Desire*, "if interbreeding among the races is so repugnant, and inter-racial sex so abhorrent, this leaves...the problem of explaining why the mixed-race population of the United States existed at all, let alone in such vast numbers."[41] Apess writes, "intermarriages...would be nothing strange or new to me; for I can assure you that I know a great many that have intermarried, both of the whites and the Indians—and many are their sons and daughters and people, too, of the first respectability." He concludes by criticizing the Massachusetts law that levies a fifty-pound fine on any church or state official who marries an Indian and a white, arguing against polygenism that such marriages rather "encourage the laws of God and nature by a legitimate union." He protests:

> I do not wonder that you blush, many of you, while you read; for many have broken the ill-fated laws made by man to hedge upon the

41. Young, *Colonial Desire*, 15.

laws of God and nature. I would ask if they who made the law have not broken it.... For I think that I or any of my brethren have the right to choose a wife for themselves as well as the whites—and as the whites have taken the liberty to choose my brethren, the Indians, hundreds and thousands of them, as partners in life, I believe the Indians have as much right to choose their partners among the whites if they wish.[42]

In spite of the efforts of the historical romance to erase the mixed-blood from the rewritten past and yet-to-be-written future of the new nation, Apess proclaims what Alice Munro, in her horror, could not bear to hear, that hundreds and thousands of Indians and whites have become partners in life, not by insanity or curse, nor by force or captivity, but, like Mary Jemison, by their own liberty. Recognizing that the amalgamation of races reveals a contradiction between the ideals and practices of Christian democracy, he invokes the right to individual liberty and the laws of God while simultaneously attacking the separatism these ideals and laws had come to justify.

In order to support his claim for the natural goodness of mixed marriage, Apess invokes a popular idea of Indian origin that would establish a common lineage of the white and Indian races and undermine the argument for polygenism and hybrid degeneracy. Assembling an exhaustive catalog of cultural and linguistic parallels between the Indians and the Jews, from jewelry design and purification rituals to names and myth patterns, Apess traces the probable migration of Semitic tribes across the Bering land bridge and grandly concludes that he and his "Native brethren" are "none other than the descendants of Jacob and the long lost tribes of Israel" (*SF,* 74). Proving a connection between the Jews and the Indians enables Apess to rationalize Indian suffering as the continuing punishment for the "heinous transgressions" of the ten tribes chronicled in the Old Testament but also to maintain his hope that the Indians "have not been altogether forsaken and will hereafter appear to have been, in all their dispersions and wanderings, the subjects of God's divine protection and gracious care" (*SF,* 53). Apess committed himself to the doctrine in anticipation of the "day not far distant

42. Apess, "An Indian's Looking-Glass for the White Man," 159–60.

when ample justice shall be done the red man by his white brother—
when he shall be allowed that station in the scale of being and intelligence which unerring wisdom designed him to occupy."[43]

The belief in the Semitic origin of the Native tribes of America also
influences Apess's religious conversion, which comes through an epiphany that "Christ died for all mankind—that age, sect, color, country,
or situation made no difference" (*SF*, 19) and that heaven, as he claims
in *The Increase of the Kingdom of Christ* (1831), is a kingdom of pure
equality, unlike earthly kingdoms, where subjects "can enslave no
man . . . oppress no man," and where the "white man, who has most
cruelly oppressed his red brother . . . pours out unavailing tears over the
wasted generations of mighty forest hunters." White oppression of "his
red brother" amounts to fratricide, and the vanishing of the "wasted
generations" is not lamented as an unfortunate inevitability, as it is in
the romance, but condemned as the sin of Cain. As Krupat suggests,
Apess employs traditional Christian typology in his narrative of personal
conversion, but this moment betrays a significant typological revision.[44]
In Genesis 4:15, God curses Cain with a mark so that others will know
his crime. In a reversal of Christian doctrine, Apess affixes this mark,
commonly interpreted as a dark complexion, on whites themselves, who
in the kingdom of Christ will answer for the same sin, fratricide, that
they attribute to the dark races, the "sons of Cain." Circulating at least
since Roger Williams published *A Key into the Language of America* in
1643 and revised in 1816 with the Cherokee Elias Boudinot's *A Star
in the West; or, A Humble Attempt to Discover the Long Lost Ten Tribes
of Israel*, the theory of a Hebrew migration during the last Ice Age was
almost as familiar and sensationalized as that of natural repugnance.

43. Apess, *The Increase of the Kingdom of Christ*, 114.

44. Ibid., 102. Krupat's analysis of Apess rests on Christian "salvationism," a
term he borrows from Sacvan Bercovitch and defines as a nationalized version of
traditional Protestant typology that sees human action in relation to God's will and
events in history as reinscriptions, or "types," of Biblical originals. Krupat claims that
Apess simultaneously emulates and struggles against this dominant early nineteenth-
century discourse. On one level, *A Son of the Forest* is "militant in its attempt to
subsume all voices into the single voice of Christian Salvationism," yet in Apess's
later essays, he "adds the voice of social justice to the voice of salvationism, integrating the two" (Krupat, *Voice*, 142–44, 171, 174).

Apess, however, appeals to the popular fascination with the Lost Tribes for the new and more urgent purpose of attacking the polygenist ideas underlying not only the antimiscegenation law but the much more portentous Removal Bill. If the races are not separate, finally, but rather "one family," all "descendants of one great progenitor—Adam" (*SF*, 4), then the scientific and religious foundations of these racist policies would crumble.[45] Apess begs this question throughout his writing: Who are the children of Adam? The answer, Apess knew well, converged with racial theory, religion, and history, discourses he simultaneously utilizes and contests first to persuade readers with his humanity then to persuade them with his policies.

Although Apess's ambitions were not fulfilled and Removal was enacted only a year after the publication of *A Son of the Forest,* this earliest of mixed-blood autobiographies had farther reaching consequences. Apess's appeal to linguistic evidence in his case for monogenesis anticipates the revolution in anthropology that would flourish at the turn of the twentieth century, when Henry Weatherbee Henshaw and Franz Boas would privilege language over physical proportion as the most reliable way to determine racial origins. Although Roger Williams undertook a comparative analysis of the Hebrew and Iroquois languages in the seventeenth century, Williams did not conceive his idiosyncratic study as a political intervention with immediate consequence, as Apess and Boas both did.

Apess's last published work, *Indian Nullification,* more clearly reveals the political agenda implicit in his autobiography. An argument for the autonomy of the Mashpees, a tribe of mixed-bloods living in southeastern Massachusetts with whom Apess closely identified, the essay claims that the white fear of miscegenation and degeneracy represents a major obstacle to the political equality America claims to embody. He

45. Despite his vehement public attacks on the legal and social prohibition of miscegenation, Apess carefully reminds his readers in *A Son of the Forest* that his own wife, Mary Wood Apess, is also a mixed-blood, "nearly the same color as myself" (*SF*, 46). In this incidental phrase at the end of his autobiography, we hear a faint apology to his more conservative readers, an echo of Sedgwick's compromise. Though he has extensively theorized the natural equality of races and the rightness of mixed marriages, he seems to suggest that, personally, he has the good manners to marry within his caste.

writes that natural law instead favors intermarriage, and sometimes, he suggests, those that preach against it in public in fact pursue it in private: "As soon as we begin to talk about equal rights, the cry of amalgamation is set up.... Were I permitted to express an opinion, it would be that it is more honorable in the two races to intermarry than to act as too many of them do. My advice to the white man is to let the colored race alone. It will considerably diminish the annual amount of sin committed. Or else let them even *marry* our daughters, and no more ado about amalgamation."[46]

Finally, he questions the basis of what is considered natural with sly mockery of the strange group of "Indians" who have usurped control of the reservation: "All the Indians I had ever seen were of a reddish color, sometimes approaching a yellow, but now, look to what quarter I would, most of those coming were pale faces, and, in my disappointment, it seemed to me that the hue of death sat upon their countenances. It seemed very strange to me that my brethren should have changed their natural color and become in every respect like white men."[47] The pale faces he sees are not fellow Indians with the hue of death like white men but in fact are white men, who seem to Apess unnatural apparitions in this place where they do not belong. In a final inversion of the romantic discourse of degeneration, Apess evokes the gothic image of living death that characterizes Mary Conant, Cora Munro, and Faith Leslie to describe those whites that assume authority over Mashpee worship. What is unnatural and degenerate in this scene is not interracial marriage, but whites' conflicting attempts to evangelize and segregate the Indians. Apess's joke hints at what whites might have feared most about miscegenation and recalls the profound and unexpressed fear evident in the initial reviews of *Hobomok*, that those like the pale "Indians" on the Mashpee reservation who did not remain at a safe distance would become indistinguishable from the Indians themselves and that racial differences held so sacred would ultimately be effaced. Such was Apess's dream of racial equality and the historical romance's nightmare of degeneracy; the more the Indian came to resemble the white man, the more frightening he became.

46. Apess, *Indian Nullification*, 230–31.
47. Ibid., 170.

A Resemblance and a Menace

In *Constituting Americans,* Priscilla Wald provides a useful comparison to Apess's argument for Mashpee autonomy, as well as his synthesis of traditional and radical voices in his writing, in her reading of the 1827 Constitution of the Cherokee Nation, a document "simultaneously modeled on and opposed to the United States Constitution." Cherokee mixed-bloods facing Removal forged the system as proof of their civilization, which would support their suit to remain on their land. This demonstration, however, seemed to have the opposite effect. As the Cherokee mixed-bloods adopted white practices of farming and slaveholding, white authorities responded anxiously. Georgia congressman and later governor Wilson Lumpkin writes: "[A] portion of the Cherokee people, composed mostly of mixed breeds and white bloods, had advanced in all the various arts of civilization to an extent that rendered it altogether impracticable to enforce the Laws of the United States passed by Congress for regulating intercourse with Indian Tribes within the United States, and for governing and restraining such tribes."[48] The cases of the Cherokees and the Mashpees raise questions that become more articulate and more immediate during the later nineteenth and twentieth centuries. Where did these mixed-bloods stand in relation to a system of laws that did not recognize any space or overlap between one race and another? How much white blood need a mixed-blood possess before laws passed expressly for "regulating intercourse with Indian Tribes" ceased to apply to him or her? How would United States law come to recognize the existence of a growing population of mixed-bloods and address the peculiar legal dilemmas they posed to a system of laws predicated on racial separation?

These legal dilemmas crystallized the problem mixed-bloods posed to the emergent national identity. Wald explains:

> Outrage [over the Cherokee Constitution] stemmed from anxieties that were exacerbated by the profound threat of Cherokee separatism to the collective identity. The Cherokee Nation's becoming like but not of the United States political entity, mirroring without acceding to its conditions, seemed to jeopardize the terms of a United States

48. Priscilla Wald, *Constituting Americans: Cultural Anxiety and Narrative Form,* 26, 27.

national identity. And the threat of a Cherokee nationalism was literally embodied by the "mixed-bloods," who represented the mixing of bloods referred to by Jefferson, but who did not fully accede to the terms of assimilation that the President had delineated, who had, that is, remained Cherokees.[49]

Cheryl Walker observes that the Cherokees who used the Constitution as a model for their own government "utilized the terms of American national rhetoric hoping to establish their own claims on a similar basis," to establish a "state within a state . . . a collective identity separate from, while remaining connected to, the United States." Walker sees this act as "deeply subversive" in its "opening up the possibility that the Constitution's meanings are not fixed but are instead a matter of interpretation," a possibility that would enable later marginalized groups, especially mixed-bloods, to "lay claim to American identity" and, more specifically, to force the issue in the courts and congressional houses.[50] The hybrid status of the Mashpees and the Cherokees reveals the fatal flaw in the attempt to legislate race: the incapacity to adjudicate or even to recognize individuals who do not fit into established racial categories. When race becomes uncertain, laws governing race also become uncertain.

Removal, which sought to accomplish geographically what romance accomplished symbolically, served more than the political and material needs of American expansion; it provided assurance against the degenerative consequences that racial mixing seemed to threaten in the national body. The fear hidden in the historical romance and in the opposition to the Mashpees and Cherokees, however, reveals perhaps surprisingly that the mixed-blood's threat was embodied not by his difference, which law and science were amply prepared to address, but by his sameness, which they were not prepared to address. Buffon's and Knox's theories shape this fear, Brown's and Seaver's portrayals of white savagery exploit it, and Child's splicing of Hobomok's progeny to the family tree of New England teases it, as assimilation itself becomes poisonous. As Jefferson suggests, miscegenation might contribute to the work of building a nation only by making Indians white. The mixed-blood Mashpees

49. Ibid., 27.
50. Walker, *Indian Nation*, 59, 113.

and Cherokees who accepted white social norms, but who also refused to renounce their tribal identity, threatened national integrity, since the polygenist-romantic concept of amalgamation entailed not racial or cultural hybridity, but rather transformation from Indian to white, not the consciousness of simultaneity and independence expressed by the Cherokee Constitution and, later, by Louis Riel, but a vacillation between two exclusive racial families and discursive positions. Figures like Apess and Jemison who cannot be easily cleansed or reduced to a singular category remain, in Homi Bhabha's description of hybridity, "at once resemblance and menace" and, even more, a menace because of their resemblance, "others" who are too much like us and we like them.[51]

The texts produced by these hybrid figures urge us toward a new understanding of early American culture and the theoretical terms we have used to describe it. Most fundamentally, they allow us to register the half-breed's presence even though it has been largely concealed in the literature itself and perceived only with difficulty in literary scholarship. Here and even more clearly in twentieth-century writing, hybridity seems less an assimilation of one discourse by another than the synthesis of these opposing voices into one independent of its two components. Edward Said's description of the consciousness of exile most clearly describes hybridity as I read it in Jemison's *Narrative* and Apess's *A Son of the Forest* as an "originality of vision . . . an awareness of simultaneous dimensions."[52] Said's exiles, like Reil's Métis, Mary Jemison, and William Apess, exist in two worlds, without being completely of one of the other, aware of their own simultaneous dimensions, collapsing the distinction between one self and the other and eroding the science of separation.

51. Homi K. Bhabha, *The Location of Culture*, 86.
52. Edward Said, "Reflections on Exile," 1123.

Homo *Criminalis* and Half-Breed Outlaws in the Dime Western

> The prairies are broad, and the woodlands are wide
> And proud on his steed the wild half-breed may ride,
> With the belt round his waist and the knife at his side,
> And no white man may claim his beautiful bride.
>
> —John Rollin Ridge, "The Stolen White Girl" (1868)

What Will We Do with Them?

Irwin Beadle and his partner, Robert Adams, founders of the great and dubious American literary enterprise known as the dime novel, very quickly learned a lesson that today only the publishers of the most lurid thrillers and shameless romances follow with wholehearted devotion: one good picture is worth thirty to fifty thousand words. Although their first edition of Ann Stephens's *Malaeska; The Indian Wife of the White Hunter,* the debut number in Beadle and Adams's first series of dime novels, sold out within a few weeks with its plain typeset cover, the publishers sought to improve returns on the second edition by adding a richly etched jacket depicting a heartrending death that occurs early in the novel. Their marketing stratagem introduced a convention that would distinguish the dime novel during its predominance from 1860 until the advent of film in the early twentieth century.[1] While early critics complained that the ubiquitous "yellowbacks"—a derisive moniker

---

Portions of this chapter are excerpted from my article " 'A Scorned, Outcast Thing': Half-Breed Outlaws in the Dime Novel," *Paradoxa* no. 19, *The Western,* and are reprinted by permission.

1. The immediate success of Beadle and Adams's publishing venture inspired dozens of publishers to follow in subsequent decades with their own cheap series.

referring to their flimsy, saffron covers—distracted young minds from more morally uplifting literature with sensational tales of outlawry and vengeance, the paperbacks attracted unprecedented numbers of readers from all levels of society and contributed to the exploding literacy rate in the later nineteenth century. The dramatic cover scenes arrested the casual glance and invited even the illiterate to learn to read so that they could more completely savor the experience of the mongrel villain, slinking behind the tree, leveling his rifle at the unsuspecting woodsman; or the renegade half-breed, his drawn blade poised over the body of his bound adversary, promising unspeakable torture; or the chivalric chieftain, eyes cast lovingly upon his white princess, adorning her in Indian finery.

Today, aficionados, collectors, and scholars value these covers as much as the texts themselves. Their reproductions supplement nearly every published discussion of the dime novel, serving both to entertain and to illuminate the culture that produced them. The cover illustration of the second edition of *Malaeska* offers revealing clues about the novel's characters, whose initial appearance deceives the careless observer. At the edge of the fatal river, dusky Malaeska clutches her mortally wounded husband as he gestures toward their infant son toddling nearby. The Indian wife, her skin and her clothing shaded as darkly as the shadows cast by the ensconcing foliage, contrasts sharply with the white hunter, pallid and beatified in the throes of death, even his buckskins shining like alabaster. A casual observer probably would not guess that the small child who reaches toward the dying man is the mixed-blood offspring of this doomed romance. The baby's skin is white like his father's. His hair, seemingly, is blond, though the text later describes its black luster. To a reader acquainted with the long tradition of American captivity narratives, he would appear more like a white innocent torn from his swaddling blanket during an Indian raid than a would-be war chief of

---

Dime novel has since become a generic term, no longer defining the original volumes in *Beadle's Dime Novels* series but all popular paperback fiction generated roughly between 1860 and 1915. Considering the sheer number and formal variation of dime novels, statements in this chapter regarding the dime-novel tradition are unavoidably generalized. In fact, I will discuss both proper dime novels and other sorts of popular Westerns published concurrently with dime novels though outside the recognized influence of the mass-fiction phenomenon.

his mother's people. Just as the cover illustration protects prospective readers from the disturbing knowledge of the cherub's Indian parentage before they plunge into the story, the child's wealthy white grandparents, we later find, raise him in ignorance of his unfortunate birth. Young William Danforth, unnamed in the novel until his full initiation into New York society, learns all that befits the proud son of a prosperous Manhattan merchant: polite manners, proper French, and hatred of Indians. While still a young man, he secures a small business empire and an engagement to a charming girl, but on the eve of his wedding, when William discovers his secret stain, none of life's happy promises can prevent him from drowning himself in the same river where, as a helpless infant, he had embraced his dying father.

This significant illustration visually reinforces the proscription against racial mixing introduced in the historical romance and developed in the dime novel. Beadle and Adams, perhaps to ensure both critical and popular appeal, spare their readers the potential disorientation and revulsion of watching a dark-skinned child grasp at his white father by graphically cleansing the mixed-blood infant of color as Lydia Maria Child metaphorically cleanses the mixed-blood Charles Hobomok Conant in the conclusion of her novel. If suspicions remain, Stephens's narrative, in the tradition of the gothic historical romance, amply repays those who have transgressed nature's boundaries: William Danforth meets a violent death; Malaeska suffers lifelong misery before finally succumbing to her grief; and young William, learning the horrible circumstance of his birth, is driven to madness and suicide. *Malaeska,* both in its cover illustration and in its tragic finale, reveals the denial of racial mixing characteristic of earlier historical romance but also portends the new ways its innumerable successors would approach this persistent problem.

In spite of the demographic reality of mixed-bloods in nineteenth-century America, nationalist fiction until the 1830s, like the cover illustration of Stephens's novel, had effectively denied their presence. The historical romance, the keystone of America's burgeoning national idea, revolted at the possibility of offspring between an Indian and a white. Such creatures belied the myth of the vanishing Indian that provided the moral and evolutionary foundation for claims of white ascendance and the expansion of the New World empire. Child, Cooper, and Sedgwick blend gothic texture into their historical romances in order to represent racial mixing as abhorrent, insane, and grotesque, a doomed union conceived in unreason, inevitably rent in spectacular violence, and informed by polygenism. Although the dime-novel tradition that follows *Malaeska* inherits and intensifies the madness and violence that earlier historical romance associated with miscegenation, later narratives could not, as the romance had done, preclude the circumstances that might lead to the mixed-blood's existence and still aspire to historical and dramatic relevance. William Scheick explains that in the fiction of the later nineteenth century, the mixed-blood "could not be treated evasively because, whereas the full-blood Indian could be restricted to America's prehistory or history, could be safely confined in the past, the mixed-blood Indian belonged very much to the present and quite possibly to the future of America."[2] As Native writers such as William Apess frequently reminded readers, the Indian-white mixed-blood, despite the willful forgetting of nationalist literature, existed in growing numbers not only on the frontier but also within the more secure confines of civilization. The dime novel confronts this problematic figure fitfully though without the paralyzing hesitation evident in the historical romance. Like Cooper, Beadle and Adams and later dime-novel publishers styled themselves as architects of a national mythology conceived in the immense historical crucible of the American West. The dime Western, however, departed significantly from Cooper's example as the infamous half-breed, inconceivable in the romance, made his skulking entrance within the first few pages of *Malaeska*.

This chapter assesses representations of the mixed-blood in a necessarily limited selection of dime novels within the contexts of literary tradition, public policy, and racialist science.[3] As earlier narratives, in their attempt to resolve the biological and political status of the mixed-blood,

2. Scheick, *Half-Blood*, 2.
3. Between 1860 and 1915, the publishing industry generated more than five hundred distinct dime-novel series. The largest collections catalog many thousands of titles. The Library of Congress, for example, contains more than seventeen thousand volumes, while the University of Minnesota boasts more than seventy thousand, including many British editions. Very few of these works, however, exist in modern, readily obtainable editions. Only recently has Bill Brown's anthology, *Reading the West*, facilitated the use of the dime western in the classroom, anthologizing four dime novels. For a list of the few reprints, facsimiles, and critical editions in existence, see J. Randolph Cox, *The Dime Novel Companion: A Source Book*, xxiv.

reacted to polygenism and the debate concerning Indian Removal, the dime novel reacts to questions posed by criminal anthropology, a refinement of nineteenth-century racialism, and the debate concerning Indian assimilation, ongoing since the passage of the Removal Act and culminating with Allotment. While Removal had attempted to banish the Indians beyond the borders of the expanding nation, Allotment conditionally invited Indians to join the United States—a significant revision in the government's response to the exasperating problem expressed succinctly by an 1883 *New York Times* editorial: "What Will We Do with Them?" Reformers proposed to grant individual Indians allotments of reservation land in the hope that a system of private ownership would stimulate socioeconomic development and facilitate, with the help of the mixed-blood, the full-blood Indian's assimilation to mainstream American society. Unable to remove the Indian from the popular imagination as the historical romance had attempted to remove him, the dime Western ponders the consequences of his assimilation.

Like earlier popular fiction anticipating the Removal Act, the frontier stories of the later nineteenth century manifest divergent responses to this proposed assimilation and its inherent threat of racial blending, each governed by the assumptions of monogenism or polygenism. The half-breed, the inevitable product of assimilation, initially emerges in popular frontier stories such as Walt Whitman's anonymously published *The Half-Breed* as a degenerate half-devil, a monstrous manifestation of the cultural fear of racial crossing inherited from earlier historical romance and informed by the polygenist supposition of a fixed hierarchy of separate races. In later dime novels, this grotesque mixed-blood evolves into a more definitive symbol of outlawry, an element of criminal instability in a historical moment when the institution and enforcement of law becomes paramount to the integrity of a nation conceived in the Enlightenment faith in order and reason and yet anxiously anticipating the integration of an irrational savage element.

The transformation of the mixed-blood from a threat to the biological order into a threat to the social order occurs in the context of the

---

In 1981, University Microfilms International compiled over three thousand titles on more than seventy clearly cataloged reels. This microfilm collection, available in many university libraries, provides the primary source for this study.

discourse of criminal anthropology. During the later nineteenth century, as the United States enacted the assimilation of the Indians into the national body, Cesare Lombroso, professor of medical jurisprudence at the University of Turin, and other members of the positivist school of criminology correlated anthropometrical measurements of earlier poly-genist studies with antisocial behavior and conceived of a *Homo crimi-nalis,* a breed of criminal man predisposed to mischief and violence and marked by certain atavistic anatomical characteristics. Lombroso and others, including several English and American researchers, observed that these characteristics appeared not only in white criminals but also in those races they believed lower in the evolutionary hierarchy: Jews, gypsies, blacks, Mongolians, and their cousins, the savages of America. Lombroso argued further that degenerate criminal traits also seemed to proliferate in hybrid civilizations such as that proposed by assimilation-ist reformers. The newly perceived link between hybridity, atavism, and criminality effectively criminalized the inherent savagism of the frontier tribes; confirmed Indian physical degeneracy, an opinion prevalent among polygenists since the later eighteenth century and manifested in early portrayals of the half-devil in frontier fiction; and predicted that racial assimilation would foster social anarchy. Condemned by science as born criminals, as threats to the progress of civilization and the growth of the American nation, mixed-bloods in the nationalist dime novels of the later nineteenth century live and die on the margins of the law, forced, in their impossible position, to suicide, as in Stephens's *Malaeska;* to unregenerate savagery, as in Walt Whitman's *The Half-Breed,* Joseph Badger's *Redlaw,* and Edward Ellis's *The Half-Blood;* or to melancholy masquerade, as in Mayne Reid's *The White Squaw.*

In my selection and discussion of these texts, which represent only a small part of the vast catalog of dime novels portraying mixed-bloods, I do not propose their stylistic, thematic, or ideological uniformity. They do not represent an aggregate of evidence for a common attitude among writers, publishers, and readers. Rather, in their divergent representa-tions of the "half-breed," they illustrate the tensions and transforma-tions in the cultural view of racial mixing during an era that witnessed significant changes in the scientific and political attitudes toward the Indian and a consequent movement toward the modern understanding of race as culture and hybridity as discursive synthesis. Originally composed by Stephens in 1839 as a serial in *The Ladies' Companion* and revised and reprinted by Beadle and Adams in 1860, *Malaeska* marks the transition from the cultural denial of miscegenation to the more explicit association of hybridity and criminality. Whitman's *The Half-Breed* also reveals the evolution of the fictional mixed-blood from a biological aberration to an outlaw figure and anticipates narratives, such as *Redlaw* and *The Half-Blood,* that appropriate a criminological vocabulary in ways that these earlier texts could not. By contrast, Reid's *The White Squaw* looks forward to more sympathetic portrayals of the mixed-blood that challenge the polygenist assumption of hybrid degeneracy and criminality. In spite of their differences, however, these novels share a genetically determined perspective in which racially mixed individuals, whether malformed imps as in *The Half-Breed,* born criminals as in *Redlaw* and *The Half-Blood,* or noble men tragically but necessarily exiled by the accident of birth as in *The White Squaw,* are cast out as threats to the tentative social order of the frontier. In their shared recognition of this correlation between biological disorder and social disorder, each of these novels precludes assimilation as a possibility for national development and anticipates Allotment with manifest anxiety.

Another tradition of frontier stories, represented by John Rollin Ridge's *Joaquín Murieta* and Helen Hunt Jackson's *Ramona,* looks forward to Allotment more hopefully and challenges the dime novels' assumptions of the biological basis of criminality. Informed by the monogenist assumptions of humanity's common hereditary origin, an idea previously explored by Apess in his linkage of the Indians with the Lost Tribes, Ridge and Jackson view assimilation as the natural course of democratic civilization. As Charles Thomson countered the polygenist arguments of Count Buffon a century earlier, Jackson and Ridge attack the determinist foundation of criminal anthropology by representing crime as the product of circumstance rather than heredity. In their sympathetic representations of racially crossed and outlaw figures, their novels demonstrate that the scourge of outlawry on the frontier derives not from ill-conceived interracial couplings but rather from ill-conceived laws. National degeneracy, Jackson and Ridge suggest, resides not in unnatural hybridization but in corrupt, undemocratic policies that function to exclude the Indians from the American polity, even as it proposes to invite them to join. By defining outlawry in political rather than biological terms, these novels absolve the mixed-blood of his criminal taint and prepare for the emergence of twentieth-century Native writing, when hybridity, partially liberated from the racialist associations of the nineteenth century, comes to represent the cultural and discursive synthesis that characterizes the modern Métis consciousness.

Malaeska

A proven favorite of audiences, Ann Stephens already had published two recent best sellers, *Fashion and Famine* (1854) and *The Old Homestead* (1855), when Beadle and Adams contracted her novel *Malaeska* to inaugurate their new series of dime novels. Stephens had also written *Mary Derwent, a Tale of the Early Settlers* (1838), a story, roughly modeled on the Jemison narrative, of a white woman adopted by the Shawnee. According to Bill Brown, Beadle and Adams chose *Malaeska,* a revision of her original serial, to "establish the American emphasis of the series with a treatment of provincial New York in the manner of Cooper," to capitalize on the story's previous popularity, and also to protect their enterprise from the objections that would likely attend *Mary Derwent,* the story of a white woman's embrace of Indian life.[4] Apparently mindful of the potential critical prejudice against their series, the publishers consistently aspired to literary respectability, advertising in the "Publisher's Notice" of the first edition of *Malaeska* that they "have made every effort to obtain such works as are, in all respects, superior for ability, and faultless in taste and morals."[5] As Beadle and Adams assure their readers, Stephens's "name upon the title-page is enough to convince the reading public that the book is in every respect interesting and worthy" (*M,* 57). The interracial romance portrayed in Stephens's novel, however, invites doubts and might have prompted the attachment of a second notice, which affirms that *Malaeska* remains "American in all its features" and "chaste" in the "character of its delineations" (*M,* 59). Although William Everett of the *North American Review* judged *Malaeska* "silly" and complained of its grammatical de-

---

4. Bill Brown, ed., *Reading the West: An Anthology of Dime Westerns,* 54–55.
5. Ann S. Stephens, *Malaeska; The Indian Wife of the White Hunter,* 57. Further citations will be made parenthetically with the abbreviation *M.*

fects,[6] Beadle and Adams's marketing gambits proved overwhelmingly successful. The publishers sold ten thousand copies within the first few weeks, sixty-five thousand within the first few months, and three hundred thousand by the turn of the twentieth century, auspiciously marking the transition between the cultural hesitancy to admit the mixed-blood's existence in the historical romance and his notorious emergence as a malicious outcast.

The novel introduces Malaeska as the typically nubile, frolicking forest maiden, with laughter "musical as a bird's song" and movements "graceful as an untamed gazelle" (*M*, 64). Her child is likewise "very beautiful" (*M*, 64). In contrast to the interracial unions portrayed in the historical romance, where white women and Indian men collide in spirals of violence and derangement, Stephens's revelation of William Danforth's secret marriage to Malaeska simmers with genuine passion. The Indian wife and the white hunter greet each other with an apparently sincere love uncomplicated by the coquetry and jealousy demonstrated by the novel's white sweethearts, Arthur Jones and Martha Fellows. Danforth embraces her wordlessly, cheek softly to cheek. Malaeska's "untutored heart, rich in its natural affections, had no aim, no object, but what centered in the love she bore for her white husband. . . . [A]s her husband bowed his head to hers, the blood darkened her cheek, and her large liquid eyes were flooded with delight" (*M*, 72). The plush warmth of this passage, while unprecedented in literary portrayals of interracial romance, dramatically sours when Danforth looks upon his child. Just as Stephens reminds the reader of the darkness of the blood flooding the Indian heroine's cheek, Danforth, brushing the straight, black hair from his son's forehead, perceives the "tinge of its mother's blood," however slight (*M*, 72). "It's a pity the little fellow is not quite white," he remarks to Malaeska (*M*, 72). Stephens further describes Danforth's shame for loving Malaeska as the indignity of an adulterer living a double life: "[Danforth] never thought of introducing her as his wife among the whites . . . or to take her among his people for shelter. . . . His affections struggled powerfully with his pride. The picture

6. Quoted in Edmund Pearson, *Dime Novels; or, Following an Old Trail in Popular Literature*, 91.

of his disgrace—of the scorn with which his parents and sisters would receive the Indian wife and the half-Indian child, presented itself before him, and he had not the moral courage to risk the degradation which her companionship would bring upon him" (*M*, 76). Her husband's attitude silently crushes Malaeska, and although she takes great pride in her son's destiny as a chief of his tribe, she remains ominously aware of the infant's "white man's blood," which will soon cause the separation of husband and wife, mother and son (*M*, 73).

Later in the novel, when the horrible consequences of this seemingly ideal wilderness romance are more fully realized, Stephens suggests that it was love blended with madness that engendered this child: "It was a blessed madness—the madness of two warm young hearts that forgot everything in the sweet impulse with which they clung together; it was madness which led [Danforth] . . . to take the wild Indian girl to his bosom, when in the bloom of early girlhood. Mad!" (*M*, 159). Like the deranged interracial desire in the historical romance, the love between Danforth and Malaeska is conceived in passion rather than reason. The careless haste of youth causes these two young hearts to enter into this "unnatural marriage," as Stephens calls it in the end, to commit this crime against reason and nature for which they and their child will pay with their lives.

Danforth faces the inevitable crisis when the outbreak of hostilities between Malaeska's tribe and white settlers forces him to side with his own race and abandon his wife and son. Before he can join the defense of the Fellows farm, however, the Indian chief, his own father-in-law, ambushes him. In the ensuing combat, Danforth kills his attacker but suffers a mortal wound and prepares for death as Malaeska carries the infant to her husband's side. Depicted on the cover of the second edition, the scene represents the critical decision that shapes the destiny of Malaeska and her son. Guilt-ridden for neglecting to instruct his heathenish wife and child in Christianity, Danforth orders Malaeska to bear the infant down the Hudson River to Manhattan, where she must commit him to the care of his wealthy parents, who will give him a Christian education. This way, he explains, the family may be reunited in the kingdom of God. Malaeska promises to honor her husband's dying wish, though she does not yet understand its consequences. Danforth's resolution to introduce his Indian wife and half-Indian child to his white family, made in the weakness and derangement of impending death, constitutes a racial transgression worse than his keeping an Indian wife or even his siring a mixed-blood child. While the white family and the Indian family might exist peacefully in distant separation, Stephens suggests, both would be destroyed when met in collision. For Malaeska, Danforth's request brings a lifetime of misery. For the child who embodies this disastrous collision, it portends death on the same riverbank. The scene, white slain beside Indian, the child clutching his father's face as it becomes hard and cold beneath him, recalls Edgar Huntly wounded and prostrate on the corpse of the savage, blood mingled with blood; or the massacre at Fort William Henry, where frenzied Hurons imbibe the blood of white refugees; moments of convulsion where miscegenation foreshadows not harmonious integration but violent apocalypse.

Danforth's fear of degradation before his white family proves justified when Malaeska and the child present themselves at the mansion of John Danforth, a prosperous trade investor, and his wife, Therese. The elder Danforth immediately blames Malaeska for his son's death and curses fiercely when he beholds his half-Indian grandson. His wife, finding traces of their son's likeness in "this poor, fatherless creature," urges compassion (*M,* 92). Danforth softens, promising to raise the child and to allow Malaeska to live with them as a servant, but he forbids that anyone, even the boy himself, know of his Indian parentage. The proud man ponders this "thing worse than death—disgrace" (*M,* 91) and the stain that will follow his descendants into posterity:

> His [son's] blood . . . had been mingled with the accursed race who had sacrificed him. Gladly would he have rent the two races asunder, in the very person of his grandchild, could the pure half of his being been thus preserved. But . . . there was something in the boy's eyes . . . which filled the void of his heart, half with love and half with pain. He could no more separate the two passions in his own soul, than he could drain the savage blood from the little boy's veins. . . . The wild blood of the boy must be quenched; he must know nothing of the race from which his disgrace sprang. (*M,* 94–95)

Malaeska lingers miserably for more than a decade in the household, watching William, finally given his father's name, as he grows into adolescence. The boy betrays obvious signs of his "Indian blood . . . strong in his young veins" as he excels at outdoor sports, but he also learns haughtiness and hatred for Indians from his grandfather (*M*, 96). Eventually usurped by a white nurse and cut off from any contact with her son, Malaeska makes a desperate attempt to abduct him and convey him back to her tribe. Although eager for adventure and affectionate to the strange Indian woman he believes merely a servant, William finally scorns her and runs to his grandfather when he arrives to rescue him. Danforth banishes Malaeska from his household following the failed abduction and sends William to Europe to finish his education beyond his mother's reach.

When William returns, he has matured, like Charles Hobomok Conant, into fine white manhood, his dark hair, lithe gait, and black piercing eyes the only hints of his Indian birth. Sarah Jones, the daughter of Arthur Jones and Martha Fellows, who have long since married and settled peacefully in the backwoods, now resides in Manhattan under the tutelage of a French mistress and the guardianship of the aging Danforths. In the weeks following William's return from Europe, Sarah wins the young man's heart and the two are engaged. At first, the romance seems as genuine as that between Malaeska and William's father, but Stephens soon reveals a darker side to William's affections. He promises himself to Sarah, a girl well beneath his own station, not entirely for love, but for the "predominating pride" and "refined selfishness" he satisfies in bestowing his noblesse oblige on the "portionless...daughter of a plain country farmer" (*M*, 149). He strides into the Jones homestead like a prince but shudders at having to fraternize with the bumpkins in his fiancée's family. He also admits that his hatred for Indians has become more acute since boyhood, telling Sarah, "I hate the whole race! If there is a thing I abhor on earth, it is a savage—a fierce, bloodthirsty wild beast in human form!" (*M*, 140). In spite of his prejudice, Sarah invites him to meet Malaeska, who in the intervening years has returned to the frontier and subsisted by selling simple Indian crafts. Startled by the apparent coincidence, William remembers the housemaid of his youth, the one Indian spared from his ire, and he agrees to meet her alone in the woods.

The reunion between mother and son propels the novel to its abrupt and fatal conclusion. Near the spot where the infant William embraced his father's corpse, Malaeska finally reveals that she is his mother. William's reaction recalls the madness attending scenes of racial crossing in earlier historical romances. With "his almost insane gaze," he contemplates repaying the Indian woman's unthinkable insult with violence (*M*, 158). As he realizes that Malaeska speaks the truth—"Great God! . . . I, an Indian? a half blood?"—William, like Mary Conant and Faith Leslie, becomes "as one in a dream," drifting between states of paralyzed numbness and violent "frenzy" (*M*, 159). When Malaeska recounts his Indian infancy, the battle in which his father had died, and her promise to conceal her identity, William "convulsed" and "trembled," lamenting finally, "I was about to be married to one so gentle—so pure—I, an Indian—was about to give my stained hand to a lovely being of untainted blood. . . . Father of heaven, my heart will break—I am going mad!" (*M*, 159–60). Already "perfectly colorless . . . like marble" in anticipation of death, William plunges into the river and drowns (*M*, 160). Malaeska herself dies of grief, sprawled over the graves of her father, her husband, and her son, finally laid side by side, all "victims," the novel concludes, "of an unnatural marriage" (*M*, 163).

Stephens's brief epilogue emphasizes the disastrous consequences of this unnatural racial crossing, and, unlike Child's *Hobomok*, her novel leaves no doubt about the fate of the mixed-blood. All progeny of this marriage, the tainted posterity that so disturbed John Danforth, vanishes. After the death of William, Stephens explains, "there had been no relative in America to claim the estate left by his grandfather" (*M*, 163). The Danforth property reverts to distant relatives in England, who dismantle the mansion and erect a "block of stores" (*M*, 164). Rendered barren, the Danforth line is terminated and dispossessed by English lords. This denouement carries the vague but significant threat that racial mixing, as it leads to degeneracy in the individual body, similarly reverses the progress of national evolution and of history itself, returning a small piece of republican America to the clutches of European aristocracy. In this degenerative scenario, property, the Danforth estate that once shared in the expansive growth of the nation now suddenly dissolved, becomes the site of these evolutionary and historical reversals. Although Allotment would not pass for another twenty-seven years, Stephens's novel registers growing anxiety as the United States, like John Danforth, considered inviting the Indian into the house, making him a ward, and promising him a share in the nation's future. The novel's ominous conclusion suggests Stephens's misgivings about assimilation.

John Danforth's worst fears are manifested in a disturbing reversal of the conventional racial hierarchy, as the Indian, having infiltrated and disgraced his house, dooms his tainted white progeny to the fate Robert Knox predicted for a weak race that blended with a stronger race: degradation and disappearance.

Like earlier historical romances, *Malaeska* fuses polygenist theory with a vision of American destiny, rejecting the marriage of races as a route to national ascendance and depicting the mixed-blood as criminally complicit in America's potential decline. William, like Cora Munro, cannot escape the curse of his own blood. The narrative evokes something sinister beneath his handsome, debonair appearance, a shadowy presence reminiscent of those moments when the historical romance, confronting miscegenation, conjures gothic specters and the noble savage becomes a degenerate abductor. With eyes like coal, aristocratic affectation, and scheming intelligence, the mixed-blood William seems suited to a villainous role in a classic gothic novel and heralds the appearance of more riotous outlaws such as Badger's Redlaw and Ellis's Kaam. His contemptuous sense of superiority, his apparent incapacity to love his fiancée genuinely, and his barely checked impulse to kill his own mother reveal his egoism, antipathy, and homicidal perversity, traits that Mark Twain would portray in Injun Joe and later anthropologists would categorize as innate in Indian blood. Although William kills himself before he can transform into the half-breed renegade common in later dime novels, *Malaeska* shares their vision of hybridity as tense dialectical struggle between white and Indian, order and anarchy. In her portrayal of William's vague villainy and violent derangement as the sad consequences of an unnatural marriage, Stephens portrays the consequences of violating the natural law ordering the fictional universe of the historical romance and creates a correlation between race and criminality that would inform the subsequent discourses of criminal anthropology and the dime Western.

Stephens ventures into imaginative territory left unexplored by Cooper, Sedgwick, and even Child. Where *The Last of the Mohicans* ends, *Malaeska* begins, portraying the survivors of racial warfare rather than the casualties. Her model of hybridity, however, functions through alternation rather than simultaneity. William transforms from Indian child to white man without any awareness of his dual identity, as Edgar

Huntly, who sleepwalks through his savage encounters, or Mary Conant, who elopes with Hobomok in a state of dumb derangement. He does not share Mary Jemison's and William Apess's double consciousness or even that of later, more complex half-breed renegades like Ellis's Kaam and Reid's Wacora. Finally confronted with the revelation, he chooses suicide; as Knox suggested, nature suffers no hybrids.

Originally conceived in 1839 and revived in 1860, the story shares more aesthetic and political ideals with earlier historical romances than with subsequent dime novels, yet it lends itself more readily to progressive interpretations than *Hobomok* or *Hope Leslie*. In spite of her apparent doubts about miscegenation and assimilationist policy, Stephens portrays Malaeska and her son with sympathy unknown in previous narratives of racial crossing, as William demands more understanding than the fanged hunchback that would shortly terrorize the pages of Whitman's *The Half-Breed*. Stephens suggests, moreover, that William's flaws result as much from the corrupting influence of his white grandfather as from any hereditary deficiency, challenging the traditional polygenist assumption that nature rather than circumstance plants the seed of degeneracy and, like William Apess, partially attributing Indian degeneracy to white abuses. In the tradition of American frontier narrative, *Malaeska* marks the transition between the end of the age of Cooper and the beginning of the age of the dime novel. Although the novel depicts with some compassion a figure reviled or simply denied in earlier fiction, it remains bound in a moral universe where racial crossing foretells individual death and national decline, invoking an image of the mixed-blood that resonates with the same conflicted emotions that divide John Danforth as he beholds his half-Indian grandson, half with love, half with pain.

The Half-Breed and the Hybrid Grotesque

Susanna Rowson and Thomas Jefferson liberally tried to imagine the mixed-blood as the embodiment of a new kind of nation taking shape in the West, a heterogeneous America where races would enter into a natural marriage and conceive a vigorous new people fit to settle the wilderness. Helen Hunt Jackson's *Ramona* would resurrect Jefferson's dream, but Francis Parkman's *Oregon Trail* (1849) provides another definition of the mixed-blood, evocatively illogical yet more readily adaptable to nationalist literature insistent upon the dialectical relationship of white and Indian: "a race of rather extraordinary composition, being, according to the common saying, half Indian, half white man, and half devil."[7] Although many writers, including Stephens, Badger, Ellis, and Reid, portray the mixed-blood as handsome and physically, though not psychologically, well-proportioned, the dime novel inherits from earlier frontier stories (like Whitman's) the image of a subhuman creature, more goblin than either white or Indian. Physically marked, in John Haller's words, as an "outcast from evolution," the grotesque half-breed inevitably emerges in American fiction as an outlaw from society.

In his frontier tale *The Mestico* (1850), M. C. Hodges describes the character of half-breed Jim Henry as a blend of "the striking moral and intellectual habitudes of the Indian, with many of the groveling, vicious propensities of those representatives of our own race with whom he had associated . . . vile, drunken, intractable in peace—cruel, base, rapacious in war." In *Lord Fairfax* (1868), John Esten Cook's half-breed villain also exemplifies the prevalent image of the mixed-blood as a grotesque outcast: "[He stands] about five feet high, with a deep yellow or sallow complexion, a gigantic breadth of a chest, long monkey-like arms, and legs which resembled the crooked and gnarled boughs of a distorted oak. His forehead was scarcely an inch in height; his small eyes, as cunning and cruel as a serpent's, rolled beneath bushy brows; his nose was crooked like a hawk's bill and the hideous mouth, stretching almost from ear to ear, was distorted with protruding tusks like those of a wild boar." Dirk Peters, the half-breed voyager in Edgar Allan Poe's *The Narrative of Arthur Gordon Pym of Nantucket* (1839), is another beastly creation, with his stocky apelike frame, phrenological deficiencies, "protruding" teeth, demonic smile stretching ear to ear, and his air of animal "ferocity."[8] In *A Tour on the Prairies* (1835), Washington Irving's narrator similarly considers the half-breed guide Pierre Beatte: "I had been taught to look upon all half-breeds with distrust, as an uncertain and

---

7. Francis Parkman Jr., *The Oregon Trail*, 362.

8. Louise K. Barnett, *The Ignoble Savage: American Literary Racism, 1790–1890*, 121, 122–23; Edgar Allan Poe, *The Narrative of Arthur Gordon Pym of Nantucket*, 49.

faithless race ... the worthless brood engendered and brought up among the missions ... [a] rabble rout of nondescript beings that keep about the frontiers, between civilized and savage life, as those equivocal birds, the bats, hover about the confines of light and darkness."[9]

William Scheick identifies Beatte, with these other half-devils of nineteenth-century fiction, as an example of the stereotypical "twilight hybrid," a malicious creature hovering in the shadow between the light of civilization and the darkness of savagery, heir to the basest qualities of both races, and manifesting American culture's "semiconscious dread that ... humanity's savage element remains very much alive and might, with a power surpassing civilized restraint, at any moment devastatingly erupt." Scheick also finds this dread in Irving's *Astoria* (1836), which echoes Buffon's and Knox's formulations of hybrid degeneracy in its comparison of the "hybrid race on the frontier" to "new formations in geology, the amalgamation of the 'debris' and 'abrasions' of former races, civilized and savage ... which apparently defies cultivation and the habitation of civilized life"; and in *Adventures of Captain Bonneville* (1837), which similarly concludes, "the amalgamation of the various tribes, and of white men of every nation, will in time produce hybrid races like the mountain Tartars of the Caucasus ... [who] may, in time, become a scourge to the civilized frontiers."[10] While Scheick somewhat vaguely attributes Irving's reaction to racial blending in these passages to a "darkening" of the writer's attitude toward the frontier, the trend of these observations more clearly suggests the developing perception among American writers of the link between "hybrid races" and frontier criminality.

An anonymously published serial novel by Walt Whitman offers one of the earliest and more interesting American expressions of the persistent dread of the mixed-blood as a threat to both the biological and social orders and represents a link between the vaguely misanthropic William Danforth and the fully criminalized half-breeds of the dime novel. Originally published as *Arrow-Tip* in the March 1845 issue of *The Aristidean*, Whitman's *The Half-Breed*, a revision of *Arrow-Tip*,

9. Washington Irving, *A Tour on the Prairies*, 14.
10. Scheick, *Half-Blood*, 17; Washington Irving, *Astoria*, 217; Washington Irving, *The Adventures of Captain Bonneville, U.S.A., in the Rocky Mountains and the Far West*, 422.

appeared in the *Brooklyn Eagle* in June 1846. Both versions of Whitman's short novel portray Warren, a frontier settlement on the upper Mississippi, and the unjust hanging of Arrow-Tip, "one of the finest specimens of the Red People."[11] The primary agent of Arrow-Tip's demise is Boddo, a deformed mixed-blood whose guileful inaction precipitates the noble Indian's wrongful execution. The tale opens with a familiarly grotesque description of the half-breed troglodyte:

> He was deformed in body—his back being mounted with a mighty hunch, and his long neck bent forward, in a peculiar and disagreeable manner. In height he was hardly taller than the smallest of the children who clustered tormentingly around him.—His face was the index to many bad passions—which were only limited in the degree of their evil, because his intellect itself was not very bright.... Among the most powerful of his bad points was a malignant peevishness, dwelling on every feature of his countenance.... The gazer would have been at some doubt whether to class this strange and hideous creature with the race of Red Men or White....[He was an] impish creature... which mocked the outlines of humanity. (*WHB*, 258, 277)

The narrative soon reveals that Father Luke, a reclusive Catholic priest who was forced to flee his native Ireland for the American wilderness, has sired Boddo. When Peter Brown, a local blacksmith, summons Father Luke to the settlement to officiate his marriage, the "monk," as Father Luke calls himself, recounts a gothic story reminiscent of Brown's *Edgar Huntly*. To avenge the despoilment of his sister by an evil aristocrat, Father Luke exacts revenge in a duel and escapes to America. He confesses further that the boredom, loneliness, and poverty he found on the frontier compelled him to receive the love of an Indian girl who soon bore his child. When Father Luke sees his son for the first time, he says, "I almost shrieked with horror at the monstrous abortion! The mother herself had died in giving birth. No wonder. Never had my eyes been blasted with so much ugliness as that hunchbacked boy!...[T]hat child even now moves among you, an object of pity and disgust....[I]t is no other than the half-idiot, half-devil, Boddo" (*WHB*, 272).

11. Walt Whitman, *The Half-Breed: A Tale of the Western Frontier*, 263. Further citations will be made parenthetically with the abbreviation *WHB*.

In spite of these stunning revelations, the village happily prepares for the wedding but soon reels at the news of the groom's supposed death. Mistaking a hunting accident for murder, a mob hastily erects a scaffold for the stoically resigned Arrow-Tip, wrongly implicated in the incident. While wandering the forest, however, Boddo discovers that Brown, though wounded and immobilized, surely lives. The young blacksmith urgently bids the half-breed to return to the village, apprise them of Arrow-Tip's innocence, and save the Indian from the noose. But rather than seizing this opportunity to redeem himself in the eyes of his neighbors, Boddo, motivated by a blend of "cunning," "natural dull-ness," and "petty resolves of evil" (*WHB,* 277, 281) decides to avenge himself on Arrow-Tip, who had earlier humiliated Boddo by exposing him as a thief. Boddo promises to Brown he will deliver the message to Warren, but he takes a slow, circuitous route to the settlement, calcu-lating his arrival just a moment too late to stop Arrow-Tip's hanging. In the end, Boddo flees Warren, "scorned and abhorred by man, woman, and child" (*WHB,* 291).

Boddo's hunched stature, his evil physiognomy, and the irrationality that motivates both his conception and his crimes signify his violation of the racial dialectic at the foundation of nationalist fiction and demon-strate the developing perception of a link between hybrid atavism and crime. Like romance heroines Mary Conant and Faith Leslie, who slip into the woods with Indian lovers, Father Luke acts irrationally, his judgment compromised by grief, fear, and loneliness. Like Injun Joe, the bastard Boddo avenges his own birth upon good folk. While deriv-ative of earlier narratives, *The Half-Breed* also anticipates the suggestion in later dime novels that, in Scheick's words, "at some level of the white American psyche there existed a vague sense that as long as half-bloods were prominent in frontier settlements, the implementation of Ameri-can Manifest Destiny would be impeded, for the mixed-blood repre-sented the persistence of both an Indian and an alien European pres-ence in America."[12] This alien presence, transformed by racialist theory into an agent of criminal anarchy, becomes a more actively disruptive presence as reformers proposed new policies that would foster his assim-

12. Scheick, *Half-Blood,* 5.

ilation into the already fragile frontier social order. Boddo, a recognized thief, proves most treacherous in his exploitation of frontier vigilantism in order to satisfy his lust for revenge and his more basic desire to create mayhem, an irrational drive that registers more sharply nearer the passage of Allotment in later dime-novel mixed-bloods such as Badger's Redlaw and Ellis's Kaam. Although Whitman does not attempt to explore the root of the outlaw's antisocial malignity as do later writers, he does offer a glimpse of the place mixed-bloods would occupy in the dime novel, where the half-devil, the grotesque imp representing the belief in an inviolable hierarchy of races and the criminal consequence of violating this order, evolves into the misanthropic doppelgänger of the dashing Western hero, the *Homo criminalis* conceived by the science of criminal anthropology.

The Half-Breed as *Homo Criminalis*

Helen Carr's *Inventing the American Primitive* illustrates the close relationship in the nineteenth century between the new science of man and the growing national consciousness in the United States. Although she does not specifically consider the dime novel as an expression of this consciousness, her analysis suggests the ways the mass-publishing phenomenon in the United States appropriated racialist thought to sustain the national idea invented in the historical romance. Carr explains that American researchers Samuel Morton and Josiah Nott adopted methods practiced by European anthropologists to establish a "hierarchy of races whose hereditary and unchanging differences proved their totally separated origin, and the superiority of the white races to all others." George Fitzhugh, another American anthropologist, deduced that the law of nature, reflected in anatomical differences among the races, "enables and impels the stronger race to oppress and exterminate the weaker. . . . The Indian, like the savage races of Canaan, is doomed to extermination, and those who most sympathize with his fate would be the first to shoot him if they lived on the frontier." George Gliddon also writes that it is "vain to talk of civilizing them [the Indians]. You might as well attempt to change the nature of the buffalo." In Carr's view, the racial hierarchy conceived by American polygenist anthropology serves a crucial ideological purpose in its reconciliation of two mutually exclusive but equally compelling national ideals: the sacred trust bequeathed by the Revolution to defend the liberty and equality of all people; and the mandate of Manifest Destiny to dispossess and eradicate the Indian tribes. Carr concludes, "scientific racism politically resolved and removed this contradiction by making liberty the preserve of the highly evolved, but inappropriate to the lower races."[13] In its apparent resolution of the tension between equality and empire, a persistent problem in American nationalist fiction since Indian Removal, scientific racism becomes indispensable in the development of nationalist fiction of the later nineteenth century.

In his capacity to undermine the oppositions that distinguish the lower races from the more highly evolved, however, the mixed-blood represents a problem in this polygenist vision of national formation. His disappearance, unlike that of the full-blood Indian, could not be resolved by the invention of a deterministic racial hierarchy. In fact, his healthy, handsome presence throughout the nation directly challenged the assumed genetic incompatibility of Indians and whites, upsetting the balanced equation that justified and guaranteed the conquest of the western wilderness in the minds of Morton, Nott, Fitzhugh, and Gliddon. Although some observers such as W. H. Emory doggedly maintained that this "hybrid integration" produces a "very inferior and syphilitic race,"[14] Buffon's theory of the diminishing fertility of mixed-race pairs seemed increasingly doubtful to many Americans by 1860. Alexander Ross, for example, who lived more than fifty years on the frontier, married an Indian woman, and raised mixed-blood children, observes in *The Fur Hunters of the Far West* (1855): "Half-breeds ... are more designing, more daring, and more dissolute [than the pure Indian].... They are by far the fittest persons for the Indian countries, the best calculated by nature for going among Indians.... They are vigorous, brave; and while they possess the shrewdness and sagacity of the whites, they inherit the agility and expertness of the savage." In *Red River Settlement* (1856), Ross writes, "when not influenced or roused by bad counsel, or urged on to mischief by designing men, the natural disposition of the

13. Helen Carr, *Inventing the American Primitive: Politics, Gender, and the Representation of Native American Literary Traditions, 1789–1936,* 114, 115, 116, 119 (includes Fitzhugh and Gliddon quotes).

14. Emory quoted in Scheick, *Half-Blood,* 11.

half-breed is humble, benevolent, kind, and sociable. . . . While enjoy-
ing a kind of licentious freedom, they are generous, warm-hearted, and
brave, and left to themselves, quiet and orderly."[15] In order to reflect the
reality of a vigorous population of mixed-bloods on the American frontier and yet to maintain the necessity of the separation of races, the
dime novel required a more rigorously scientific confirmation of polygenesis, and it found such support in criminal anthropology.

In the middle nineteenth century, European racialist theory began
to confirm the American dread of the mixed-blood as an explosive, anarchic force only uncertainly perceived in *Malaeska* and *The Half-Breed*.
Through their correlation between the anatomical characteristics of the
savage and the predisposition to criminal behavior, anthropologists
warned that miscegenation would reverse the progress of evolution toward these beastly forms and trigger, as Scheick called it, the devastat-
ing eruption of "humanity's savage element." As David Jones explains,
the publication of Charles Darwin's *The Origin of Species* (1859) and
The Descent of Man (1871) provided for the founding of criminal anthropology, a discipline that drew from evolutionary theory in its proposal that "criminals are 'born' as 'atavistic' or biological 'throwbacks'
to an earlier and lower form of life."[16] In England, for example, Henry
Maudsley's *The Physiology and Pathology of the Mind* (1867) ventured
to call crime the product of disease, arguing, "no effort of the will,
however strong, will avail to prevent irregular and convulsive action
when a certain degree of instability of nervous element has, from one
cause or another, been produced in the spinal cells. It would be equally
absurd to preach control to the spasms . . . of epilepsy . . . or gentleness
to the hurricane."[17]

Francis Galton's "Hereditary Talent and Character" (1865) connected this instability to the "innate" character of the "savage," in
which nature had evolved a "wild, untamable restlessness."[18] In "The
Hereditary Nature of Crime" (1870) and "The Psychology of the

15. Alexander Ross, *The Fur Hunters of the Far West*, 96, 98; Alexander Ross,
The Red River Settlement, 23, 193.
16. David A. Jones, *History of Criminology: A Philosophical Perspective*, 82.
17. Maudsley quoted in Martin J. Wiener, *Reconstructing the Criminal: Culture, Law, and Policy in England, 1830–1914*, 168.
18. Galton quoted in Stocking, *Victorian Anthropology*, 95.

Criminal" (1870), Scottish prison surgeon James Bruce Thomson also concluded that concentrated populations of criminals, left to their own devices in the jail or in the urban "thieves' quarter," inevitably "degenerate into a set of demi-civilized savages, who, in hoards [*sic*], prey upon society... have no respect for the laws of marriage... [and] beget a depraved and criminal class hereditarily disposed to crime."[19] Maudsley, Galton, and Thomson represent the majority of criminal anthropologists of this era who generally equated civilized crime with savage custom. As historian of anthropology George Stocking explains, Victorian scientists perceived both as "governed more by impulse, deficient in foresight... [and] unable to subordinate instinctual need to human rational control."[20]

Although Cesare Lombroso relied heavily on the work of these earlier positivist criminologists, his landmark study, *L'uomo delinquente* (1876), most famously introduced the formal principles of criminal anthropology and the description of *Homo criminalis,* a distinct taxon of man predestined by biology to criminal behavior. Autopsies performed on 383 Italian prisoners revealed to Lombroso that all of the convicts shared certain physiological idiosyncrasies, a generalized "asymmetry of the head and face,"[21] and, more specifically, an enlarged middle occipital fossa in the skull and an overdeveloped vermis in the brain, two known characteristics of lower primates.[22] Lombroso declared the importance of his discovery in his dramatic characterization of the "born criminal":

> I seemed to see all of a sudden, lighted up as a vast plain under a flaming sky, the problem of the nature of the criminal—an atavistic being who reproduces in his person the ferocious instincts of primitive humanity and the inferior animals. Thus were explained anatomically the enormous jaws, high cheekbones, prominent superciliar arches, solitary lines in the palms, extreme size of the orbits, handle-shaped or sessile ears found in criminals, savages, and apes, insensibility

19. Thomson quoted in Robert Fletcher, "The New School of Criminal Anthropology," 229–30.
20. Stocking, *Victorian Anthropology,* 229.
21. Fletcher, "New School," 219.
22. Marie-Christine Leps, *Apprehending the Criminal: The Production of Deviance in Nineteenth-Century Discourse,* 32.

to pain, extremely acute sight, tattooing, excessive idleness, love of orgies, and the irresistible craving for evil for its own sake, the desire not only to extinguish life in the victim, but to mutilate the corpse, tear its flesh, and drink its blood.[23]

Lombroso further correlates race with criminality, drawing explicit parallels between criminal degeneracy and race traits observable in American savages: "Many of the characteristics found in savages, and among the colored races, are also to be found in habitual delinquents. They have in common, for example, thinning [facial] hair, lack of strength and weight, low cranial capacity, receding foreheads, highly developed frontal sinuses . . . darker skin, thicker . . . hair, large or handle-shaped ears . . . facile superstition . . . and finally the relative concept of the divinity and morals." In the skull of this atavistic being, Lombroso found evidence of a species of criminal man, proving, he believed, the hereditary basis of criminality and, more significantly, a biological connection between criminal man and primitive humanity.[24]

Providing new validation for traditional racialist theories of hybrid degeneracy introduced by Buffon; for the scientific racism of Nott, Morton, Gliddon, and Fitzhugh; and for the association of savagery and criminality among English researchers such as Maudsley, Galton, and Thomson; Lombroso's ideas were readily adopted by American anthropologists such as Robert Fletcher, president of the Anthropological So-

---

23. Quoted in Jones, *History of Criminology,* 83. I borrow here excerpted translations from David Jones's *History of Criminology* and Piers Beirne's *Inventing Criminology: Essays on the Rise of "Homo Criminalis."*

24. Beirne, *Inventing Criminology,* 149. Almost as soon as Lombroso published his extensive findings, critics called attention to faults in his documentation and reasoning, effectively discrediting by the turn of the twentieth century his claim that heredity alone determines criminality. His original study of 252 pages eventually grew to a formidable three-volume fifth edition of nearly 2,000 pages (1897), in which Lombroso considered an ever-increasing list of anomalies that contradicted his models and attempted to answer mounting criticism of his own methods, conclusions, and those of the positivist approach in general. By the end of his career, when the anomalies seemed to outnumber his proofs, he grudgingly admitted that social forces as well as heredity account for criminality and that "an entirely normal person could become a criminal . . . under exceptional circumstances," signaling the end of purely positivist criminology (Jones, *History of Criminology,* 87).

ciety of Washington. In an 1890 lecture, reprinted the following year in *American Anthropologist* as an introduction to "The New School of Criminal Anthropology," Fletcher approves the "resemblance" between the criminal and the "savage man" in their "atavistic" physiology, their "absence of the moral sense," their "enormous" egoism, their "adoption of the most direct and violent means to obtain [their] end[s]," and their inability to restrain "unkindly or inconvenient instincts." In "The Ascent of Man," an address delivered to the American Association for the Advancement of Science in 1890, Frank Baker similarly concludes that Indians frequently exhibit "ape-like" characteristics of bone structure and musculature, and atavistic "peculiarities" that demonstrate the biological affinity between the "lower races of man" and the "criminal classes." Fletcher's conclusion that neither the criminal nor the savage has the capacity to "accommodate himself to the society in which he must live" betrays the doubt, prevalent among these anthropologists, about the success of Allotment, passed only three years before Fletcher and Baker presented their lectures.[25]

This perception of an anatomical relationship between habitual delinquents and the colored races developing in both Europe and the United States over several decades suggested not only the dangers of miscegenation and other forms of integration but also the need for new, harsher methods for dealing with both born criminals and their kin, the savage Indians. Lombroso believed, for example, that *Homo criminalis*, "impervious to any kind of reform," necessitated sentences of "death, transportation, life imprisonment, [or] sterilization," and that "social defense required that born-criminal children also be institutionalized."[26] The association of Indians with such born criminals mandated similar penological policies of Indian removal and reform: extermination, exile, internment on reservations, and the forced reeducation of Indian children in schools far from home, measures that ensured the protection of social development on the frontier from this virulent sociopathic element. According to Rosa del Olmo, who chronicles the reception of European criminology in the Americas, the criminal man and the Indian

25. Fletcher, "New School," 209, 214–15; Frank Baker, "The Ascent of Man," 305, 316–17.
26. Leps, *Apprehending the Criminal*, 32, 59.

similarly represented a "direct challenge to order and progress....
[Their] limitations were not only moral, but also morphological. [They]
belonged to an inferior species, a 'different race,'" and thus required
parallel responses of isolation and punishment.[27]

The association of hereditary criminality and madness that Maudsley
evoked as early as 1867 reveals a connection between the historical romance and the dime novel, between heroines driven by madness to
Indian lovers and the atavistic, innately criminal half-breeds the dime
novel imagines as their unnatural progeny. Since the *North American
Review* first urged the creation of a national literature, novelists such as
Brown, Child, Sedgwick, and Cooper identified miscegenation with a
form of madness in which racially crossed characters, bereft of their
reason, degenerate into animal-like insensibility. Criminal anthropology,
in its definition of criminality as a genetic disease, represents the continuity of the association of racial mixing with the corrosion of health
and social order. Lombroso himself continued to assert the disruptive
potential of interracial contact throughout his career. His last major
work, the posthumously published *Crime: Its Causes and Remedies*
(1911), specifically addressed a North American audience and, summa-
rizing many of his earlier claims, identified "hybrid civilization," the
interaction and interbreeding between civilized and savage races, as a
cause of criminality.[28] This idea seemed to forebode that assimilationist
policy such as Allotment, in its proposed creation of a hybrid civilization, invited prolonged social instability and conflict, reversing the parallel courses of evolution and Manifest Destiny. Threatening to throw
open the doors of the jailhouse and set loose these born criminals on
American society, the proposed policy understandably disquieted a national culture founded on a deterministic sociobiological hierarchy.

27. Rosa del Olmo, "The Development of Criminology in Latin America," 1.
In *Crime and Punishment in American History,* Lawrence M. Friedman describes a
military commission's trial and execution of more than three hundred Dakotas,
defeated combatants in a war with Minnesota settlers. Friedman considers the case
"unusual" and "irregular" in its substitution of criminal proceedings for Indian
policy, a historical irregularity that suggests a developing penalogical approach to
savagery as early as 1862, the year of the mass execution (Friedman, *Crime and
Punishment,* 97).

28. Jones, *History of Criminology,* 87, 90.

The mixed-blood thus emerges in the nationalist fiction of the later nineteenth century as the dark double of the frontier hero, bearing the significant traits of Lombroso's criminal man: the dark skin and, darker still, the sadistic and "irresistible craving for evil for its own sake."

Redlaw

Although American culture did not fully absorb Lombroso's terminology until the last two decades of the nineteenth century, well after the dime novel had begun to flourish, *L'uomo delinquente* only represented the most notorious expression of a criminological discourse that had engaged Anglo-American anthropologists since Darwin introduced evolutionary theory. Rosa del Olmo identifies Lombroso's participation in the Third International Penitentiary Congress held in Rome in 1885 as the first formal introduction of American criminologists to Italian positivism. Other documents, however, suggest that American culture had appropriated these ideas earlier through British sources. For example, in his address recapitulating the claims of "The New School of Criminal Anthropology" to the Anthropological Society of Washington in 1891, Robert Fletcher explains that although "[n]othing has been published in the United States in relation" to Lombroso's "criminal man," American scientists have become familiar with the idea of crime as a "taint . . . in the blood" through earlier "well-known" and "frequently quoted" works by Thomson and Maudsley. Fletcher's remarks suggest that while American scientists and writers might not have been familiar with Lombroso's specific terminology until 1885 or 1890, the positivist tenet that "crime . . . becomes decisive only when the anthropologic and physical factors are found . . . [in] the organic constitution and the abnormal brain . . . [a] hereditary taint" already had been an anthropological commonplace for two decades. A series of criminological conferences, held throughout Europe and the United States in the 1870s, helped to define the new discipline as Lombroso would later envision it. Del Olmo explains that around this time American anthropologists came to consider the Indians as "America's first criminals. . . . They were defined as degenerate, with racial and mental limitations, and their ignorance and backwardness were attributed to innate, inferior traits."[29] This innate criminality, inherited by the mixed-bloods from their degenerate Indian parent, consistently manifests itself in dime-novel half-breeds such as Joseph Badger's Redlaw, an unfortunate product of hybrid civilization and a warning against the assimilation envisioned by Allotment.

Badger boasts the sort of reputation, relatively common among dime-novel authorial personae, blended from fact, rumor, and public fictions constructed by themselves and their publishers. His biography reads like one of his novels, and he was, in fact, the subject of several dime novels depicting him as a Western hero. Less romantic accounts show him as one of the most methodical and professionally conscientious dime-novel authors, regularly producing Westerns for Beadle and Adams for twenty-five years before his suicide. In the estimation of some critics, Badger stood above his peers as one of the most talented of the great multitude of dime-novel writers, perhaps because he couched his tales in a more complex historical context than his peers did, although *Redlaw* strikes the reader as more elemental, more ambiguous in its historical and geographical setting, brief, confusing at some turns, and starker in its characterization. Like John Rollin Ridge, Badger seems more interested in the villain than the hero, conceding the requisite triumph of the stock, square-jawed champion but roving more gleefully in the rogue's bloodthirsty scheming.[30] In his irrational treachery and violence, the half-breed villain, Polk Redlaw, serves to test the law, its formation, its function, its limits, and its abuses, embodying the criminal man in his dogged opposition to the just frontier hero, Clay Poynter.

Somewhere in settlements west of Fort Leavenworth, a vigilance committee gathers to discuss a mysterious outbreak of counterfeiting and horse theft. Through the instigation of Dement, who later emerges as the novel's evil mastermind, suspicion quickly falls on Poynter, a fair-haired and well-muscled young man with an admittedly shady past.

29. Fletcher, "New School," 202, 217, 204; del Olmo, "Development of Criminology," 5.

30. In addition to writing nearly a dozen novels with the mixed-blood outlaw at the core of the narrative, Badger also published a series of books dramatizing the legend of Joaquín Murieta, the "gold rush Robin Hood" introduced in John Rollin Ridge's 1854 novel.

The band of vigilantes elects as their judge Neil McGuire, a tough and prosperous farmer and the father of Poynter's secret sweetheart, Nora. Badger depicts McGuire as honest though self-important and too hasty to administer "Kentucky law," the rough border justice that dispenses with the inconveniences of due process and pronounces only two forms of sentence: flogging or hanging. Badger introduces Redlaw lurking on the edge of the mob. With a stature "tall and straight as an arrow... a lithe suppleness in every movement... [a] swarthy complexion, and long, straight, black hair," Redlaw does not resemble the half-breed grotesques of earlier fiction, but in his dusky vigor appears as Poynter's dark double: robust, skilled in tracking, shooting, and fighting but criminally motivated by greed, vengeance, and the simple and inexplicable will to anarchy.[31]

Throughout the narrative, Redlaw wages personal warfare on Poynter, picking a fight at the Twin Sycamores tavern, shooting him through the shoulder and, in turn, accusing Poynter of attempted murder when the young hero repays these assaults with a sound beating. Already suspected in the counterfeiting scheme, Poynter finds himself before the committee. Redlaw introduces phony evidence, inflames the "fiercest, basest passions" of the vigilantes—"wolves, not men"—and speeds Poynter's trial to its expected conclusion. Found guilty of both counterfeiting and attempted murder, Poynter is sentenced to flogging and hanging, an unprecedented judgment (*RL*, 40). McGuire finally objects, arguing that only torturous savages would lash a condemned man before his execution. He resigns as judge and washes his hands of the proceedings but makes no effort to delay Poynter's lynching or to discover the truth behind Redlaw's obviously bogus accusations. The hopeless scene, of course, only sets the stage for Poynter's daring escape and the opportune appearance of a band of outlaws led by the mysterious old-timer White Crees. Redlaw narrowly escapes the wrath of Poynter's rescuers and vows revenge: "The traits inherited from the Indian cross in his blood were aroused and in full play.... The mongrel was not satisfied.... His hatred was too intense; he required a death of shame—of degrada-

---

31. Joseph E. Badger Jr., *Redlaw, the Half-Breed; or, The Tangled Trail*, 16. Further citations will be made parenthetically with the abbreviation *RL*.

tion; a death that would destroy the life and honor of his foe," but for a short time the "villainous mongrel" retreats to the shadows of Badger's story (*RL,* 49).

In the tradition of the dime-novel plot, Badger reveals a string of old secrets and true identities at the end of the novel's tangled trail. White Crees is unmasked as Poynter's long-lost father who had also miraculously escaped execution but was prevented by his status as a condemned felon from returning to his family. Dement is likewise unmasked as Meagreson, the ignoble outlaw who had originally framed Poynter's father and doomed him to exile, and who now orchestrates the pursuit of Poynter himself, slaking his old hatred for the father upon the son. Meagreson meets his deserved end writhing in a horrible death-agony, a bullet shattering his spine. McGuire reasserts control of the committee and declares both Poynter and his father innocent. Nora, long forgotten, reappears in the final pages to take her place beside Poynter at the altar. Redlaw remains the only unresolved problem. No longer in Meagreson's service, the "mongrel cur" now seeks his own irrational revenge in a suicidal assault on Poynter's wedding celebration. Thwarted by Poynter's friends in his attempt to slash Nora's throat, he fires a shot that grazes Poynter's head before the wedding guests finally kill him in a flurry of return fire. With "the mangled form of the mongrel assassin, Polk Redlaw" cleared from the dance floor, the festivities resume, Poynter's "slight headache" the only harm done (*RL,* 95).

Badger's novel underwent several reprints in subsequent decades as publishers continued to capitalize on readers' apparent desire to witness Redlaw shredded by bullets again and again. A later revision of the title, *The Half-Breed Rival,* emphasizes his role as Poynter's evil doppelgänger. In one sense, this mirror imaging recalls Edgar Huntly's violent communion with savages. Like Brown, Badger offers sensational imagery but comparatively little psychological insight into the dark adversary, much less, in fact, than *Malaeska, The Half-Blood,* or *The White Squaw.* At first, the half-breed renegade appears merely greedy, but he continues his campaign against Poynter even after Meagreson no longer compensates him. He claims vengeance, but Badger furnishes no background and no reason to explain his wild personal animosity for the winsome white hero. Critics generally attribute such "illogical," "incomplete" characterization to the lack of exposition symptomatic of the dime novel's inherently jerky, action-packed plot. In this fundamentally dialectical novel, however, understanding Redlaw depends on understanding Poynter.

Badger imagines the frontier as an inversion of an orderly, lawful society, a perverse world where vigilantism cloaks itself as justice, criminals prosecute victims, and innocent men hang on the false testimony of the guilty. From the first pages of the novel, Poynter represents law on the lawless frontier. He does not swagger in the more familiar costume of the silver-starred sheriff but stalwartly asserts rationality and judiciousness against the irrational and corrupt forces represented by Redlaw and the vigilantes. Upon his arrest, Poynter claims his constitutional right to due process, demanding that his trial "shall be according to the law," that the charges against him be clearly and publicly stated, that he may answer them publicly, that he may have "counsel" and the "time to procure witnesses" on his behalf (*RL*, 28–29). When he captures Wesley Sprowl, another man Meagreson pays to fabricate damning evidence against him, Poynter spares his life, moved by Sprowl's remorse and by pity for his innocent wife. He pardons and releases the captive, his sense of justice tempered by the mercy the vigilantes had not shown him. In contrast to their wolfish drive to punish without deliberation, Poynter stands for reason, prudence, and a form of justice that seeks not to punish the guilty but to protect the innocent. McGuire and his vigilantes, in their belief in the unwritten law "that justifies a man in killing a snake, or ridding the community of a scourge" (*RL*, 26), are well intentioned but ignorant, foolishly misled by more malicious, more clever agents, and ultimately destructive rather than protective of the public welfare. Badger rejects their Kentucky law but seems also to recognize its necessity as a step toward the inevitable development of civilization on the frontier. McGuire remains an honest if temporarily deluded man, eventually recognizing and enforcing true justice. In the meantime, Poynter and White Crees bear their unjust pursuit with confidence in their own innocence and their idealistic view that justice must ultimately prevail over villainy and ignorance, reason over madness and savagery.

Redlaw, finally, represents the darker instinct that rules the backwoods, the criminal antithesis to the Enlightenment ideals that buttress the nation. Like Whitman's Boddo, he speaks falsely, instigates the mob, and exploits frontier vigilantism to sate his irrational urge for revenge. By protecting and acting in the service of horse thieves, Redlaw undermines the order of rightful ownership that sustained assimilationist arguments for Allotment during the later decades of the nineteenth century, signifying a threat to the development of civilized life in the West more dangerous even than vigilantism or the mischief perpetrated by White Crees, who admits to the rash of counterfeiting and horse theft but defends these deeds as habits of "free living" rather than crime. In this series of confessions, Badger establishes the racial basis for real villainy, distinguishing the cause of the white criminal's behavior from that of the innately criminal man, the atavistic half-breed Redlaw. While White Crees, a naturally law-abiding man, is driven to mischief by external circumstances, Redlaw's actions arise from an innate flaw in his tainted heredity. This distinction between heredity and circumstance—the point of contention between Jefferson and Buffon and the key evidence in William Apess's case for Indian redemption—also forms the foundation of Ridge's sympathetic portrayal of Murieta and his explanation of the Mexican outlaw's deeds as reactions against unfair laws and cruel mistreatment by Americans rather than as inherent evil. For Badger and for readers anticipating the assimilation of the Indian into mainstream society, however, Redlaw's outlawry is logical in its illogic. It needs no explanation, no reason, because it is born and impelled in the absence of reason, the province of only the more highly evolved races. The Indian cross in his blood naturally disposes Redlaw to criminality. According to the familiar tenets of criminal anthropology and the description of the criminal man that Lombroso would popularize shortly after the publication of Badger's novel, Redlaw's desires "to extinguish life" and to do "evil for its own sake" are innate. With the half-breed villain's long-awaited destruction, Badger restores law to the renegade's anarchic world and ensures the success of the civilizing project, offering a formula for national ascendance in the wholesale acquittal of the innocent; the cathartic purging of the criminal, mixed-blood element; and the nuptials of the formerly wild, free rover, symbolically heralding civilization in the wilderness. "What is a novel," Badger finally asks his reader, "without that?" (RL, 95).

The Half-Blood

Only nineteen years old and working as a teacher in Trenton when he sold *Seth Jones*, his first novel, to Beadle and Adams in 1860, Edward Ellis seemed a born dime novelist. The book proved extraordinarily successful, far outselling the previous seven Beadle's Dime Novels and firmly establishing the fledgling series as a highly profitable enterprise. Ellis undoubtedly benefited from Beadle and Adams' innovative promotional campaign. During the summer of 1860, mysterious posters appeared on barn walls and fences throughout New York: "Who is Seth Jones?" Weeks later a picture of a frontier hunter clad in buckskin proclaimed, "I am Seth Jones." Subsequent advertisements announced: "Seth Jones is from New Hampshire"; "Seth Jones understands the redskins"; "Seth Jones takes an observation"; "Seth Jones can't express himself." During his subsequent career, Ellis prodigiously published more than 150 volumes of adventure tales and popular history and maintained an impeccable reputation even among critics who remained persistently hostile to the dime-novel venture. He adopted more than twenty pseudonyms, including James Fenimore Cooper Adams, an homage to the dime novel's patron saint, and, like Cooper, won both commercial profit and critical distinction among prestigious reviewers such as William Everett, who praised *Seth Jones* for its "human portrayal of the Indians."[32] *The Half-Blood* similarly presents a more human picture of the mixed-blood than *Malaeska, The Half-Breed*, or *Redlaw*, exploring his alienation in more depth than these previous novels. While the half-breed in Ellis's novel, discovering his origin, experiences the same crushing melancholy that drives William Danforth to suicide and enacts a retribution on the white race more criminally sadistic than even Boddo or Redlaw might imagine, he also seeks his place among those whom he considers his native people, manifesting the double consciousness that previous fictional mixed-bloods could not and anticipating the conflicted, more sympathetic characters in *The White Squaw* and *Ramona*.

When an Arapaho hunting party snares trappers Edward Murtel and Harry Harmer, the Indians prepare to sacrifice their captives as compensation for the spirits of two braves recently fallen in battle with the

32. Pearson, *Dime Novels*, 91.

hated Pawnee. Murtel and Harmer seize their only opportunity for salvation by improbably flirting with two Indian girls, Yana and Kouna, the young widows of the braves for whom the trappers will be sacrificed. Although the hapless mountain men do not realize it, the widows alone can stay the executions, according to the vague but "irrevocable laws of custom."[33] In another reenactment of the Pocahontas drama, Yana and Kouna, smitten by the comical white men, defy the bloodthirsty warriors and command that Murtel and Harmer be spared. Murtel weds Yana, who bears a son, whom they name Kaam, or "Daylight." Harmer weds Kouna, and though the two do not conceive a child, the aging trapper grows to love his young Indian wife. Both men, however, long to return to civilization and plan their escape once they have gained the trust of the Arapaho. When the two sisters try to stop them, Murtel, in an act of inhuman brutality, slays both women and abducts his own mixed-blood son, planning to sell him as a Negro to cover his expenses for the failed trapping expedition. Avenging his beloved Kouna, Harmer kills his partner, rescues the infant Kaam, and returns with the child to St. Louis, where he claims paternity and provides for the child's education with a Catholic priest while he continues his adventures in the West.

The first half of Ellis's story resembles *Malaeska* in its portrayal of a half-breed child conceived in an unfortunate union, orphaned in frontier conflict, and commended to civilization, where he grows into "a fine, dark, intelligent stripling," tentatively content under an affectionate guardian yet ignorant of his origin. Kaam inherits the refined "intellectual countenance of the European races" but, like the narcissistic William Danforth, exhibits sinister evidence of the "hot blood of his nature." He devours histories of the Crusades but sympathizes with the Muslim infidels, a people, he imagines, "battling against the combined upholders of . . . oppression, treachery, ambition, and bloodshed"—the Europeans (*EHB*, 9). Despite his aloofness and disdain for the herd of humanity, Kaam falls in love with Julia Severance, a fellow orphan. Although the girl cares for him, his brooding personality repels her. Like William Danforth, he affects an unusual sense of superiority, the enormous egoism anthropologist Robert Fletcher would shortly identify as an innate

---

33. Edward S. Ellis, *The Half-Blood; or, The Panther of the Plains*, 6. Further citations will be made parenthetically with the abbreviation *EHB*.

characteristic of the born criminal and the savage, feeling himself "heir to the right rule," above the "common multitude . . . which great minds live to control, scourge when they rebel, and . . . drive to toil like the cattle to the fields" (*EHB*, 10).

The Half-Blood, like *Malaeska*, reaches its crisis when the mixed-blood hero, addled by internal turmoil, learns of his Indian parentage. Kaam's hauteur, like that of William Danforth, only guarantees more acute trauma when he discovers his true "degenerate" nature. When Harmer returns to St. Louis, Kaam confronts the aging trapper and begs him to disclose the unknown truth about his parents. Harmer dutifully tells of Murtel's fatherhood and treachery as Kaam sinks beneath the realization: "like some fair ship struck by the tempest and reft of everything, he yielded his heart to the storm's billows of passion and wept long and bitterly." Tears soon give way to "a moody melancholy" and his painful acceptance of himself as a "scorned . . . outcast thing." His former belief in his own natural predominance over the slavish multitude collapses and he resolves to shun the white man forever: "Raised by civilized society, and educated in its distinctions, he felt that he, the half-breed . . . held but a questionable place among those with whom he had mingled; and fancying himself, as it were, in an amphitheater, gazed upon by the assembled world, who all were possessed of his story, he shrunk from the gaze of human eyes" (*EHB*, 10).

Adding to his humiliation, Adolph Murtel, Edward Murtel's previous son by a white woman and thus Kaam's half-brother, swaggers into town and wins Julia's affection. As reminder of his father's cruelty, a rival suitor to Julia, and a representative of the entire white race, a civilization he had always believed oppressive and now recognizes as the confirmed "foe of his native people," Adolph becomes the object of Kaam's intense hatred. The half-breed swears vengeance upon Murtel and all "those who crossed his path," severs his friendship with the kind priest who raised him, and sets out to find his fortune in the western wilderness as an avowed renegade. He soon encounters the Arapaho and discovers that his mother, whom he and Harmer believed murdered by Murtel, had in fact survived the vicious attack. The scene represents another departure from *Malaeska*. While Danforth shrinks in denial from Malaeska as she tries to embrace him as her lost and beloved son, Kaam declares, "Mother, I am Kaam, thy son" (*EHB*, 11), locks her in his arms, and, befitting one of superior blood, assumes command of the tribe.

The novel moves toward its sensational conclusion as Kaam and Adolph cross paths in the mountains during a blizzard. Kaam gives food and shelter to Adolph who, exhausted and on the brink of starvation, lies completely at Kaam's mercy. Although Kaam recognizes Adolph, the white man fails to identify his Arapaho benefactor as the young, brooding gentleman he had known in St. Louis. Adolph's inadvertent confession that he has left Julia pregnant and slandered her in order to deny his paternal responsibility whets Kaam's appetite for revenge. He pretends friendship and nurses Adolph until his strength returns, but only so that his hated rival and half-brother might longer endure the horrible tortures Kaam secretly plans, a method of revenge commensurate with his "perfect hatred" for "the whole white race" (*EHB*, 13). Ellis does not delay the delicious execution. In the glow of the rising sun, Kaam strips and binds Adolph upright to a tree and with the point of his knife opens a dozen surgical wounds in Adolph's veins, condemning him to an agonizing death by slow bleeding.[34] Kaam finally reveals his identity, and even as Adolph begs, "stab me to the heart at once . . . but do not torture me with this slow murder as if you were a fiend," the half-breed exults, "No . . . by doing so I would forego my dearest revenge—cut short the enjoyment of seeing death infold you in its cold embrace. . . . You *die*, and by the hand of Kaam, the Arapahoe half-breed" (*EHB*, 14).

With this chilling declaration, Ellis transforms the victim of white injustice—a criminal like Badger's White Crees and Ridge's Murieta who reacts to hostile circumstances—into an unregenerate outlaw, an embodiment of the sadistic *Homo criminalis* who desires, as Lombroso observes, "not only to extinguish life in the victim, but to mutilate the corpse, tear its flesh, and drink its blood."[35] Although Ellis represents Kaam's vengeance on Adolph as ostensibly justified, the savagery of the torture and the vicious pleasure Kaam derives from it blurs the distinction between heroism and villainy, between the fully evolved, moral man and the atavistic savage. Watching the dying Adolph beg for his

34. The cover illustration depicting the scene shows Adolph fully clothed.
35. Quoted in Jones, *History of Criminology*, 83.

life and then for his death, the reader suspects that Kaam lacks mercy, the most divine Christian virtue that Clay Poynter bestows on Wesley Sprowl. The scene demonstrates that Kaam's Indian half—his thirst for revenge, his unchecked rage, his all-consuming race hatred, his animalistic blood lust—has usurped his white half, the aspirations and refinements of civilization that had nourished his youth. When he later learns that Julia has died from the grief Adolph has caused her, Kaam "registered an oath of vengeance between himself and the white race forever. He swore to be their foe until death—to hold no faith with them, but, with treacherous revenge, to visit on all alike an indiscriminate hatred," and thus vomits his last trace of civilization (*EHB*, 15). Having satisfied his perceived chivalric duty toward Julia in killing Adolph, he no longer has justification for the rage that has finally become treacherous, no longer manifested as revenge upon a deserving scoundrel but rather as indiscriminate warfare on all white men, guilty and innocent alike.

While he anticipates mixed-blood characters that embrace Indian life by qualified choice rather than default, Kaam remains, like Boddo and Redlaw, doomed to exile and criminality by the unfortunate cross in his blood. His embrace of his Arapaho identity seems, as he punctures Adolph Murtel's writhing flesh, less the happy affirmation of Indian life that we will witness in Jackson's *Ramona* than the rancorous rejection of white civilization that we witness in *Redlaw*. In Kaam's egoistic conviction of his own superiority, in his ultimately savage and indiscriminate violence, Ellis hints at the mixed-blood's criminal taint and a tyrannous narcissism that, when stripped of civilized refinement, reveals itself as a sadism so inhuman that it must be branded in his criminal, half-animal nature.

Although Kaam's motivation is more individualized, more human, than Redlaw's, Ellis, like Badger, conceives the half-breed a more generally pervasive threat to the civilized order. The kinetic narrative, typical of the dime novel, where one bloody action scene follows rapidly upon another, slows in an unusually long interlude when Kaam considers his origin and comes to accept his outcast status. In his careful meditation on Kaam's acceptance of exile, Ellis emphasizes the necessity of the separation of the half-breed from white society, a separation, the narrative suggests, mandated by a natural racial antipathy that precedes and perhaps facilitates the individual crimes that whites commit against Kaam and that Kaam commits against whites. Even before Kaam has a good reason to hate whites, before he knows the betrayal of his white father, the treachery of his white half-brother, and the disfavor of his white lover, when he had known only the kindness and devotion of Harmer and the priest, he expresses an instinctual loathing for the hypocrisy of white civilized order, a criminal bent similar to Redlaw's innate, unreasoning hatred of Clay Poynter. Reading of the medieval battles between the Saracens and the Europeans, the youthful Kaam allies himself with the infidels, the ancient enemies of Christianity and civilization. In this attempt to reimagine the Crusades (the historical antecedent, Ellis suggests, of the present Indian wars) from a nonwhite, non-Christian point of view, Ellis ventures cautious criticism of the nationalist ideology that Reid, Jackson, and Ridge subvert with greater conviction. Yet, while Jackson and Ridge suggest that the barriers to assimilation are not biologically determined but rather politically arbitrary and thus surmountable, Ellis's criticism veils an admonition against hybrid civilization that echoes Lombroso's, a hint of an innate racial antagonism that cuts deeper than politics or sentimentality. Ellis portrays Kaam's outlawry less as a reaction against individual circumstances, as Jackson and Ridge would, than as an inevitable manifestation of the latent antisocial bent of the schoolboy who roots for the villains, the born criminal. Ellis does not seek to absolve white cruelties and invites the reader to sympathize with Kaam. He even hints that Kaam inherits his innate bloodlust not from his Indian mother but from his white father, who sought to butcher his Arapaho wife and sell his son into slavery. Ellis, however, strenuously warns readers to fear the half-breed. When Kaam's instinctual mistrust of the white race explodes into violent hatred, Kaam declares war not only upon his evil rival, Adolph Murtel, but also upon the entire white race and on the readers themselves. Although Ellis complicates Badger's representation of the irrationally evil Redlaw by providing his character with a sympathetic history and a loathsome white foil, Kaam ultimately becomes the familiar half-breed devil who, in spite of his white blood and white education, cannot overcome his hereditary predisposition to violence, an "acknowledged savage," by his own account, who renounces the "Daylight" his name signifies and adopts the name Mo Kah, "Night," the name that marks the "settled gloom . . . on his brow" and frightens even his fellow Arapahoes (*EHB*, 16). Ellis, unlike Child, Stephens, Whitman, and Badger, does not purge the savage element through education, exile, or death. He alone has the stage at the conclusion of the novel, vowing not to disappear like the Indian of old romance but to pursue like a savage Ahab his vengeance until he draws his last breath. This half-breed outlaw who would not disappear embodies most frightfully Injun Joe's ghost, the residue of romance, the destructive potential of assimilationist experiments.

The White Squaw

Mayne Reid's portrayal of the mixed-blood Wacora significantly departs from *Redlaw* and *The Half-Blood* in its suggestions that race war and other forms of social disorder arise as much from circumstance, from white vice, as from racial taint, and that chaos and degeneracy need not attend the hybrid civilization proposed by Allotment. The novel thus anticipates *Ramona* and Native writing of the twentieth century that challenge not only the biological basis of crime but also the biological interpretation of race in general. While Reid rejects the idea that Indian blood might degrade the white man to an atavistic state, he nevertheless maintains the parallel racialist idea, also suggested by Thomas Jefferson and Robert Knox, that white blood may elevate the Indian to a more enlightened state. The novel, though not as closely allied to criminal anthropology as other dime novels, remains reluctant to abandon the assumption of a racial hierarchy that ultimately precludes integration. Like many of the earlier romances of the vanishing Indian, the narrative concludes that the accident of Wacora's Indian birth tragically necessitates his separation from the white settlements and casts doubt on the project of assimilation enacted less than a decade later.

The White Squaw is set in the years immediately preceding Florida's Second Seminole War (1835–1842) and represents the conflict attending the Indians' imminent removal in the drama of two communities, a settlement of white colonists led by the imperious and greedy governor Elias Rody and a Seminole band led by the aging chief Oluski. Former friends, these two patriarchs now vie for control of a particularly valuable hill coveted by Rody as a potential site for a mansion overlooking Tampa Bay and venerated by the Seminoles as an ancestral burial ground. When Oluski refuses to sell the land, Rody swiftly moves a group of armed settlers onto the hill and constructs a plantation house fortified by a stockade. Wacora, a young mixed-blood war chief and nephew of Oluski, assembles the scattered Seminole bands into a small but well-coordinated army and plans an attack on Rody's settlement.

In the shadow of the impending storm, two interracial romances develop. Warren Rody, the foppish heir of the expansive estate, secretly lusts for Sansuta, Oluski's beautiful but foolish daughter. Both children fall disappointingly short of their fathers' lordly expectations, echoing Sedgwick's characterization of Faith Leslie and Oneco in *Hope Leslie*. Warren is "of small stature, effeminate countenance, restless shifting eyes and a vacillating expression of mouth. . . . [H]e did not look like the son of the hard, rugged man who stood beside him," Elias Rody.[36] Sansuta is a lovely "wood-nymph . . . innocent as a child, but inordinately vain . . . nothing but a frivolous child," whose lack of discernment provokes Warren "to the accomplishment of her ruin" (*WS*, 47, 63–64). The degenerate Warren pursues Sansuta not with "manly, loving passion" but with "a covert gambler's lust for possession without labor" (*WS*, 36). He cultivates a false friendship with Nelatee, Sansuta's equally naive brother, and enlists Crookleg, a deformed Negro, to deliver messages to Sansuta and arrange secret trysts. His open condemnation of the shame of interracial desire barely conceals his "base treachery" (*WS*, 37). Her vanity inflated by the prospect of becoming the wife of a prominent white man, Sansuta easily falls prey to Warren's false promises and agrees to elope with him.

In contrast to this debased form of miscegenation, Reid offers a true romance, conceived in mature love and right judgment, between Alice Rody, Warren's "frank, fearless" sister, and Wacora, the son of a Seminole chief and a Spanish captive who, like Mary Jemison, grew to love her Indian captor. While Warren appears to be the heir to Elias Rody's meanest qualities, his covetousness, dishonesty, and brutality, Alice inherits her father's physical robustness and commanding intelligence. The reader meets her astride a horse, riding through wild Gulf Coast swampland, her "hair in a rich, golden shower of curls," her "neck and

36. Mayne Reid, *The White Squaw*, 83. Further citations will be made parenthetically with the abbreviation *WS*.

shoulders admirably rounded," and her figure "graceful and striking" (*WS*, 66). Initially enamored of Sansuta, Wacora delays courtship until he has succeeded in destroying Rody's plantation.

Unlike the chaotic mischief innate in the half-breeds depicted in *The Half-Breed*, *Redlaw* and *The Half-Blood*, Reid represents Wacora's aggression against whites not as irrational self-hatred but rather as a "great ambition . . . nobler than that of revenge" for the unification and "regeneration of the Indian race" (*WS*, 103–4). Applying the superior education he received in a Spanish mission and the natural good judgment of his mother's race, Wacora cautions his warriors against their customarily random retaliation and organizes a timely, coordinated offensive. Using superior white tactics against whites themselves, the mixed-blood general accomplishes the complete devastation of the white settlement, the recapture of Seminole burial grounds, and the death of the hated governor. Alice, the sole white survivor of the battle, becomes the Seminoles' captive.

During the battle, the cowardly Warren hides with Sansuta in a distant cave. Although the narrative is politely hazy, Reid hints that the planned elopement has become an abduction, and that Warren has rapaciously satisfied his lust for the Indian maiden. When Nelatee rescues Sansuta and kills Warren, he finds that his sister has succumbed to the familiar fate of white women who indulge unnatural passions in the historical romance: "Her wild, staring eyes, with the unmeaning smile upon her lips, told the sad tale. Her reason had departed!" (*WS*, 130). She refuses to believe that Warren, whom she still cherishes as her lover and savior, is dead, and eventually her delusions give way to "violent madness," "silent . . . melancholy," and "rapt . . . bewildered thoughts" (*WS*, 150). Like the miscegenated white women of earlier historical romance, she loses her former nymphal vitality: the "poor girl's form had wasted away, and her features become shrunken" (*WS*, 157).

Unlike Child, Sedgwick, or other dime-novel writers, however, Reid conceives a more successful possibility for racial mixture. His formula, like the one some critics identify in Jackson's *Ramona*, depends on effacing the Indian half of his mixed-blood hero. Wacora exemplifies an interracial ideal presented in some dime novels and, later, in *Ramona*, a hybrid form of noble savagery that Reid calls "savage chivalry." In this hopeful vision, which Jefferson had once considered as a path toward the assimilation of the red race into the white nation, superior white blood cleanses the savage blood through succeeding generations; where education, religion, legislation, and warfare fail, selective breeding might yet succeed. Although Reid portrays Wacora as a nativist messiah in the mold of Pontiac, Cornplanter, and Tecumseh, his vision, intelligence, and ability to command the naturally impulsive and fractious Seminoles derive from his white parentage and white education. The "influence of the white blood flowing in his veins" causes him to feel remorse for the victims of his campaign against the settlement, a twinge of mercy "strangely inconsistent" with his Indian nature and clearly lacking in the renegades Redlaw and Kaam (*WS,* 39). Such evidence of humanity piques Alice's interest in her captor. She baits him, "savages must act according to their instincts," evincing his reply, "Savages, yes! but men who know right from wrong should act from judgment" (*WS,* 146). Although Wacora does not explicitly identify "men who know" as white men, readers conditioned by captivity narratives, historical romances, and dime novels would recognize reason and judgment as white qualities. The exchange demonstrates that Wacora's white half predominates over his Indian half, his innate criminal irrationality, confirming his natural leadership of the wild and ungoverned pack of Indians and his suitability as a partner for Alice.

As romance blooms in the final chapters of the novel, Reid inverts traditional notions of Indian captivity. In order that his interracial marriage and consummation do not disturbingly resemble the abductions and rapes conventional in captivity narratives, Reid emphasizes both Wacora's whiteness and Alice's consent. In the months following the attack, the captive woman gradually accepts the deaths of her father and her brother and, "by one of those marvelous transformations of which the human heart is capable, Alice Rody... became reconciled to her residence among the Indians... even to the awakening of pleasant thoughts" (*WS,* 155). This "marvelous transformation," the awakening of love for her Indian mate, is the same experienced by Mary Jemison and denied by Child, Sedgwick, and later romantic writers such as Walter Edmonds. Significantly, before the chivalric Wacora presumes to express his love openly, he offers Alice her chance to return, as the Seneca offered redemption to Jemison. Like Jemison, Alice declines and, in turn, captures Wacora's heart: "The girl was free—her jailer had become her prisoner.... [H]is white captive ... had made him a captive" (*WS,* 155, 190). From his unusual superiority to other Indians, Alice senses that "he had white blood in his veins," but she regrets that he had not been "brought up among her own race." She wonders, "What might not a man of his intelligence, chivalric courage, and purity of thought, have become in a society where civilization would have developed all these mental qualities?" (*WS,* 156) Wacora nevertheless proves more noble than "civilized" men like her father and brother, who "approach[ed] ... barbarism [with] the selfishness and rapacity" characteristic of whites (*WS,* 156). Alice concludes, "No *preux chevalier* could be more courteous in his bearing. No prince more calmly conscious of his own birthright.... Whether thinking so or not, he was one of nature's noblemen.... His mind was of his mother's race" (*WS,* 157). Her lengthy deliberation on Wacora, as unusual in the dime novel as Kaam's slow brooding on his own mixed origins, signals Reid's care in establishing the healthy basis of the interracial romance, conceived in liberty rather than captivity, in reason rather than derangement, and Wacora's moral superiority to the savage abductors familiar in captivity narratives. Bound to the tribe neither by force nor by the inconvenient birth of mixed-blood children, Alice enjoys an autonomy that "white squaws" such as Mary Conant and Mary Jemison do not. Reid demonstrates that her pleasant thoughts of her Indian mate do not rise unnaturally from grief or madness but rather from many months of reflection and reconciliation to her situation. With a "heart like a pure flower," unblighted by the "accident of [Indian] birth," Wacora likewise does not desire Alice by the instinctual lust thought to draw Indian men to white women (*WS,* 194–95).

While Kaam represents the darkest fear of assimilation, Wacora represents its most hopeful dream. Although he answers the troubling questions handed him by the traditions of the captivity narrative and historical romance, Reid maintains an ominous irresolution in his short epilogue explaining that the Seminole War forces Wacora, his young white bride, and their people to flee to reservation lands beyond the Mississippi. Although respected as a great war chief even in defeat, Wacora continues to suffer an acute identity crisis. As much as Alice becomes the "white squaw" of the Seminoles, Wacora remains their white chief, superior to his people in both breeding and education but tragically bound to them by the accident of birth. Anticipating further warfare between Seminoles and whites, Wacora soliloquizes on the difficulty of his position as a mixed-blood leader, anticipating the internal conflicts of mixed-bloods in twentieth-century fiction: "I, an Indian savage as white men call me, would gladly lay down this day and forever the rifle and the knife, would willingly bury the war hatchet, and abandon this sanguinary contest! Could I do so with honor? . . . No! To the end I must now proceed, half assured that my early enthusiasm [in the attack on Rody] was but a flash of conscious right, and not the result of reason and knowledge" (*WS*, 189). Although rightness and reason, those white qualities that predominate in Wacora and remain absent in the criminal half-breeds in *Redlaw* and *The Half-Blood*, demand that he sue for peace, cede the land he had won from Rody, and accept the white presence on the frontier, misguided Indian honor and enthusiasm inevitably draw him and his people into an uncompromising struggle that his reason assures him cannot be won. Although he recognizes what is right and reasonable, his race and his duty to his people determine that he must act unreasonably. For Reid, the mixed-blood is not, as Allotment imagined him, a facilitator of racial accord but simply an Indian exile who, because of his innate white intelligence and sensitivity, feels the pain of dispossession more acutely.

We see in these dime novels spanning more than two decades a progression from polygenist attitudes about the innate degeneracy of the mixed-blood and the inevitable extinction of the Indian toward a more compromising picture of racial blending. *The Half-Blood* and *The White Squaw*, published nearer the passage of Allotment than *Malaeska* and *Redlaw*, resist the cultural tendency to purge the hybrid element, and although Kaam and Wacora are banished as certainly as Boddo and the generations of Indians who followed the Trail of Tears, Ellis and Reid invite readers to interrogate the reasons and consequences of their exile. Their half-breed characters themselves manifest the double consciousness evident before the 1870s only in exceptional documents like *A Narrative of the Life of Mrs. Mary Jemison*, *A Son of the Forest*, and Ridge's *Joaquín Murieta*.

Several significant ideas, however, locate these novels in the romantic nineteenth century and distinguish them from modern explorations
of hybrid consciousness. Each remains bound to the positivist view that
race, savagery, and criminality are writ in human biology. Though
Stephens, Ellis, and Reid variously test the limitations of these views,
they ultimately agree that nature itself, not politics or injustice, poses
the greatest difficulty to assimilation. They further envision hybridity as
a process of discursive alternation, where one must live in one world or
the other, speak as a white man or as an Indian, alternately one or the
other, perhaps, but never as both. William Danforth and Kaam first
live as fully fledged white men unconscious of their origins. The crisis
in both Stephens's and Ellis's novels arrives with the mixed-blood's
knowledge of his divided self, and the necessity of having to sacrifice
the life he has known either by suicide or by transformation into a fully
fledged savage. Although conscious of the ironies of dual identity and
the incapacity of racial policy to adequately dispense with the enlightened mixed-blood, Reid likewise sees no option for Wacora and Alice
Rody but to take their place among the dispossessed tribes. In order to
see the way writing of the later nineteenth and early twentieth centuries
begins to liberate race from biology and to synthesize Native and white
consciousness into an independent hybrid discourse, we turn to one
with intimate experience of Removal and a personal stake in Allotment,
one who simultaneously bore the brunt of separation and reaped the
reward of assimilation.

John Rollin Ridge and *Joaquín Murieta*

Ridge's father, uncle, and grandfather, who led the Treaty Party of
Cherokees, the largely mixed-blood elite faction that reluctantly supported removal, were assassinated during a single night by members of
the opposing party led by John Ross. Ridge and his mother watched
helplessly as assassins repeatedly stabbed his father before their eyes.
Throughout his life, Ridge, like his relatives, maintained that assimilation would prove Indians' only means of survival, a view that continued to alienate him from many of his fellow Cherokees. Following an
undocumented incident involving Ross Party members, Ridge, not yet
twenty, fled Arkansas as an accused murderer. In Missouri he attempted

to raise funds to finance a fair trial and, failing that, to raise a private army that he would lead into Arkansas, he fantasizes in a letter to his cousin Stand Watie, to slaughter the entire Ross Party.[37]

These colorful biographical details lead most scholars to speculate that Ridge's experience "living in an alien country [following the Cherokee removal], conditioned by violence and sudden death in his boyhood, writing with thoughts of revenge buzzing in his head," perhaps led him to seek psychological and pecuniary relief in creating his heroic Mexican outlaw, Joaquín Murieta. Ridge's *The Life and Adventures of Joaquín Murieta, the Celebrated California Bandit* tells the story, very loosely based on actual events, of a Mexican miner who is brutally mistreated by American settlers and becomes a sensationally vicious bandit in his fight to oppose the incursions of American forty-niners into California. The short, kinetic, and bloody tale anticipates the dime novel in its haphazard narrative and financial motive, though Ridge apparently saw no profit from it.[38] The book, however, achieved a celebrated notoriety almost entirely independent of its author and the critical establishment. Although ignored by the San Francisco press, *Murieta* ignited a folk tradition that has since spawned hundreds of revisions and translations worldwide.

The immediate and mythic relevance of Ridge's novel lies in its peculiar vision of Joaquín's outlawry as an expression of democratic protest rather than racialist criminology. In spite of Ridge's belief in compro-

---

37. Joseph Henry Jackson explains, "Accounts of the incident are generalized and imprecise, but there seems reason to believe that Ridge acted in self-defense; the man he killed may have been sent deliberately to provoke a quarrel and thus provide an excuse to do away with the third-generation Ridge as well" (Jackson, introduction to *The Life and Adventures of Joaquín Murieta, the Celebrated California Bandit*, xiv).

38. Ibid., xlix. Ridge himself vaguely speculated that his San Francisco publisher, W. B. Cooke, had somehow cheated him and destroyed a number of copies. He wrote in a letter to his cousin and financial supporter Stand Watie, "I have expected to make a great deal of money of my book, my life of Joaquin Murieta . . . but my publishers, after selling 7,000 copies and putting the money in their pockets, fled, bursted up, tee totally smashed, and left me, with a hundred others, to whistle for our money." Ridge himself claimed that the first edition sold seven thousand copies, although Joseph Henry Jackson suspects that Ridge might have publicly exaggerated sales figures to ensure continuing financial support in his literary ventures (ibid., xxxii).

mise and assimilation as a route to survival, his novel heralds a figure that resists assimilation and, like the mixed-blood, defies the imagined political boundaries that constitute national identity. Ridge also implies a criticism of policies like Allotment that promised economic redemption through private property, represented in *Murieta* as a very tenuous proposition in which land rights are arbitrary, tenuous, and favorable to California's gringo ruling class.

The Foreign Miner's Tax Law, passed by California in 1850, four years before Ridge published his novel, ensured that only citizens of the United States could benefit from mining claims by imposing a crippling series of fees and taxes on foreign miners. "Foreign," however, actually denoted Mexican, as the law exempted German, Irish, French, and Australian immigrants and implicitly encouraged persecution of nonwhite Californians. Among these "foreigners," for whom the half-legendary outlaw "Joaquín" was a symbolic champion, "patriotism" quickly became "equated with outlawry."[39] This pervasive sense of injustice lent Ridge's violent story its emotional and political immediacy and represents the institution of private property not as a utopian solution to race conflict, as Allotment imagined it, but rather as a seizure of resources by white governmental authority. Ridge portrays Joaquín as resisting this seizure, manifesting itself in the novel as the Foreign Miner's Tax Law. Even in acts of savage brutality committed against sometimes innocent Americans, Ridge's Joaquín arouses sympathy, not because he demonstrates an innate sensitivity and savage chivalry evident in some dime-novel mixed-bloods, but because Joaquín himself has also been wronged. Like the delinquent behavior Apess confesses in *A Son of the Forest*, Joaquín's criminality is not marked by any cranial abnormality but rather arises as the unfortunate final recourse of a man forced to abide by intolerable, unjust circumstances. Ridge provides Joaquín with a list of grievances equal to his offenses: American miners beat him, bind him, and rape his beloved mistress before his eyes; claim jumpers drive him from his own lawfully acquired dig; and a lynch mob hangs his half-brother on false charges and flogs Joaquín himself for good measure. No longer able to bear such "prejudice" and "wanton cruelty," Joaquín confesses to an old friend "as he brushed a tear from

39. Ibid., xvii.

his eyes, 'I am not the man that I was; I am a deep-eyed scoundrel, but so help me God! I was driven to it by oppression and wrong.'"[40] In Ridge's California, where justice is divorced from law, outlawry, like Apess's "nullification," is justified, and unjust laws must bear responsibility for crime as heavily as the outlaw who cannot accept them.

Ridge ostensibly conceives Joaquín, who is not explicitly identified as a mixed-blood, as an emblem of Spanish dispossession, but the novel associates the plight of Mexicans with Indian removal. Published during the era of the half-breed grotesque before popular writing turned from a model of physical degeneracy to one of mental defect, *Murieta* disguises its hybrid figure as a Mexican bandit, perhaps conceding to readers who could not yet accept the half-breed in the role of a dashing outlaw hero. The publisher's preface speaks of Indian dispossession rather than Mexican persecution, reminding readers of "that terrible civil commotion which followed the removal of the Cherokee Nation from the east to the west of the Mississippi" and also of the great individual tragedy Ridge and his family suffered in "retaliation and revenge." The preface also instructs that "the author is ... born in the woods— reared in the midst of the wildest scenery—and familiar with all that is thrilling, fearful, and tragical in forest life," offering these biographical notes as proof that Ridge is "well fitted ... to portray in living colors the fearful scenes which are described in this book." While these prefatory remarks anticipate the audience's doubtful estimation of "Indian literary talent,"[41] they also establish sympathy between the Mexican bandit and the Indian mixed-blood, both Ridge himself and those fictional corollaries that would follow in the dime novel.

In his poem "The Stolen White Girl" (1868), Ridge more clearly associates the "wild half-breed" with the celebrated outlaw in his novel:

> The prairies are broad, and the woodlands are wide
> And proud on his steed the wild half-breed may ride,
> With the belt round his waist and the knife at his side,
> And no white man may claim his beautiful bride.

40. John Rollin Ridge, *The Life and Adventures of Joaquín Murieta, the Celebrated California Bandit,* 50.
41. Ibid., 2.

Though he stole her away from the land of the whites,
Pursuit is in vain, for her bosom delights
In the love that she bears the dark-eyed, the proud,
Whose glance is like starlight beneath a night-cloud....

The contrast between them is pleasing and rare;
Her sweet eye of blue and her soft silken hair,
Her beautiful waist and her bosom of white
That heaves to the touch with a sense of delight;

His form more majestic and darker his brow,
Where the sun has imparted its liveliest glow—
An eye that grows brighter with passion's true fire,
As he looks on his loved one with earnest desire.

Oh, never let Sorrow's cloud darken their fate,
The girl of the "pale face," her Indian mate!
But deep in the forest of shadows and flowers,
Let Happiness smile, as she wings their sweet hours.

Although the poem exemplifies the sort of verse that even Ridge's most committed apologists admit is hackneyed, its lively narrative, sensational as any dime novel, uniquely and surprisingly employs Romantic conventions to eulogize an Indian abduction, the occasion for the most intense horror in the historical romance and the dime novel. While Lydia Maria Child, Catherine Maria Sedgwick, and Mayne Reid represent Indian elopement more distinctly as abduction, Ridge casts the dark abductor here as a heroic rescuer and the typically wilting, witless, white prey as a willing, buoyant bride rapidly and physically awakening to her desire for her Indian mate. His dark eye, the night-cloud hanging on his brow, do not, like the chilling darkness of Kaam's visage, foreshadow apocalyptic race war, nor does it brand him as Lombroso's *Homo criminalis,* but rather, like dawn starlight, promises happiness. The white man who would reclaim the stolen white girl pursues in vain, as the wild half-breed, the "scorned, outcast thing" inexorably and brutally punished for his transgressions in the historical romance and the dime novel, makes his final, triumphant escape in the slapdash rhyme of an exiled half-Cherokee.

Such fortunate inversions of familiar stereotypes during a generation dominated by popular depictions of half-devils like Boddo and Dirk

Peters reveal the limits and potential alternatives to the polygenist mandates of much nineteenth-century nationalist literature. Their popularity suggests a culture more sympathetic to Indian assimilation, especially as previous policies of removal had only yielded decades of warfare and recrimination. To hopeful reformers in the decades following the publication of Ridge's novel, Allotment seemed a harbinger of integration. The new legislation would foster assimilation, essentially closing the frontier by finally embracing the Indian adversary within the borders of the American polity. The novel's chaotic revelry signifies a democratic optimism that envisions outlawry as the transformative force capable of effecting such reform. Ridge himself viewed California as a country rife with new social possibilities, writing to Watie, "California still goes ahead, reversing the old order of things . . . the beggar of today is the prince of tomorrow."[42] In his novel Ridge imagines these "princes of tomorrow" as the mixed-bloods and outlaws who would hold an increasingly commercial and aristocratic American society true to the ideals of its nobler forebears and lead the way to the future. While Ridge expresses fear that promises of assimilation would be perverted into policies of exclusion, his utopian imagination of Joaquín's California briefly resurrects Rowson's dream of a racially blended nation and urges American fiction toward a more inclusive understanding of hybridity. For Ridge, California is the America of tomorrow, a synthesis of races and cultures in constant political flux, where communal and legal boundaries are indefinite and permeable, a picture much different from the rigidly dialectical frontier imagined in the historical romance and the dime novel. Reformers of the next generation, such as Helen Hunt Jackson, made it their purpose to actually create the democratic utopia only dreamed of in Ridge's wild novel.

Ramona

At the crisis of Helen Hunt Jackson's protest novel *Ramona*, the half-Indian heroine, fired by young love, announces her plans to defy her stepmother, the imperious Señora Moreno, and run away to marry the Indian sheepshearer, Alessandro Assis. The señora, having exhausted

42. Quoted in Walker, *Indian Nation*, 134.

her appeals to Ramona's sense of duty to family and to Church, basely attempts to bribe her stepdaughter with a treasure of jewels, a secret inheritance left to Ramona by her former guardian but expressly forbidden to her if she should she marry unworthily. Untying the long-hidden bundle, Ramona shakes the stones from the aged handkerchief: "The pearls fell in among the rubies, rolling right and left, making the rubies look still redder by contrast with their snowy whiteness."[43] In this symbolic moment, this contrast of red jewels among white—of radically distinct yet equally dazzling nature—reflects the young mixed-blood woman who might possess them. Faced now with the choice of love or riches, Ramona, lest we ever doubted, remains immune to the hypnotic power of this fortune laid before her. "I will marry Alessandro," she tells her seething stepmother, and begins her path toward poverty and undying love.

This metaphor of dappled treasure represents Jackson's apparent attitude, similar to Reid's, toward racial mixing and Indian assimilation. While the rubies and pearls might remain inviolably distinct, an uncanny beauty emerges in their contrast. Dimmer in separation, the red stones and the white stones glow with enhanced luster as they tumble together, just as cooperation and blending invigorate California's Spanish and Indian races. Jackson's novel remains bound to the model of hybridity as alternation; like the miscegenated women and mixed-bloods in earlier fiction, Ramona may choose to be white or to be Indian though never both. The contrast she embodies, however, does not predestine her to criminality, nor does it warrant her exile or destruction as it does for Danforth, Redlaw, Kaam, and Wacora. Like Mary Jemison, Ramona represents an alternative vision of hybridity in which miscegenation does not yield grotesque half-devils or sociopathic outlaws but a frontier heroine who is stronger, more adaptable, and more comely in the synthesis she embodies than either of her composite races in separation, an idealized image of the mixed-blood informed by the monogenist assumption of the essential kinship of all races.

Although critics such as Michael Dorris and Valerie Sherer Mathes remain bound to the dialectical understanding of hybridity, focusing

---

43. Helen Hunt Jackson, *Ramona*, 134. Further citations will be made parenthetically with the abbreviation *R*.

solely on Jackson's superficial separation of rubies and pearls and assuming from this the novel's political failure, the brilliance that each gem lends to its opposite—the alchemy of combination—seems more significant of the vision and influence of *Ramona*. In her mixed-blood character, more akin to those in twentieth-century Native American fiction than those in the dime novel, Jackson inverts the discourses of nationalism and criminal anthropology that reinforce the justice and inevitability of Indian decline and the morbid fear of racial blending, appropriating the conventions of sentimental romance in order to challenge the polygenist foundation of the romance tradition. In this way *Ramona* speaks with two voices and represents a discursive simultaneity like that of Jemison's *Narrative,* Apess's autobiography, and Ridge's *Murieta.*

Jackson's campaign for the Indians began famously in Boston in November 1879. After witnessing a heartrending series of speeches by Ponca representatives relating their story of deportation, exploitation, and legal impotence, she resolved that she would devote the rest of her life to combating government injustice toward America's Native population. Within two years she published *A Century of Dishonor* (1881), a hastily researched though passionately rendered account of the United States' "shameful record of broken treaties and unfulfilled promises" made with the Indians. Like many scholars, Michael Dorris evaluates this unprecedented document as "unimpressive either as history or literature," but highly important as a watershed of public opinion toward Indian policy. The book, Dorris says, "offered a strikingly contrastive perspective in which Native Americans were victims, not aggressors."[44] As a result, Jackson, already a renowned writer, became an influential political spokesperson and won a stint as Commissioner of Indian Affairs in California, where she prepared her *Report on the Condition and Needs of the Mission Indians of California* (1883). Her testimonial argued, as Charles Thomson, William Apess, and John Rollin Ridge had, that the alarming decline in Indian population and prosperity derived from adverse conditions rather than biological deficiencies, and this argument served as the basis for her novel.

44. Helen Hunt Jackson, *A Century of Dishonor: The Early Crusade for Indian Reform,* 339; Michael Dorris, introduction to *Ramona,* ix.

Between November 1883 and March 1884, Jackson feverishly composed *Ramona*, a novel that paints a sentimental picture of the decline of Spanish culture in an increasingly Americanized California.[45] The American usurpers, at best greedy and at worst murderous, redraw property lines to the advantage of American enterprise, diminishing Spanish possessions and completely displacing the Indians, who are forced to adopt a rootless, impoverished existence. In the midst of these terrible changes, Ramona, the orphan stepdaughter of Señora Moreno, the widowed mistress of a once sprawling but now rapidly declining ranch, falls in love with the Indian Alessandro. In defiance of her stepmother, Ramona elopes with the Indian and for a few years lives as a Temecula wife, sharing the mounting sorrows of the tribe and giving birth to two daughters. The first, named Eyes of the Sky in the Temecula language because Ramona's father's blue Anglo-Saxon eyes dominate her features, dies of pneumonia when a lazy agency doctor refuses to ride thirty miles to help her. The second, named after Ramona, possesses Alessandro's dark brown eyes. Hardship finally robs Alessandro of his wits and, when he mistakenly steals a horse from an American rancher, he is brutally gunned down before he may offer explanation. Beaten but still proud, Ramona and her infant daughter rejoin her supportive stepbrother, Felipe, who has assumed control of the Moreno estate following the señora's death. Although Ramona will not relinquish her love for Alessandro, she agrees to marry Felipe in celibate companionship. The two decide they will never be happy in American California, sell the ranch, and immigrate to Mexico, where older, nobler ways of life survive.

Before beginning work on the novel, Jackson wrote in a private letter to Thomas Bailey Aldrich, editor of the *Atlantic Monthly,* "if I could write a story that would do for the Indian a thousandth part that Uncle

---

45. Apparently, Jackson drew the plot for *Ramona* from the story of an impassioned daughter of a proud Spanish American family who eloped with an Indian herder. During Jackson's tour of southern California, Juan Diego, an unarmed Mission Indian, was killed by Sam Temple, a white rancher. Scholars assume that Diego's widow, Ramona Lubo, inspired Jackson's character. In contrast to Jackson's narrative of love triumphant, however, the lovers were caught, the Indian flogged, and the young woman expeditiously married to a Spanish American caballero. For an extensive discussion of the genesis of *Ramona,* see Ruth Odell, *Helen Hunt Jackson,* 170–211.

Tom's Cabin did for the Negro, I would be thankful the rest of my life."[46] To Jackson's great personal disappointment, however, *Ramona* did not effect immediate political upheaval. Although the novel splashed into the market with a success that rivaled the most popular dime novels, selling seven thousand copies within the first three months of its publication and more than fifteen thousand copies within its first year, readers, apparently, loved the novel for the wrong reason. Critics did not express indignation against Indian displacement but rather melted in the sumptuous heat of an exotic romance.[47]

Valerie Sherer Mathes argues that the novel's "romantic myth" defuses the more radical implications of Jackson's story, that *Ramona* did not effect the desired reforms or public awareness of Indian issues because it adopted too well the sentimental model that was to serve only as a vehicle for protest. In her explanation of the novel's failure to generate popular support for the Indian cause, Mathes cites Jackson's apparent hesitancy to violate traditional racial barriers and her ambiguous characterization of Alessandro and Ramona, neither of whom seem particularly Indian.[48] In contrast to the dreary Temecula "squaws," Ramona is "sunny," "joyous," and dearly loved by everyone who knows her. She is assiduous in her studies, though not ungirlishly so, a perfectly typical romance heroine. Alessandro likewise "makes one forget he is an Indian" (*R*, 101). Afforded a Franciscan education equal to that of privileged Spanish boys, he demonstrates unusual talent in music and speech and proves "for one of his race, wise and farseeing" (*R*, 52). In "things of the soul, and of honor," (*R*, 74) Alessandro surpasses even Felipe, the young master of the Moreno house. Like the chivalric, mostly white Wacora, Alessandro pledges his love to Ramona in a woodland grove but dares not kiss her until she has accepted his proposal to marry,

46. Valerie Sherer Mathes, *Helen Hunt Jackson and Her Indian Reform Legacy*, 77.

47. An initial review in the *Critic* called the novel "one of the most tender and touching [love stories] we have read for a considerable period." Milicent W. Shinn of the *Overland Monthly* called it "a prose Evangeline . . . a sweet and mournful poetic story." An anonymous reviewer in the same magazine wrote more critically that Jackson's novel had fallen short of its intended purpose and offered "no burning appeal, no crushing arraignment. . . . [It was] no such book as 'Uncle Tom's Cabin' . . . an idyll—sorrowful, yet never harsh" (Mathes, *Indian Reform*, 82, 83).

48. Mathes, *Indian Reform*, 81, 84.

exhibiting a degree of sensitivity and self-control that distances him from the innately criminal half-breeds in the dime novel. He loves Ramona at first sight, not lustfully or rapaciously like the savage abductors of traditional frontier stories, but with a romantic infatuation characteristic of sentimental white heroes.

While Mathes finds Ramona all too white, Michael Dorris conversely finds her all too Indian. Dorris finds nothing transgressive in the romance between Ramona and Alessandro, since Jackson, compulsively reminding her readers of Ramona's Indian blood and her ethnic compatibility with Alessandro, maintains the integrity of racial boundaries. When Felipe learns of Ramona's origins, the potential romance between the heir of the Moreno estate and his mysterious stepsister quickly vanishes like the "unnatural" attraction between Everell Fletcher and Magawisca. Having previously fantasized about marrying Ramona, Felipe quickly distances himself from her, reasoning with his mother in favor of her union with Alessandro, "I don't see anything disgraceful in it, nor anything wrong, nor anything but what is perfectly natural. You know, mother, it isn't as if Ramona really belonged to our family; you know she is half Indian" (*R*, 143). Felipe finally confesses that he would not like to see Ramona marry an Indian if she was truly his sister, and not "half Indian" (*R*, 145). As Dorris suggests, Jackson risks less in pairing the half-Indian Ramona with the Indian Alessandro than she might have if the sunny señorita boasted pure Spanish descent. Ramona's Indian blood certainly makes her transformation more plausible. Her wholehearted acceptance of Alessandro's proposal, her own declaration of love for the Indian, and her instantaneous willingness to reject family and fortune, impossible sentimental contrivances for Mathes, seem, for Dorris, inevitable. Ramona's love for Alessandro prompts an easy assimilation to tribal life and awakens the dormant "Indian" within her. Dorris argues that nineteenth-century "readers were unlikely to have accepted an interracial love story. . . . Any suggestion of impropriety would have destroyed the atmosphere of romance, so the novel remained cautious and broke no new ground."[49] The novel's popularity, Dorris concludes, rests in its careful avoidance of miscegenation, its suggestion that the marriage between Ramona and Alessandro is not, ultimately, interracial.

49. Dorris, introduction to *Ramona*, xiv.

Jackson's unromantic portrayal of Ramona's ill-fated parents supports Dorris's claim. Blue-eyed Angus Phial and the anonymous Temecula woman represent a more radically mixed pair than Alessandro and Ramona do, yet Jackson depicts their coupling as the traditionally unfortunate if not unnatural consequence of a white lover driven to madness by the loss of his or her true, racially compatible love. Angus, a Scottish seaman, desperately falls in love with the young Ramona Ortegna. When his Spanish sweetheart marries a debauched Mexican army officer instead, Angus becomes a "man bereft of his senses," a condition that Jackson offers as the "only excuse ever to be made" for his retreat into marriage with the Temecula woman (*R*, 26). The unfortunate union produces a beautiful baby named for her father's lost love, Ramona, but in spite of his infant daughter's beauty, Angus, like Father Luke in Whitman's *The Half-Breed*, considers the child a punishment for his wrongheaded coupling with the Indian. He surrenders the baby to Señora Ortegna as a tribute to the love they once shared and vanishes in self-imposed exile. Señora Ortegna loves Ramona as her own child, but when her abusive husband drives her to misery, illness, and early death, she entrusts Ramona and her inheritance to her sister, Señora Moreno, who never forgets the child's stain and never grows to love her. Señora Moreno explains her lack of affection for the child Ramona: "If the child were pure Indian, I would like it better. . . . I like not these crosses. It is the worst, and not the best of each that remains. . . . Base begotten, base born, she has carried out the instincts of her nature" (*R*, 30, 125).

Although Mathes and Dorris interpret Jackson's characterization of Ramona from different perspectives, these scholars share a fundamentally dialectical approach to *Ramona*. Like Richard Vanderbeets and Susan Walsh, who respond to a similar rift in Jemison's *Narrative*, they insist upon racial and discursive singularity. Ramona is, alternately, essentially white or essentially Indian; she is not, as Jackson herself suggests, simultaneously white and Indian. Although *Ramona* borrows certain suppositions of polygenist science and romantic fiction, especially in its description of Angus Phial and his Temecula "squaw," Jackson's novel also demonstrates significant reversals of these suppositions, urges a reconsideration of the biological argument for Indian degeneracy, and moves American fiction toward the synthesis of Native and Western discourses witnessed in Indian writing of the twentieth century.

In contrast to the snarling half-breed hunchbacks, degenerate villains, and tragic exiles of the dime novel, Ramona, though the progeny of an unfortunate match, emerges as a more luminous figure than any of Jackson's racially pure characters, a significant change from the dime novel, where the mixed-blood is most frequently measured as the shadow of a triumphant white hero whose racial cross predestines him to outlawry. Ramona's reaction to the knowledge of her Indian parent offers another significant contrast. Unlike William Danforth, who hurls himself to his death when he learns of his parentage, or Kaam, who vows slaughter upon the white race, Ramona blooms with happiness, confidence, and vigor when Señora Moreno tells her that her mother is a common Indian. In a narrative moment equal in consequence to Mary Jemison's unabashed affirmation of her love for Sheninjee, Ramona shockingly declares, "Oh, I am glad I am an Indian!" reversing the pattern of self-loathing and vengeance in previous dime-novel mixed-bloods. The knowledge confirms her devotion to Alessandro and steels her will against the Señora: "It was the first free moment her soul had ever known. She felt herself buoyed up as by wings in the air. . . . The tables were being turned. . . . Ramona seemed to tower in stature, and to have the bearing of one of authority" as she stands before the uncharacteristically "constrained" Señora Moreno (*R*, 129, 133).

Perhaps even more subversive than this celebration of Ramona's Indian parentage, Jackson's revision of the national idea represents racial hybridity not as degenerative but as transformative and celebrates the prospect of cultural and racial assimilation that the dime novel dreads. *Ramona* imagines American expansion from the point of view of the West Coast rather than the East, of a border moving backward rather than forward, of the dark foils of Manifest Destiny rather than its white vanguard. Like the historical romance, Jackson's novel is set in a troubled past, a time of violence and political flux. Unlike Cooper, Child, or Sedgwick, however, she does not arouse sympathy for the United States, a great nation on the verge of ascendance, but rather for Spanish California, a happy land on the verge of dissolution. The Moreno estate symbolizes the passing age, "the half barbaric, half elegant, wholly generous and free-handed life led there by Mexican men and women of degree in the early part of this century.... It was a picturesque life, with more sentiment and gayety in it, more also that was truly dramatic, more romance, than will ever be seen again on those sunny shores" (*R*, 11–12). While reminiscent of the elegies for the passing primeval wilderness rife in nationalist romance, Jackson's sentiment conceals a protest. Her heroes do not have white uncrossed complexions, nor do they trace their faith to Calvinist New England, nor do they speak English, nor do they see the American advance across the continent as the providential fulfillment of a grand historical destiny. They are a dark, passionate race driven by love and revenge rather than material gain; they revere the Catholic saints; they wince at the arrhythmic English language; and they view the immigrant wave of American traders, prospectors, and bureaucrats sweeping California not as the vanguard of civilization but as an invasion of heathens.

Jackson locates Ramona and Alessandro's struggles within the complex political landscape of a territory in swift and radical transition. In a place where American law has supplanted Mexican law almost overnight, Spanish Californians like Señora Moreno find themselves aliens on rapidly shrinking possessions. In the past, the Indians flourished economically and culturally because the viceroys and friars honored their hereditary land claims. A verbal promise alone could validate lines drawn on a map, and "no Mexican proprietor ever broke faith" with his Mexican or Indian neighbors (*R*, 52). The changing regime has the most severe impact on the Indians. Although the new American administration has commissioned Indian agents to facilitate assimilation and mediate disputes with whites, Indian homes and farmlands are confiscated and sold to American settlers by the Washington-based Land Commission before the Indians can file a complaint with the lazy and indifferent agents. Spanish gentry, Franciscan monasteries, and Indians, all prosperous and relatively autonomous for generations, thus regard the new law as arbitrary, unjust, and hostile: "Any day... the United States Government might send out a new Land Commission to examine the decrees of the first, and revoke such as they saw fit.... Nobody need feel himself safe under American rule. There was no knowing what might happen any day" (*R*, 13). As Alessandro is driven from Temecula to San Pasquale to Saboba, into more desperate poverty with each eviction, he becomes increasingly frustrated with a law that is inscrutable and remote: "It was the law... and nobody could go against the law.... [The Americans have] got all the papers to show it.... But they never did in those days [under Mexican rule]. Nobody had papers. The American law is different.... They have made a law which will take the land from Indians; from us who have owned it longer than any one can remember... will take that land and give it to themselves and say that it is theirs" (*R*, 179, 258–59). Alessandro's eloquent diatribes eventually become mute rage, despair, and dementia, hinting at Jackson's fears that Allotment, soon to institute a similar system of property redistribution across the entire continent, would drive all of America's tribes to similar extremes.

From Jackson and Ridge's perspective, the dispossessed outlaw is not predestined to crime by his Indian heredity, nor does he refuse to accept the newly constituted law. Rather, he is unable to accept it, because the law, as it regards him, does not allow him to do otherwise. It recognizes neither his rights nor his existence, demonstrating the perceptual flaw, characteristic of both removal policy and current academic discourse, which allows the Land Commission to sell entire Indian villages as "vacant" rangeland. Because they do not have the papers to force even a preliminary hearing, Alessandro and the other Temeculas cannot take their case to court and thus become invisible to the government. Any unofficial declaration of their presence, such as Alessandro's defiant lurking about the adobe house once his father's and now belonging to drunken American settlers, amounts to criminal aggression punishable with a shotgun blast. As William Apess had argued fifty years earlier in his landmark case for the Mashpees, disobedience of the law in such extreme cases is not crime but nullification, a form of civil disobedience that recognizes the injustice or inapplicability of certain laws.

In her role as a protest writer, Jackson seeks to ensure that Allotment does not replicate the flaws of Removal, demanding that the legislation does exactly as it proposes: to welcome the Indians as partners in America rather than protectively isolate them as its wards. Although critical of American policy and embarrassed at the administrative behavior that shames the ideals upon which the United States was founded, Jackson remains committed to those ideals. The pure heart of America is redeemed in Jeff, Joshua, and Maria "Aunt Ri" Hyer, a family of itinerant white farmers who vocally empathize with California's downtrodden Indians. When Ramona laments to Aunt Ri, "It's all cheating . . . but there isn't any help for it. . . . The Americans think it is no shame to cheat for money," Aunt Ri retorts, "I'm an Ummeriken! . . . an' Jeff Hyer and Jos! We're Ummerikens! 'n we wouldn't cheat nobody, not ef we knowed it, not out er a dollar. We're pore, an' I allus expect us to be, but we're above cheatin'; and I tell you, naow, the Ummeriken people don't want any of this cheatin' done, naow!" (*R*, 291). Jackson, too, blames government and bureaucracy, not the innocent entity of the "Ummeriken people" for whom she speaks. Outlawry, the disavowal of laws unworthy of the nation's Constitutional trust, does not represent the criminal corrosion of America's Enlightenment ideals, as it does in the dime novel, but rather the bravest and most sincere affirmation of these ideals.

As other books, assuming a naturally inviolable racial hierarchy, portray grotesque and villainous half-breeds and thus fitfully attempt to reconcile egalitarianism and expansionism, Jackson's novel emphasizes the fundamental incompatibility of the two ideologies. In contradiction to Knox's polygenist assumptions of hybrid degeneracy, Eyes of the Sky, Ramona's predominantly white daughter, succumbs to the harshness of frontier life, while Ramona, her predominantly Indian daughter, proves stronger and more adaptable. The elder Ramona's own nobility and vigor, though bland and contrived to some critics, nonetheless suggests, as monogenist writers such as William Apess had previously suggested, that the natural barrier between the races is simply an illusory ideological construct designed to facilitate American commercial interests within conquered territory, that a racially hybrid civilization will produce not a nation of troglodytes or born criminals but rather a hybrid race embodying the fulfillment of the nation's most sacred, most fundamental promise of progress and profit for all and to the exclusion of none.

At the conclusion of the novel, Jackson provides a symbol for this racially blended utopia in the homespun rag carpet of Aunt Ri:

> It was of her favorite pattern, the "hit-er-miss" pattern, as she called it, no set stripes or regular alternation of colors, but ball after ball of the indiscriminately mixed tints, woven back and forth on a warp of a single color. The constant variety in it, the unexpectedly harmonious blending of the colors, gave her delight, and afforded her a subject

too, of not unphilosophical reflection. . . . "It's jest a kind er hit-er-miss pattern we air all on us livin' on. . . . The breadths does fit heaps better 'n yer'd think; come ter sew 'em, 't aint never no sech colors ez yer thought 't wuz gwine ter be, but it's allers pooty, allers." (*R*, 349)

In her novel, Jackson attempts to weave a similar rug of disparate, unpredictable, yet always pretty colors, a vision of a nation woven together from indiscriminately mixed tints into a similarly harmonious blending of races. The end of the novel witnesses the death of Alessandro and his father, Ramona's dispassionate marriage to Felipe, and the exodus of Spanish Californians to Mexico, and seems, like the dime novel, to represent the impossibility of assimilation. Jackson's seemingly hopeless resolution, however, in the context of her overt protest, does not constitute a warning against reform but rather a plea for its swift enactment. The death and exile of her Spanish and Indian characters parallel the ending of *Uncle Tom's Cabin,* the novel that inspired Jackson, where Stowe's black characters meet similar fates. Ramona, Felipe, and the younger Ramona, the surviving child of Alessandro, flee to the edge of the continent and finally beyond America's borders, the only place, Jackson seems to suggest, where such mixed tints are suffered to exist, at least in the present, unforgiving age. Yet this sorrowful ending, like Stowe's, implies that tomorrow's reforms might indeed reverse yesterday's dishonors, revive America's most revered democratic ideal, and embrace the mixed-blood as the synthesis of America's unjustly divided colors.

The Problem of Assimilation

The passage of Allotment in 1887, only three years after the publication of *Ramona,* might have convinced Jackson that politicians and common readers were indeed moved by her protest of governmental injustice against the Indians. Although she died in 1885 and we cannot know her reaction to Allotment, she would likely have celebrated the legislation. In its sweeping ambition to assimilate the tribes through the institution of private property and the dissolution of collective tribal authority, Allotment attempted to weave Indian culture into the fabric of the United States in the fortuitous "hit-er-miss" pattern that Jackson had envisioned in her novel. Reformers hoped that such a change would lead to further economic, legal, and educational enfranchisement and sought to enlist the mixed-blood as an interracial ambassador who might facilitate the exchange. Jackson's involvement with the Women's National Indian Organization, the group Senator Henry Dawes himself credited as the "nurse" of the legislation he authored, almost certainly guarantees that she would have joined the organization's applause of Allotment as the welcome end to the "Century of Dishonor."

Reformers who sponsored the legislation adopted a fundamentally monogenist position in their belief that the degraded tribes could be improved through increased interaction with civilized society. In a lecture delivered to the Anthropological Society of Washington in 1886, John Wesley Powell, director of the U.S. Bureau of Ethnology, carefully outlined those practices that distinguish savagery from civilization, and although Powell does not remark on the impending legislation, his formula for the advancement of uncivilized tribes expresses the hope of those who authored and supported Allotment. Agriculture, "the cultivation of the soil and the domestication of animals," represents the first and most important step toward civilization, while "personal property" held in "severalty" rather than collectively by a clan or a tribe marks the ultimate institutional advance from a barbaric to a civilized society. The adoption of such practices, Powell claimed, might be accelerated through the interaction of savage tribes with a more advanced civilization. He noted that the "advent of European civilization on this continent" awakened the Indians, mired in a perpetual stone age, to the use and manufacture of iron tools and weaponry, that several tribes had organized governments "modeled somewhat after the civilized governments of the States," that "savage peoples" who associate with "civilized peoples . . . learn the civilized language . . . and the power of expression of the savage is greatly improved thereby." In all cases, Powell concluded, "activities borrowed from a higher by a lower culture result in progress."[50] Although Powell's reasoning lies in the same hierarchical assumptions that grounded polygenist arguments, his convictions that savages could be improved, and that exchange between unequal races and cultures would result in the progress of the lower race rather than the degradation of the higher race distinguish him from determin-

50. J. W. Powell, "From Barbarism to Civilization," 106, 114, 100, 101–2.

istic polygenist theorists like Lombroso, who predicted that hybrid civilization would result in the degeneracy of both peoples. Powell's address articulates the characteristically monogenist belief of assimilationist reformers, who viewed the commingling of the Indian and white races as a natural, invigorating, and democratic rather than perverse, atavistic, and anarchic. In their view, the mixed-blood is not an agent of villainy but a harbinger and an embodiment of the harmonious blending that would characterize America's future.

In her analysis of the tribal constitution proposed by Cherokee mixed-bloods prior to their removal beyond the Mississippi, Priscilla Wald identifies the group as physically as well as legally "uncanny," an indefinite threat to the "United States political identity."[51] The mixed-blood's defiance of the established racial boundaries that served as the scientific, political, and moral foundation for expansion created significant problems for the legal and military administration of the frontier, where successive policies continually redrew property lines according to strict racial divisions. All such policies that sought to legislate civilization among the Indians assumed four "specific legal conceptions central to the transformation that had produced modern civilization: inheritance, property, contract, and crime."[52]

The mixed-blood complicated all four of these distinctive legal conceptions of civilized society. The Chippewa treaty (1826) stipulates that "half-breeds, scattered through this extensive country, should be stimulated to exertion and improvement by the possession of permanent property and fixed residences." This treaty anticipates Allotment for all tribes and represents one of the first documents to acknowledge the special problem that mixed-bloods posed to segregationist Indian policies that reserved clearly defined lands for Indians and opened the rest to white settlement. Within a decade of the Chippewa treaty, mixed-bloods exploited this division by claiming land as both Indians and whites, effectively "reaping financial benefits by violating the integrity of the reservation [boundaries]" and undermining the system of property redistribution eventually instituted by Allotment. Subsequent treaties expressly prohibited mixed-blood land claims on the reservation. Others

51. Wald, *Constituting Americans*, 89.
52. Stocking, *Victorian Anthropology*, 123.

granted mixed-bloods reservation land rights but stipulated that they may not also claim additional land beyond the borders of the reservation where they might, as a revised Chippewa treaty (1855) states, "follow the pursuits of civilized life, and ... reside among the whites." Mixed-bloods might also abandon Indian life and carry on the work of white civilization, claiming reservation land if they provide missionary service such as founding churches, schools, or mills.[53]

In effect, mixed-bloods, like the tragically conflicted half-breeds in the dime novel, could choose to live alternately as Indians or as whites but not as both simultaneously. The racial dialectic founded in polygenism and predominant throughout the nineteenth century thus served crucial mythical, moral, and political functions. The continuing efforts of Indian policies either fully to Indianize or fully to assimilate the mixed-blood reflect both their insistence on racial separation and their inability to implement it effectively. The presence of the mixed-blood revealed the essential permeability of both the geographical and economic borders of the reservation and the imaginary border between the whites and Indians, mandating the mixed-blood be sanctioned as an outlaw by policies, such as the Chippewa Treaties and Allotment, that granted specific and separate property rights to whites and to Indians. These rights, like the identities of mixed-blood characters in nineteenth-century fiction, could not be compromised, combined, or exchanged.

Jackson might have been thankful that she would not live to see the passage of the Allotment Act, had she been able to foresee its effects. The decades following Allotment confirmed the apprehension of Ridge and Jackson that assimilationist policy might be perverted to white gain, as the distribution of private property initiated an economic decline that would lead tribes to the brink of extinction. Rather than establishing a firm and legal land base for the tribes, as reformers proposed, Allotment led to a decrease in total Indian holdings from 138 million acres in 1887 to 47 million acres in 1934. While previous treaties prevented the sale of reservation land held in common by members of the tribe, the severalty of real estate entitled individual Indians to dispose of their allotments independently and freed white investors and settlers to bargain for valuable land and resources that had previously remained non-

53. Scheick, *Half-Blood*, 7–8.

negotiable. This process continued until the Indian Reorganization Act effectively reversed Allotment in 1934. Racialist views of the nineteenth century suggest that the fundamental failure of the legislation arose from the cultural mistrust of the mixed-blood, the physical embodiment of assimilation, who remained a problematic figure, simultaneously antithetical and emblematic of this new polity, but, significantly, no longer invisible as he had been in the imagination of the early republic. Ridge and Jackson, anticipating the evolution of the mixed-blood in twentieth century fiction, invert dime-novel stereotypes, recasting the half-breed *Homo criminalis* as the "prince of tomorrow," humanizing the subhuman grotesques, and revising their villainy as democratic heroism.

From Biological to Cultural Hybridity in *Cogewea, Sundown,* and Twentieth-Century Magazine Fiction

You wait and watch. . . . The day will come when the
desolate, exiled breed will come into his own; when our
vaunting "superior" will appreciate our worth.

      —Mourning Dove, *Cogewea* (1927)

Yukon Burial Ground

In the summer of 1978, a bulldozer operator in Dawson, an old Yukon boomtown determined to rebuild itself as a modern tourist destination, began his day digging the foundation for a new recreation center. His work soon unearthed a bizarre cache of artifacts. Half-frozen in the basin of a swimming pool long since condemned and buried under the permafrost lay reels and reels of film. Soon the Public Archives of Canada rescued the unprecedented discovery from the mud of the construction site. The archivists salvaged 510 reels of thirty-five-millimeter nitrate film, a collection of more than one hundred feature motion pictures dating from the years 1903 to 1929.

The mystery then unraveled. In 1903, the Dawson Amateur Athletic Association introduced American film, a form of entertainment still in its miraculous infancy, to the raucous mass of prospectors come to the Yukon in search of gold. Dawson stood at the end of the distribution

Portions of this chapter appeared earlier, in different form, in Peter G. Beidler, Harry J. Brown, and Marion F. Egge, eds., *The Native American in Short Fiction in the* Saturday Evening Post (Lanham, Md.: Scarecrow Press, 2001), and are reprinted by permission.

line, and because studios valued the prints less than the cost of shipping them back to California, the discarded films were cataloged at Dawson's public library, where hundreds of reels accumulated over the next three decades. In 1929, the library, fearing the flammable nitrate stock to be a fire hazard, "donated" the collection to a local landfill, where they were deposited in the condemned swimming pool, covered by earth and a new skating rink, and forgotten for the next forty-nine years. In 1978, the preservation specialists marveled that 425 of the reels survived their interment intact, protected by the cold. Most of those that could not be rescued had become waterlogged in the process of thawing after they had been removed from the ground. With 190 reels of American productions transferred to the Library of Congress, the Dawson City Collection, an extensive record of the silent-film era, survives today and contains the only existing prints of many early films, which might have been lost forever.

This odd episode in the annals of film preservation provides a fleeting but significant glimpse of American culture's representation of the Native American mixed-blood in the early twentieth century. Among those reels salvaged from the Dawson construction site, archivists found *The Half-Breed* (1916), an early Douglas Fairbanks star vehicle directed by Allan Dwan, and *The Place beyond the Winds* (1916), a romance directed by Joseph De Grasse featuring Dorothy Phillips and Lon Chaney. *The Half-Breed,* loosely adapted from Bret Harte's novel *In the Carquinez Woods* (1883), features the smoldering, statuesque Fairbanks as L'eau Dormante, or "Lo Dorman," a half-Cherokee driven out of town and forced to live with his adoptive Indian grandfather in a hollow redwood tree. Lo finds a friend in Nellie Wynn, a coquettish preacher's daughter who encourages him to rejoin the white community. Lo's return to town upsets belligerent Sheriff Dunn, who not only claims Nellie as his girl but also guards the terrible secret that he is Lo's father. Dunn accuses the half-breed of horse theft and plans to kill him, forcing him to leave town once again. Lo joins a traveling medicine show where he meets Teresa, a burlesque dancer on the lam for stabbing her lover, Dick Curson. The two retreat to Lo's woodland sanctuary, where together they survive a forest fire and find true love in mutual exile.

Lon Chaney, the "man of a thousand faces," cuts a much less romantic profile in *The Place beyond the Winds,* adapted from the novel of the same title (1914) by Harriet Comstock and released in November 1916, only four months after audiences first beheld Fairbanks as the handsome and heroic L'eau Dormante. In revolting contrast, Chaney, as the hunched and disfigured half-breed Jerry Jo, attempts to rape Priscilla Glenn, the young heroine. Although she escapes Jerry Jo with her virginity intact, Priscilla's father believes that she has been shamed and cruelly banishes her from her beloved home in the woods. Distraught but undaunted, Priscilla goes to the city, where, in time, she becomes a nurse. By chance, she again encounters Jerry Jo, still menacing but now weakened and destitute. As Priscilla repays the half-breed's former violence with efforts to redeem him, this reunion scene most obviously portrays Priscilla's generosity and prepares the viewer for the expected resolution, where the angelic heroine receives her just reward of true love. But audiences at the Dawson Amateur Athletic Association and elsewhere must have sensed something more sour and irresolvable as they beheld Chaney in his final, slavering ugliness. Although the half-breed might be reformed by Priscilla's tender mercies, he remains scarred and hopelessly foul. Like all of Chaney's thousand faces, Jerry Jo becomes irresistible in his foulness, stealing the silent screen from the simple, sunny heroine and emanating all the fears that attended the prospect of Indian assimilation in the American imagination in 1916.

Even as motion pictures such as these supplanted the dime novel as America's favored medium for stories of the Wild West and brought an end to the golden age of the yellowback, the two images of the mixed-blood prevalent in the era before film remained fixed in the popular consciousness. The grotesque sociopath embodied by Walt Whitman's Boddo and Cesar Lombroso's *Homo criminalis* and the noble but tragically crossed hero embodied by Mayne Reid's Wacora and Helen Hunt Jackson's Ramona found new life through the two biggest stars of silent film. Archetypal in their difference, the screen personae projected by the Adonis Fairbanks and the goblin Chaney converged in 1916, as both manifested the Indian mixed-blood for an American viewing audience weaned on the dime novel and accustomed to thinking about racial blending with deep ambivalence. The stark contrast between Fairbanks's Lo Dorman and Chaney's Jerry Jo visually represents the divided image of the mixed-blood in the dime novel at the end of the nineteenth century, reminding audiences of his uncertain potential as an agent of both invigoration and corruption in the national body. Shortly, however, these traditional representations of the mixed-blood would be transformed by radical changes in Indian policy, anthropology, and the nation's idea of itself. Lo Dorman, Jerry Jo, and the ideas they embody would be entombed together on the frozen fringe of civilization as new images of the mixed-blood would come to represent new ideas about the frontier.

This chapter examines popular representations of the mixed-blood in the era between the passage of Allotment and its reversal by the Indian Reorganization Act in 1934. In the years following Allotment—a policy that promoted assimilation through the institution of private property on formerly tribal lands—new questions arose concerning the ethnic identity and political status of the Indians and the increasing number of mixed-bloods on reservations who claimed Indian status and Indian benefits. For the majority of the nineteenth century, political and literary discourse concerning the Indian reiterated the pervasive question expressed in an 1884 *New York Times* editorial: "What Shall We Do with Them?"

This question assumed a natural opposition between "us" and "them," reflecting the dialectical perception of the Indian-white relationship established by polygenist theorists and replicated in current thinking about mixed-blood writing. Although some nineteenth-century fiction encouraged readers to see Indian hybridity as a function of synthesis rather than division, the assumption of Indian otherness lingered in arguments favoring the separate hereditary origins of the races, the diminishing fertility of mixed-race pairs, and the atavism and inherent criminality of hybrid progeny. Many writers conceived Indian hybridity as a process of alternation in which the crossed individual wavers between two selves but must, in the end, be white or Indian, must choose one or be chosen by one. Nineteenth-century fiction offers a range of such figures: Charles Hobomok Conant, raised as an Indian brave before attending Harvard College and becoming Charles Conant, repressing the memory of his Narragansett father; the white captives, so perplexing to readers, who remain with the Indians even when offered redemption; and William Danforth, Kaam, and their kin, embracing death or bitter exile when confronted with their own mixed origins. Few seemed comfortable being both. Even Mary Jemison, *Dehgewanus,* Two Voices Falling, who spoke the language of the Iroquois with an Irish lilt, loved

the Seneca only knowing her children bound her to them; and though
nature made Ramona as a glittering blend of rubies and pearls, nature
too seemed bent on correcting its beautiful mistake, giving her first a
child whiter than herself, then one darker, as if dividing one half of the
mother from the other.

Allotment, however, posed a problem to these traditional representations of hybridity. While Removal was the political expression of polygenism, separating the races geographically as they had been seemingly
separated by nature itself, the new policy encouraged socioeconomic
interaction between newly propertied Indians and their more "civilized"
white neighbors; through this process the ethnic identity of the Indian
began to change. Indian mixed-bloods began to outnumber full-bloods,
and the very meaning of these terms became confused. The formerly
anomalous and detestable racial hybrid assumed a demographic and
political prominence, changing the face of the frontier in the twentieth
century and collapsing the traditional, comforting distance between the
white man and the Indian. "What Shall We Do with Them?" no longer
seemed relevant, since assimilation had made it more difficult to determine who "they" were. Inspired by the ideological and economic necessity of revising national Indian policy and by significant changes in the
scientific conception of the Indian, legislators, anthropologists, and writers raised a question both more fundamental and more complex: What
is an Indian?

Although twentieth-century policy, like that of the nineteenth century, nevertheless depended on the preservation and enforcement of
racial boundaries, the ascendance of the mixed-blood in the twentieth
century required a radical redefinition of these boundaries. Anthropologist Franz Boas initiated this process of redefinition by proposing that
racial difference consists not in heredity or physical proportion, as positivist anthropology suggested, but rather in language and cultural practice. For the first time, science defined the Indian as a culture or a group
of cultures rather than as a species, and classified these cultures not in
racial families descended from common bloodlines but in language families bound together by words, myths, rituals, or social structures. Most
fundamentally, Boas disputed the traditional claim that race determines
culture, that the Indian is biologically predestined to barbarism and
hereditarily incapable of assimilating to civilized beliefs and practices.

On the contrary, Boas believed that culture determines race, arguing in numerous studies the irrelevance of physical type to the capacity for civilization. Boas identified the study of language as the most reliable way anthropology could overcome its inherent ethnocentric biases and argued for the first time that those who would investigate Native cultures should learn their languages. This fundamental rejection of the positivist, social-Darwinist model of Indian inferiority in favor of a linguistic model tended to privilege primitive cultures as autonomous, integrated, and, perhaps, more healthy than an increasingly corrupt and alienated Western civilization.

John Collier, Franklin Roosevelt's commissioner of Indian Affairs, informed by Boas's work, adapted this ideological revaluation of primitive culture in authoring the Indian Reorganization Act, but he remained conflicted by the legal necessity, inherited from the failure of previous Indian treaties, of strictly defining the persons to whom this enlightened policy would apply. Reorganization thus adopted blood quantum as the criterion for Indianness, naturally assuming that the more Indian blood one possessed, the more Indian one was. Although the policy drew from twentieth-century anthropological developments that directly rejected the positivist logic of race as biology, it nevertheless established what it accepted as a necessary biological measure of differentiating an Indian from a white man. This continued insistence, in both public policy and romantic fiction, on being either Indian or white but not both, represents the source of the mixed-blood identity crisis prevalent in twentieth-century Native fiction, and it continues to influence current scholarly perceptions of the Indian.

There has been little written on the mixed-blood as an independent figure because scholars, like the well-intentioned reformers of the Roosevelt administration, too frequently fail to distinguish the mixed-blood from the Indian in general and fail to recognize that the mixed-blood, which Louis Riel hailed as Métis, embodies a separate set of problems and a separate consciousness. In the imposition of blood quantum as the criterion of ethnic and cultural identity, the modern redefinition of the Indian created a hierarchy of the "more Indian," legally conceived as wholly Indian and thus entitled to the benefits of government policy, and the "less Indian," legally conceived as wholly white and thus exempt from policy. In either case, the policy, even as it upset traditional racialist assumptions, banished the mixed-blood to his familiar place on the shadowy fringe of American society. While nineteenth-century culture assumed that an Indian cross inevitably corrupted the mixed-blood's nobler white nature, the primitivism of the early twentieth century, inspired by Boas, witnessed an inversion of this hierarchy, evaluating white blood as a mark of the corrupt influence of modern civilization. In both cases, the mixed-blood remains tainted and ultimately condemned: by his Indian half in the nineteenth century and by his white half in the twentieth century.

Magazines such as the *Saturday Evening Post, Overland Monthly,* and *Harper's,* sometimes contracting writers who themselves had graduated from the dime-novel fiction factory, reflect these changing political and scientific views of the mixed-blood in two ways. First, their stories manifest nostalgia for the older, more familiar image of the Indian, for a past glorified in the mythic adventures of historical romances and dime novels, for a vanishing Indian that provides comforting reassurance of national ascendance. Second, although magazines naturalize racial difference and consequently resurrect the degenerate half-breed of nineteenth-century fiction, many stories demonstrate the more modern consciousness of simultaneity glimpsed in earlier fictions such as Mayne Reid's *The White Squaw* and Helen Hunt Jackson's *Ramona,* a recognition of the more complex problems and possibilities of existence as something other than fully white or fully Indian. These stories do not turn back to traditional national mythologies but rather look forward to the modernist critique of such mythologies, portraying civilization as corrupt and assimilation as alienation. Within both of these paradigms, however, the mixed-blood is similarly banished, stained, and exiled by his Indian blood in the traditional view or by his white blood in the modernist view.

In an attempt to reverse the alarming long-term effects of Allotment, the Indian Reorganization Act halted white investment in Indian lands, offered the tribes large land grants to replace reservation territory that had been sold over the past four decades, and instituted more autonomous tribal governments that allowed the Indians themselves to control reservation economies. For the first time in the history of U.S.-Indian relations, the new policy recognized the potential ill effects of assimilation and sought to protect the rapidly disappearing traditional cultures. While Reorganization, in one way, reinforced the old biological definition of hybridity evident in magazine fiction by mandating new benefits only to those individuals who could demonstrate the required quantum of Indian blood, it conversely fostered a new intellectual openness to Native tribalism and provided a healthy climate for the germination of the contemporary tradition of Native American literature in Mourning Dove's *Cogewea* and John Joseph Mathews's *Sundown,* two novels that adopt many of the conventions of American popular fiction and yet challenge many of its nostalgic, nationalistic myths as represented in the *Saturday Evening Post.* Through linguistic and rhetorical variations within their narratives, these first mixed-blood novelists revise the concept of hybridity from biological terms to cultural terms, evoking a Native identity more fluid and more inclusive than that envisioned by the test of blood quantum, perceived in their work as politically arbitrary and irrelevant to lived experience. These revolutionary but curiously forgotten fictions anticipate the Native literary renaissance of the later twentieth century, in which hybridity assumes its significance as discursive simultaneity and, as Gerald Vizenor imagines it, as the capacity for survival, resistance, and renewal.

Like the dime novel of the nineteenth century, magazine fiction of the first four decades of the twentieth century presents an impossibly large field of study, and, as in the last chapter, generalizations must be weighed against more detailed examination of specific texts. While we will refer to stories in a range of magazines and collections, the readings will focus on the *Saturday Evening Post,* not solely because we must limit the scope of the discussion but because the magazine is uniquely appropriate to the aims of this study.

The most popular magazine in America during the first half of the twentieth century, the *Post* remains virtually unexplored by scholars. Nonetheless, it represents an invaluable resource for understanding the images of the Indian and racial mixing within the context of twentieth-century American popular culture. During the heyday of its publication, the *Post,* available for only "five cents the copy" and covered with graceful, good-humored artwork by J. C. Leyendecker and Norman Rockwell, could be found on millions of coffee tables throughout the nation. In the context of Native American history, the fiction published in the *Post* occupies the troubled interval between the 1890s, the decade that saw the widespread institutionalization of private property on the reservations, and the 1960s, the decade that saw the rebirth of Native literature. During this period, even as scientists and legislators conceived radical new ideas of the Indian, the *Post* helped to satisfy the American reading public's strong appetite for traditional narratives that made strong appeals to nationalist pride and resurrected in prolific fashion nineteenth-century images of the vanishing Indian and the monstrous half-breed. White, middle-class Americans' apparent appetite for Indian fiction, especially during the first four decades of the twentieth century, grew from their need to reaffirm the character of a nation that seemed to be crumbling before their eyes.

Nostalgia and Degenerationism

In an era that witnessed catastrophic depression, labor riots, and the rise of fascism, the *Post* offered its audience, week after week, reassuring images of certainty, victory, and prosperity couched in formulaic frontier adventure tales. The popularity of traditional Westerns during this time perhaps arises from the sense of desperation in the readers with whom they resounded so powerfully, and from a more explicit political response of the magazine to the crises of the times. As depression mandated socialist changes in Roosevelt's public policy, including the granting of aid and autonomy to Indian reservations, the *Post* reacted by strongly evoking nostalgia for a happier, half-imagined past. As Jan Cohn, a surveyor of the magazine's artwork, explains, this nostalgia appeared perhaps most vividly in the celebrated cover illustrations, poignant images of old men wistfully recalling the days before the steamship replaced the three-masted schooner or the motorcar replaced the horse-drawn coach. As fascism spread in Europe, the *Post*, just as it had before the First World War, sponsored a strict policy of isolationism. Seeming to deny the social, economic, and political problems of the present, cover art throughout the Depression depicted nineteenth-century families in holiday finery caroling around a piano, romantic profiles of sailors, soldiers, and ivy-league sportsmen, demure bathing beauties, ebullient vacationers, and children on carefree hayrides. In one of the rare covers demonstrating a consciousness of the underclass, a black hobo hitchhikes on the mythical U.S. Highway 1 (October 19, 1935). Although his clothes are tattered, his rucksack is full, and his face, as he looks down the road, beams with all the hope and American fellow-feeling of Nigger Jim as he floats the Mississippi.[1]

The fiction offered by the magazine recalls the glory days of old, colorfully remembered in these celebrated illustrations, as these "historical" stories reassure the Depression-era audience of better days ahead. In Stewart Edward White's "The Long Rifle—The Statesman" (1931), Andy Burnett, White's frontiersman hero, sets out to blaze a trail to the newly acquired New Mexico territory. Missouri senator Thomas Hart Benton, the proponent of western expansion popularly credited with the term "manifest destiny," toasts Burnett's efforts with a grand speech: "To the mountain men . . . and those who come after them! And to our country—one people, one flag, a mighty civilization that shall extend, that must extend, from sea to sea!" In F. Britten Austin's "Toward the Millennium" (1929), published shortly after the stock market crash, the Union Pacific Railroad likewise becomes a symbol of prosperity and possibility. As Abraham Lincoln sits alone in his office on the eve of the Civil War, he comforts himself with the idea of far-flung peoples bonded by the imminent construction of the transcontinental line: "It was a vision—a vision of shining rails stretching beyond sight into the Western distance—a vision of peoples yet unborn filling the intermediate empty spaces—the people of the United States."[2]

The future so happily promised in these stories' invented past becomes the present that so many middle-class *Post* readers either enjoyed or desired. A large volume of Western fiction is visually linked with cartoons, illustrations, and, most obviously, advertisements depicting the "good life." Cigarettes, liquors, automobiles, insurance policies, chocolate cakes, refrigerators, electric timers, vacation packages, storm windows, cleaning products, and other accoutrements of American middle-class life are juxtaposed with stories of wagon trains, buffalo hunts, and bloody Indian battles, associating stories of American conquest with images of economic prosperity, demonstrating most vividly Ernst

1. Jan Cohn, *The Covers of the* Saturday Evening Post, 133–34, 138.
2. Stewart Edward White, "The Long Rifle—The Statesman," 83; F. Britten Austin, "Toward the Millennium: The Railroad Builders," 39.

Renan's idea of nationalism as nostalgia, an expression of popular memory and popular forgetting. In its attempt to make a better future by celebrating the past, the magazine recalls the strategies of the historical romances of the early nineteenth century, nationalist narratives that similarly, in Renan's words, forged a strong national idea through the invention of "a heroic past, great men, glory."[3]

The evocative power of nostalgic magazine fiction in the 1930s relies not only on its appeal to history but also in its renewal of romantic racialism. In *Gunfighter Nation,* Richard Slotkin cites Theodore Roosevelt's monumental history, *The Winning of the West* (1885–1894), as a primary influence on the twentieth-century Western, especially in its argument for Anglo-Saxon ascendance. In Roosevelt's version of racial history, Slotkin explains, the conquest of the American West begins with the Teutonic invasion of the Roman Empire:

> The Teutons triumph because of their martial virtues, their love of independence, and their tribal patriotism (the germ of nationalism). But their conquest of Rome is followed by a racial and cultural inter-breeding that corrupts . . . their blood and culture. Only in the British Isles (says Roosevelt) is a "lasting addition to the Germanic soil" achieved; for only in the isolation of the European periphery can their racial germs develop without admixture. . . . In the settling of America this paradigm of ethnogenesis is reenacted. The most vigorous off-spring of that British "race of races" return to an environment very like the one that produced their original ancestors: a wilderness, isolated from civilization, in which the forces of nature and the hostility of native barbarians compel them to renew their latent capacity for self-government and military conquest. . . . The American character that emerges in the wilderness is a recrudescence of German racial traits.

Slotkin traces the influence of Roosevelt's myth of American origin in various political movements through the 1920s "to limit the role of immigrants in politics and to halt, or radically restrict, immigration by peoples of 'inferior' racial stock." Celebrated Western writers such as Owen Wister and Frederic Remington, Slotkin explains, shared Roosevelt's anxiety that America's innate Teutonic vigor and global ascendance could be corrupted by waves of immigrants who were "so fundamentally dif-

3. Renan, "What Is a Nation?" 19.

ferent from Anglo-Americans (or Teutonics) that their capacity for 'man-liness,' productivity, and 'Americanization' is extremely problematic."[4]

As Cooper viewed Indian assimilation as an accelerant of national decline in the nineteenth century, so did Roosevelt and his adherents view immigration in the twentieth century. Publishing his first anthropological papers contemporaneously with the final installments of *The Winning of the West,* Franz Boas attacked the scientific foundation of Roosevelt's thesis with a gambit no less ambitious than Roosevelt's invocation of the disinheritors of the Caesars. Muddling and measuring among the tribes of the subarctic and the Pacific Northwest, Boas called into doubt a conviction older even than Rome: that civilization betokened superior blood. Anthropologists then began to reconsider their fundamental assumption of hybrid degeneracy at the same time that racialist historians affirmed hybrid degeneracy with new renewed force.

Magazine fiction at the turn of the twentieth century confronts this dilemma with manifest nostalgia in its characterizations of the mixed-blood, affirming the racial dialectic of the preceding century. Remington's half-breed Sun-Down LeFlare, who appears in a number of anecdotal tales appearing in *Harper's Weekly* in 1898, recalls the scheming, opportunistic Boddo from Whitman's *The Half-Breed,* although the stories feature a more benign incarnation of the sociopathic mixed-bloods of the dime novel. LeFlare cheats at poker, trades girlfriends as he trades horses, and deceives more-naive Indians with white men's tricks, as when he uses field glasses to convince them that he has magical vision. In his collection *Frontier Stories,* appearing in the same year as Remington's series, Cy Warman similarly depicts half-breeds as a lot of dirty, drunken, inept bandits, with just "enough 'white blood' to make them ambitious, and enough red to make them kill a man for a new saddle."[5]

While Warman's and Remington's rascals comically embody the haplessness and venality in both races, Flora Haines Loughead's "In the Shadow of the Live-Oak" (*Overland Monthly,* 1899) and Owen Wister's "A Kinsman of Red Cloud" (*The Jimmyjohn Boss,* 1900) offer the more banal mixed-blood murderers familiar in the dime novel. Loughead's José Gomez ravages the Sierra Madre and massacres an innocent family

---

4. Richard Slotkin, *Gunfighter Nation,* 44–45, 189, 190.
5. Cy Warman, *Frontier Stories,* 61–62.

before he is gunned down by a settler, and Wister's Toussaint, when he is caught cheating at poker, kills two innocent white men and flees to his uncle, the respected Sioux chief Red Cloud. After negotiating with the posse in pursuit of Toussaint, Red Cloud surrenders his nephew to be hanged. Neither white men nor noble Indians brook the half-breed, nor do Remington, Warman, Loughead, or Wister. Although nature may indeed produce mules, despite Robert Knox's protestations half a century earlier, the cultural and hereditary degeneracy they embody cannot be suffered by a nation heir to Teutonic vigor. The romantic racialist philosophy recited by Cooper, Knox, Roosevelt, and these writers links racial blending with physical and national degeneracy and mandates that the heroic past, if it would serve the present, must enforce the separation of the white and the Indian. At a time, then, when more progressive ideas of the Indian were shaping new federal policies, the *Saturday Evening Post* featured a series of stories that in their subject and rhetoric harkened back more than a century.

In the spring of 1937, only a few months after the Democrats had won four more years in the White House despite the magazine's anti-Roosevelt campaign, the *Post* ran a series of five stories by Walter D. Edmonds portraying the destruction, captivity, and redemption of the New York frontier settlement of Dygartsbush by a band of Seneca Indians. Less than a year before, Edmonds had published his novel *Drums along the Mohawk* (1936), an epic chronicle, originally serialized in the *Post* during the spring of 1936, of the Mohawk Valley pioneers who bravely battled Tories on one front and bloodthirsty Indians on the other. In his Dygartsbush series, Edmonds confronts the problem of racial mixing on the frontier more directly than he had in his novel, though only to reinforce more strongly the nostalgic ideals he represented in *Drums along the Mohawk*.

The series opens with "The Captives," set in the spring of 1778, when a band of Senecas raid Dygartsbush as part of a unified British-Indian campaign against American forces in New York. The Indians descend quickly on the small community, killing and scalping most of the men, capturing many of the women and children, and burning the village to the ground. Edmonds's series tracks the fates of these various captives, among whom is Delia Borst, whose husband, John, had been away trading when the Indians attacked. Faced, like Cora Munro, with the horror of becoming a Huron wife, Delia shudders when she learns that the Indians plan to convey her to a distant village, where she will be "made squaw" of a Seneca warrior. She does not, however, despair, holding on to the hope that her husband will come to her rescue. In "Delia Borst," the third story of the series, Delia is brought to Onondarha, a large Seneca village on the Genesee River, and adopted into the tribe as the wife of Gasotena, a powerful Seneca chief. As Delia feels her white identity slowly ebbing away, she repeats to herself, as Mary Jemison repeated the prayers of her childhood during her captivity, "My name is Mrs. John Borst."[6] But time passes and she gradually despairs of rescue. She learns to live like a Seneca woman and makes many friends among the tribe, including Uesote, her Indian mother-in-law, and Deowuhyeh, the young wife of a Seneca brave.

As in *Hobomok* and *A Narrative of the Life of Mrs. Mary Jemison,* Delia's story reaches its crisis when the white captive conceives a child by her Indian husband. Although Delia realizes that the child will likely make her return to her husband impossible, she maintains, like many of the steadfast captives, her "pride of blood" and refuses to forget her life in Dygartsbush. Uesote advises Delia to accept her fate, and because she has conceived an Indian child, Delia feels that she is right. Not only does the baby growing inside her make Delia herself part Indian, but she also realizes, as Jemison did, that the white community would meet her and her half-breed child with shame and rejection. In the winter of 1779, as American forces strike back at the Seneca nation, Delia gives birth to a son, whom she names Ha-ace, or "Little Panther." A midwife prophesies that the unusually spirited infant "will be a great warrior against the white people," but Delia herself remains strangely detached, looking at her newborn as "a shapeless hard small lump."[7]

In "Dygartsbush," the final episode of Edmonds's series, a handful of settlers return to the site of the destroyed frontier town and begin to rebuild. Seven years have passed since the Indians raided the village. The Continental army has defeated the British, gained independence for the United States, and negotiated a treaty that secures the release of all white prisoners held by the Indians. John Borst nervously awaits

6. Walter D. Edmonds, "Delia Borst," 14.
7. Ibid., 45, 48.

news of Delia. He has not heard from his wife in the time since the raid, but, unlike many other men whose wives had been captured, he does not give up hope or remarry. One evening when he returns from the fields, John finds Delia tending the hearth, as if she had never left and the years of war and separation had not passed between them. The only differences John observes in his wife are her clothing and her hair, which she now wears in Indian fashion. After a subdued but affectionate greeting, the two briefly recount what had happened to them after the initial raid. Delia, however, remains silent about her years in the Indian village, revealing only vague or inconsequential details.

Mrs. Cutts, a good-hearted and perceptive neighbor, visits with Delia one afternoon while John is out and guesses from Delia's anxiousness the younger woman's horrible secret. "Delia Borst," Mrs. Cutts advises, "just remember that there's some things a man is a lot happier for not knowing." Delia considers Mrs. Cutts's words but decides instead to relieve herself of the guilt and tell her husband that she had borne an Indian son. Because the child had kept her from returning to her white husband, Delia confesses that she never loved the baby. "Providence," thankfully, had brought the deaths of both her Indian husband and her child during a famine, making it possible for her to return to John. Although he has suspicions, John, like Charles Brown on hearing of Mary Conant's Indian marriage and motherhood, is nonetheless confused and disappointed by Delia's revelations. Over the next few days, Delia notices coldness in John's behavior and feels "whipped and humiliated." As the series closes, John remains troubled by his wife's past, but in his inner heart he forgives her. He resolves to look to the future instead, happy to have his wife alive and to have the chance to begin life again.[8]

The Dygartsbush series bears thematic resemblance to nineteenth-century historical romance, linking national ascendance with racial separation, portraying interracial liaisons as a debased condition of chaotic frontier circumstance, and, while not entirely denying the existence of mixed-blood offspring, quickly eradicating such aberrations through the hand of providence, which sets things right by reuniting white wife with white husband to begin the work of nation building. Edmonds's

8. Walter D. Edmonds, "Dygartsbush," 82–83.

narrative itself seems to follow Mrs. Cutts's advice to repress those past events that are most shameful. Edmonds, like Child, Cooper, or Sedgwick, seeks not only to glorify the past but also to remake it according to dreams of the present. In his author's note to *Drums along the Mohawk,* Edmonds elevates his novel above more mundane historical accounts: "A novelist, if he chooses, has a greater opportunity for a faithful presentation of a bygone time than a historian, for the historian is compelled to a presentation of cause and effect and feels, as a rule, that he must present them through the lives and characters of 'famous' or 'historical' figures. My concern, however, has been with life as it was; as you or I, our mothers or our wives, our brothers and husbands and uncles, might have experienced it."[9] Edmonds sees his fiction as a broader and more reliable record of "life as it was" than plain fact, exemplifying Renan's argument that the heroic past at the core of a national idea is more frequently imagined than remembered, more prone to fictionalizing, forgetting, or denying actual history than bringing it to light.

This resurgence of nationalist fiction in the *Saturday Evening Post* grew in part from the general erosion of national self-confidence during the 1930s and more specifically from the magazine's editorial opposition to New Deal policies, including Indian Reorganization and its implicit reevaluation of orthodox ideas of race.[10] Passed only three years before Edmonds's stories appeared, Reorganization explicitly adopted a revised, more critical approach to the old myths of racial hierarchy and Manifest Destiny, especially to the Anglo-Saxonism theorized by the former president Roosevelt and celebrated by well-heeled writers such as Remington, Wister, and Edmonds. These writers' reaffirmation of the Anglo-Saxon mystique integral to nineteenth-century nationalism constitutes an attack on the progressive social policy of the present. Edmonds's picture of "life as it was" represents instead life as it should be, celebrating those early nationalist ideals of the United States and

---

9. Walter D. Edmonds, *Drums along the Mohawk,* ix.

10. The *Post* used its cover art to advertise colorfully its opposition to New Deal policies, especially during the 1936 campaign. On one of Leyendecker's preelection covers (October 17, 1936), a diminutive Democratic donkey mounted by an inexpert professor in academic robes races futilely to overtake a magnificent Republican elephant decked in luxuriant caparison and steadily piloted by a gray-suited businessman.

willfully forgetting troublesome facts such as racial mixing and other "things a man is a lot happier for not knowing."

Race as Biology in the *Saturday Evening Post*

Although stories like Edmonds's would, like the historical romance, erase the mixed-blood from the national memory, more realistic stories offered by magazine fiction could not conveniently kill the half-breed. Like the dime novel or *The Place beyond the Winds,* the nostalgic stories of the early twentieth century variously banish him as a cheater, a poacher, a thief, a gun runner, a whiskey trader, or, like the mixed-blood *Homo criminalis* of the dime novel, a murderer, a ruthless pariah, cast out by both white and Indian societies and redeemable only as he cultivates his white half over his Indian half. In consciously conservative magazines such the *Saturday Evening Post* and *Overland Monthly,* the prospect of hybridity, yet seen as a condition of alternation and conflict between two ineluctably riven identities, continued to unsettle the paradigm of racial purity and national ascendance that gained renewed relevance in the wake of Roosevelt's *The Winning of the West.*

In Rufus Steele's "Scar Neck" (*Saturday Evening Post,* 1912), two Shoshone half-breeds, Matt and Jess, belly through the alkali flats of Nevada stalking a group of wild mustangs for their hides. The mixed-bloods shoot and butcher all but two of the horses, one escaping with a broken leg, the other grazed by a shot that leaves a large scar on his neck. Within a year, "Scar Neck" gains a reputation for unrivaled speed and strength, becoming the coveted prize of cowboys and Indians alike and a symbolic reflection of what the story depicts as their respective racial values. White horse traders see Scar Neck as a rich quarry both for his own value as a bronco and for the numerous mares, colts, and fillies that follow their "lord." Indians like the Piute Illipah see the horse as a furious spirit, pursuing him with reverence and fear. Matt and Jess, exhibiting the revenge lust witnessed in Boddo, Injun Joe, Redlaw, and Kaam, see Scar Neck as an opportunity to prove themselves better than Pete Barham and his ranch hands who continually fail to corral the beast.

Following Cooper's concept of racial gifts, as well as Lombroso's and Roosevelt's theories of innate racial character, "Scar Neck" uses the horse hunt to emphasize the respective race traits of the white, the full-blood, and the mixed-blood. While slightly critical of the acquisitiveness of Barham and the superstitiousness of Illipah, respective shortcomings that ultimately prevent their capture of the wild mustang, Steele seems to reserve his harshest judgment for Matt and Jess, who resemble Whitman's Boddo, Badger's Redlaw, and Ellis's Kaam in their sadistic slaughter of the noble horses and in their irrational lust for revenge on the white race. The continually drunk pair spends more time foiling the efforts of Illipah and Barham than trying to capture Scar Neck themselves, but when they succeed in trapping the horse (through chance rather than skill), they meet their well-deserved and sufficiently sensational demise. When they attempt to saddle him, the wild stallion shatters Jess's skull with a kick and tears out Matt's throat with his teeth. Scar Neck escapes, never to be tamed.

Steele's story, though set in the present day, exemplifies the nostalgia that would become more explicit during the Depression in Edmonds's Dygartsbush series, both in its celebration of the untamed spirit of the West and in the more subtle concept of innate racial character that had defined positivist anthropology and Roosevelt's myth of the frontier. In the broad narrative lines drawn by Steele, Barham's calculating capitalism and Illipah's primitive pantheism are inevitably branded in the blood, as are Matt and Jess's wanton cruelty and criminality.

Several early stories conversely portray, like Mayne Reid's *The White Squaw,* mixed-bloods whose atavistic Indian nature has been elevated by superior white blood. Mary Alden Carver's "The Indian Who Was a White Man" (*Overland Monthly,* 1908) begins with a situation like that in Ellis's *The Half-Blood.* Spurned by a white woman, the half-breed plots revenge against the white man who has stolen his sweetheart. In Carver's story, however, the vengeful mixed-blood, Silent Pete, is torn between his desires to do right for his beloved Nora and to kill the interloper, Adolph. When Adolph is injured, Pete secretly rejoices but ushers the grieving Nora to Adolph's bedside, so that she may console him. When Adolph recovers, Pete sabotages a bridge Adolph will cross, but guiltily returns to repair it when he sees Nora's joy at Adolph's recovery. Emma Seckle Marshall's "An Infusion of Savagery" (*Out West,* 1908) represents a comparable situation, as Robert, a half-Apache, is rebuffed by Emma, a white woman, when she learns of his Indian blood.

Years later, despite his lover's betrayal, Robert gives his own life to save Emma's child by other man. Silent Pete's mercy and Robert's sacrifice emerge as a function of their white blood, elevating them above the likes of Boddo, Redlaw, and Kaam.

The revival of Anglo-Saxonism prompted in part by Roosevelt's *The Winning of the West* finds its clearest expression, however, in the *Saturday Evening Post,* which seemed to sponsor more overtly racialist language in its fiction. Edwin Balmer's 1914 serial "A Wild-Goose Chase" dramatizes a series of ethnological expeditions to the Greenland coast, sites of an Eskimo community whose dwellings bear signs of medieval Norse architecture. Otto Koehler, a German American whose character appears to have been inspired by Franz Boas and his own expedition to Baffin Island in 1883, speculates from the runic inscriptions on some of the Eskimos' weapons and the fair features and the noble carriage of the tribesmen, that the unique architecture, like the islanders themselves, descends from the Vikings who originally explored and settled the region. Balmer attributes the tribe's superior hunting and building skills, their uncommon physical beauty, and their generally noble nature to the heredity of their Nordic colonizers. Bret Harte's "The Mermaid of Lighthouse Point" (*Saturday Evening Post,* 1900) features Olooya, a northern California Indian with white skin and blonde hair. Lighthouse keeper Edward Pomfrey notes her distinctly European appearance and learns that she belongs to "a distinct and superior caste of Indian... [with] certain privileges within the tribe...[and] unmistakable Anglo-Saxon characteristics" likely inherited from the deserters of Francis Drake's expedition to northern California.[11] Emerson Hough's "My Lady's Furs—What They Cost" (1907) similarly represents Derinoff, an Aleut fur trapper of "better class" blessed with Russian blood, who distinguishes himself as the most skilled hunter in his community and a suitable partner of Anasteek, daughter of the richest Aleut family. Hough's story, like Harte's and Balmer's, manifests a fundamentally positivist or biological concept of race, as the Nordic blood in Derinoff, Olooya, and the noble Palugmiuts distinguish them as more highly evolved than their Indian fellows.

11. Bret Harte, "The Mermaid of Lighthouse Point," 6.

Magazine fiction at the turn of the twentieth century, however, already shows evidence of an inconspicuous but important transition between this traditional understanding of race as a biological category and the more modern understanding of race as a cultural or linguistic category. In 1905, *Overland Monthly* published two stories, Della Neal's "A Strife in the Blood" and Bert Huffman's "Ah-lo-ma," in which young mixed-blood women confront the knowledge of their origins and retreat into exile. Their alienation, however, does not derive from a hereditary stain, as does Boddo's, William Danforth's, or Kaam's, but rather from the bigotry of white society. John Neihardt's perverse but touching "The Alien" (*Indian Tales and Others,* 1926) likewise represents a half-breed doomed not by blood but by social prejudice, echoing nineteenth-century reformist writing by Apess, Ridge, and Jackson. Fleeing white men out to hang him, the half-French, half-Osage Antoine hides in a cave and befriends a she-wolf, whom he names Susette. He is betrayed even by her, unfortunately, when she brings a male wolf to her den to kill her human companion and take his place. Like the notorious half-breed outlaw in *Tom Sawyer,* the dime novel, and contemporaneous writing by Frederic Remington and Owen Wister, Antoine is exiled to the borderlands, where he finds more in common with beasts than with men. But Neihardt's story, while it adopts the familiar plot of the half-breed on the lam, also demonstrates a significant inversion of this plot. The half-breed outcast here is innocent of wrongdoing. The crazed posse pursuing him recalls the "vigilance committee" in Badger's *Redlaw,* but Neihardt transforms the mixed-blood from instigator to victim of injustice, casting him in the role formerly played by the white hero Clay Poynter.

Stories such as Neihardt's, Neal's, and Huffman's show signs of the growing dissatisfaction among writers with the racialist romantic idea of hybridity and anticipate its eventual rejection by writers of the later twentieth century. The *Saturday Evening Post* offers a story perhaps most modern in its racial sensibility prior to the work of La Farge, Mourning Dove, and Mathews. Joseph Hergesheimer's "Scarlet Ibis" (1920) portrays Lynn Graves, a white man who, although settled into the comfortable conservatism of middle age, becomes puzzled by the sudden feelings of discontentment he experiences during a summer holiday in the

Ontario woods. He feels increasingly stifled among his hypercivilized friends and begins to resent their witty banter and fashionable ways, preferring instead the quiet company of his Indian fishing guide, Wesley Beaver. As Beaver paddles the canoe over the calm surface of the lake, Graves scrutinizes his guide's physical features in minute detail. His "sinewy figure," broad "Mongolian" face, and strong jaw seem to Graves indicative of Beaver's "original heritage." Only his soft mouth and large red lips betray the fact that he, like many other inhabitants of the nearby Ojibwe village, is a mixed-blood. His indefinite features arouse in Graves an attitude of ambivalence toward the Indians. Although Graves senses that Beaver is "closely knit into his setting and life . . . in harmony with the elements of his life and death," he grudgingly agrees with his friend Sanford Bassett, who reiterates the Anglo-Saxonist argument that for all their stoic nobility, the Indians are inevitably "condemned by civilization to swift oblivion."[12]

Graves's inner turmoil is aggravated when he suddenly falls in love with Margaret Tyler, a half-Ojibwe servant hired by Sanford's mother. He realizes that he is drawn to Margaret simply because she appears, like Beaver, more white than the other villagers. He is attracted to her intangible Indian qualities, but, more than that, he views her as an escape route from his smothering civilized environment. Margaret likewise sees Graves as a way out of the poverty and stagnation of her village. She has been educated in Peterboro, she tells him, and cannot bear to settle down and "be a squaw." The two unhappy, impetuous lovers become secretly engaged. On the afternoon they plan to tell their families, Beaver abruptly reveals to Graves that Margaret was previously engaged to him, but that she refused to marry another Indian, and Graves begins to have second thoughts. When he goes to the village to meet Margaret's mother, he suddenly realizes that his love for Margaret was nothing but an "inexcusable infatuation." Margaret is deeply hurt by the rejection, which she feels is rooted in Graves's racism. As Graves, Margaret, and Beaver paddle across the lake to the Bassett camp, Beaver confesses that he, like Margaret, once "wanted to be white," but he was wrong to ever think such a thing. Beaver then intentionally sinks

12. Joseph Hergesheimer, "Scarlet Ibis," 6.

the canoe, drowning himself and Margaret. Graves swims to shore, more disturbed than ever. For him, the scarlet ibis, a gaudy fishing lure, is symbolic of his own life, "an affair of glittering colors concealing only the coldness, the cruelty, of death."[13]

Hergesheimer's dark antiromance expresses modernist despair in the moral bankruptcy of civilization and progress. Like the primitivist artists and writers (such as Oliver La Farge) who retreated to Taos between 1915 and 1930 and appropriated Pueblo culture as a holistic remedy to the alienation and atomism they perceived in modern life, Graves seeks meaning and harmony in the Ontario backcountry. Although he considers his own ideas on the Indian more thoughtful and sympathetic than the intellectualized racism voiced by his friends over martinis, he fixates on the "Mongolian" physiognomy of his mixed-blood guide and reads in Beaver's broad features, like the anthropometrists of the nineteenth century, signs of his innate racial character. While suited to the slow, pastoral existence of the reservation, Beaver's features seem to Graves to mark his unsuitability to contemporary civilized life, a sense shortly confirmed by Bassett's brutal though, Graves feels, honest assessment of Indian character. Graves's attraction to Margaret is also self-deluding. While her earthy Indianness represents a refreshing alternative to the increasingly unbearable wit of his white friends, Graves is consciously gratified that her hybrid beauty outshines the commoner homeliness of full-blood women. As these feelings are revealed, Hergesheimer suggests, Graves's ultimate sacrifice of Margaret to propriety seems predictable, and his false sympathy with the Ojibwe seems evidence of racism more subtle and destructive than that of his openly snobbish friends. Even in the end, as he imagines himself a sympathetic bystander to the tragedy, he remains oblivious to his own complicity in the deaths of Margaret and Beaver, blaming them instead on some vague cosmic antipathy symbolized by the scarlet ibis.

Like *Malaeska* in the previous century, Hergesheimer's story represents a transition between two distinct understandings of hybridity. His portrayal of an obtuse cultural interloper who imagines himself enlightened anticipates La Farge's warning against white bungling in fragile

13. Ibid., 62, 68, 6.

tribal cultures, which Reorganization explicitly meant to stop. His portrayal of the tragedy of two mixed-bloods who "wanted to be white" likewise shares the primitivist view of hybridity as infectious to traditional tribal society. His characterization of Margaret and Beaver, however, derives from the romantic idea of hybridity as a state of destructive conflict rather than from that most evident in the work of Mourning Dove, Silko, and Erdrich, as synthesis and liberation. Margaret longs for escape from reservation life, but her nineteenth-century half-breed self-hatred fuels her desire for the white man. Having gained nothing by her education, Margaret plans to escape from the reservation through marriage to a white man, an aspiration based on her belief that her white blood makes her superior to other Indians, a familiar racialist idea that Hergesheimer never dismisses. Her failure to achieve this marriage dooms her to a sad fate like that of the uncivilizable Wesley Beaver, whose impulsive murder-suicide aligns him with the criminally deranged half-breeds of the dime novel. Hergesheimer's apparent doubt about the social viability of miscegenation recalls the nationalist fiction of the nineteenth century, but his modern sensitivity to the intense pains caused by dispossession and the subsequent compulsion to assimilate foreshadow the advent of modern Native American fiction in *Cogewea* and *Sundown*.

Despite the rife romanticism evident in Edmonds's stories and in earlier narratives of biological corruption, magazine fiction also manifests a modern cynicism, a slight, somewhat reluctant consciousness that the restorative images of a heroic past offered in the Dygartsbush series are merely illusions, that the ascendance of the Anglo-Saxon is a veneer that only temporarily enables us to forget the present historical condition. Norman Rockwell's May 24, 1930, *Saturday Evening Post* cover, depicting a movie cowboy having makeup applied to his mouth, hints at the thinness of this nostalgic veneer that the magazine maintained most colorfully and persistently during the assault on orthodox notions of race and the myth of the frontier. Another *Saturday Evening Post* cover painted by Rockwell depicts a somber reservation Indian wrapped in an old red blanket opening his rusted, lopsided mailbox to find a sunny travel brochure inviting him to "See America First" (April 23, 1938). The implied irony of the illustration demonstrates awareness that the Indian had not wholly vanished, that the happy privileges of middle-class vacationers come at the expense of a dispossessed race, and that the assimilationist drive begun with Allotment had ended in the abject failure personified by this sad, shabby Indian. These hints provided by Rockwell's paintings betray a deeper trend in magazine fiction that cast doubt on the nostalgic myths and that aligned more definitely with new anthropological theories than with the polygenism of the nineteenth century.

The Test of Language, Redefinition, and Reorganization

In the era following Allotment, as whites invaded reservations seeking to invest in newly privatized Indian property, the full-blood population began to decline while the number of mixed-bloods increased dramatically. In a lecture delivered to an interdisciplinary delegation at the National Museum in 1889, anthropologist Henry Weatherbee Henshaw posed the definitive question necessitated by these changes: "Who Are the American Indians?" Aware of the blurring of racial lines occurring on the reservations, Henshaw immediately rejected conventional positivist views of Indian cultures and origins. Although he considered the physical tests of race such as skin color, hair color, eye color, and structural proportion reliable scientific indicators of racial origin, he ultimately found the method's inability to reach a consensus on race traits or a racial taxonomy to be "disappointing." Henshaw devoted the majority of his lecture to a consideration of the "test of language" that anticipates Boasian inquiry of the twentieth century. While Henshaw considered the task of tracing Indian language families to a likely prehistoric geographic origin too complex for himself and perhaps even for his entire generation of anthropologists, he closed his lecture with a promise: "Linguistic science is still in its infancy, and its future may contain possibilities far exceeding the dreams of the most sanguine. As science has revolutionized the world's processes and has made the impossibilities of a hundred years ago the common-places of today, so like wonders may be achieved in the domain of thought, and the science of language . . . may yet answer the unanswerable questions of the present." Henshaw dismissed physiological observation as the privileged means for discovering truth about the Indian in favor of language, inaugurating only two years after Allotment the fundamental epistemological shift that would soon lead to Boas's more extensive revision of the idea of the Indian and of racial blending.[14]

In one of his earliest studies, "Physical Characteristics of the Indians of the North Pacific Coast" (1891), Boas approaches his Indian subjects conventionally, logging precise measurements of physiological and physiognomic proportions, yet he concluded that physical differences among various Northwest tribes derive less from inherent "racial characters" than from environmental influences such as habitat and occupation. Similarly, in "Remarks on the Theory of Anthropometry" (1893), Boas suggests that mathematical laws, the tools of positivist anthropology, cannot explain all aspects of human physiology and behavior. Boas instead proposes an integrated system of the examination of race traits, a consideration of "each measurement as a function of a number of variable factors which represent the laws of heredity and environment." Pure anthropometry, limited to the inference of race traits from highly speculative methods of statistical analysis, proves satisfactory to an untrained public easily misled by the apparent certainty of numbers but remains "highly objectionable for theoretical studies." In this essay, Boas identifies the "half-blood race of Indian and white parentage" as a particularly "concrete case" in which the "method of averages" often belies the "type of a series," an anomalous group whose numerical measurements do not fit their assumed race traits. In anthropology as in Indian policy, then, the mixed-blood forces a reconsideration of fundamental categories.[15]

Boas's early conclusions were revolutionary only insofar as they contradicted anthropological orthodoxy. In fact, Boas reiterates the claim made variously by Jemison, Apess, Ridge, Jackson, and others that circumstance rather than nature causes hybrid degeneracy. In a later paper, "Instability of Human Types" (1911), published in the same year that Lombroso identified "hybrid civilization" as a cause of crime, Boas contradicts the claim of inherent race traits that supported the criminalization of "primitive" types:

14. Henry Weatherbee Henshaw, "Who Are the American Indians?" 203, 213.
15. Franz Boas, "Physical Characteristics of the Indians of the North Pacific Coast," 30, 25; Franz Boas, "Remarks on the Theory of Anthropometry," 81, 79–80.

When we try to judge the ability of the races of man, we make the silent assumption that ability is something permanent and stationary, that it depends upon heredity, and that, as compared to it, environmental, modifying influences are, comparatively speaking, of slight importance.... [This] assumption of an absolute stability of human [racial] types is not plausible. Observations on growth have shown that the amount of growth of the whole body depends upon more or less favourable conditions which prevail during the period of development.... It follows from this consideration that social and geographical environment must have an influence upon the form of the body of the adult.[16]

Although Boas shared the methods of anthropometry, the most significant of the variable factors that Boas proposes in his early methodological discussions became Henshaw's test of language. This emphasis exemplifies, in Stocking's terms, Boas's "embracive conception" of anthropology, a philosophical and methodological merging of the traditionally distinct studies of "anthropology," the study of human physical characteristics; "ethnology," the comparative study of human cultures; and linguistics.[17] This basic methodological divergence from earlier anthropologists led Boas to challenge the positivist belief in inborn race traits and to contribute to a redefinition of race itself that would shape subsequent Indian policy. In 1887, the same year that saw the passage of Allotment, Boas declared his intention to show that the mind of the "savage" has evolved equally with that of the white man, signaling a revolution in the way science perceived the Indian. He was perhaps the first anthropologist to use the term *savage* self-consciously, ironically, and subversively. His awareness of the subjective position constitutes an even more basic refusal to assume absolute scientific truth and the cultural superiority of the civilized observer to the savage subject, marking the beginning of the pluralist consciousness that would liberate Native American writing from romantic racialism.

Although Boas's early attention to physical characteristics seems to resemble more conventional racialism, he consistently resisted the biological interpretation of racial difference and its most fundamental sup-

16. Franz Boas, "The Instability of Human Types," 214–15.
17. George W. Stocking Jr., ed., *The Shaping of American Anthropology, 1883–1911: A Franz Boas Reader,* 14.

position of white ascendance. In "The Anthropology of the North American Indian" (1894), for example, Boas analyzed the "measurements of about 17,000 full-blood and half-breed Indians which are distributed all over the North American continent" and proposed "to pay particular attention to the question regarding the anthropology of the half-breeds." Boas first refuted the polygenist belief in the "diminishing fertility" of mixed-race pairs, assembling evidence of "hybrid vigor":

> It appears from these statistics that Indian women . . . have on an average, approximately, six children, while half-breed women have on average seven to eight children. . . . It appears that the smaller numbers of children are very much more frequent among the Indians than among the half-breeds, while the higher numbers of children are much more frequent among the half-breeds than among the Indians; that is to say, we find the rather unexpected result that the fertility among half-breed women is considerably larger than among full-blood women. . . . The increased fertility among half-breed women would tend to show that the mixture of races results in increased vitality. . . . I believe the cause of this fact must be considered to be wholly in effects of the intermixture, as the social surrounding of the half-breeds and of the Indians are so much alike that they cannot cause the existing differences.

He also notes "the remarkable fact that . . . the half-breed is always more alike to the Indian than to the whites," inverting Anglo-Saxonism by redefining assumed primitive traits as the stronger, more vigorous traits and suggesting that racial blending would result not in a race of Aryans tinged with weaker Indian blood, as Buffon and Knox believed, but in a race of Indians tinged with Aryan blood, a view that would characterize primitivist artists and writers such as Oliver La Farge.[18]

In an address to the American Association for the Advancement of Science, "Human Faculty as Determined by Race" (1894), Boas suggests that physiological difference does not mark racial superiority or inferiority, a central tenet of Lombrosian criminology and of racialism in general. In order to show that cultural or technological "achieve-

18. Franz Boas, "The Anthropology of the North American Indian," 192, 194, 195.

ment is not necessarily a measure of aptitude" and that primitive races were indeed equally capable of "rising to higher levels" of development, Boas identifies intercultural exchange facilitated by linguistic blending, lacking in the Americas, as the primary reason for the ascendance of European civilization. Whereas Knox, Lombroso, and Roosevelt argued that such cultural cross-fertilization produces hereditary and social degeneracy, Boas argued the opposite, that intercultural blending stimulates both physical robustness and intellectual achievement. In another address, "Race Problems in America" (1908), Boas specifically returned to the old fear of racial blending as a cause of national degeneracy, more acute than ever as immigrant hordes reached American shores. As Slotkin observes, the immigrants caused great anxiety in Roosevelt "about the ability of his own class to maintain its power and values against the numbers and ambitions of the lesser breeds." In his "Race Problems" address, Boas assured that "the concern that is felt by many in regard to the continuance of racial purity of our nation is to a great extent imaginary." Overwhelming evidence, Boas suggested, should silence "advocates of the theory of a degradation of type by the influx of so-called 'lower' types" and show that "looking for a general degradation, for a reversion to remote ancestral types," as Lombroso and the positivist criminologists had, is motivated by "fancy or personal inclination."[19]

Within two decades after the publication of Boas's earliest work, his fundamental redefinition of race and inversion of the long-held standards of civilization and savagery began to contribute to progressive development in the artistic view of the Indian. In 1915, Taos, New Mexico, became a colony for a group of avant-garde artists known as the Taos Society of Artists, who, in their repudiation of modern industrial society, adopted an ideal they characterized as primitivist. Among these artists, Helen Carr observes, "Americanism no longer seemed necessarily a higher, or more mature, form of life. 'Mental and moral' progress was failing as a convincing narrative for mankind. The modern world did not point unequivocally to 'future betterment.' "[20] The replacement of the paradigm of evolutionism and white ascendance that informed the

19. Franz Boas, "Human Faculty as Determined by Race," 222–23; Slotkin, *Gunfighter Nation,* 170; Boas, "Race Problems in America," 322, 323, 326.
20. Carr, *Inventing the American Primitive,* 197–98.

racialist discourse of the nineteenth century with the cultural relativism introduced by Boas supported new views of the Indian, of his integration into the national body, and of his blending with the white race.

This apparent rejection of the evolutionary model that provided the ideological foundation for expansionist policy and maintained the essential incompatibility of races masked, however, a more conservative view of miscegenation. Mary Austin and Mabel Dodge Luhan, founders of the Taos Society, represented the belief held by many who embraced primitivism as a means to the wholeness and harmony lost in modern society. Carr writes, "the essentialism of this period . . . [was] in itself a form of racism; the 'real' . . . traditional, Indian was mythicized, while the Indian of mixed origins, racial or cultural, was scorned as much as ever." While nineteenth-century racialists viewed the mixed-blood as debased because he bore the taint of savagism, modern primitivists viewed him as debased because he bore the taint of civilization. According to this modern idea of the Indian, the "truly Indian was what had been there in the past, untouched by the modern world. It could only be preserved in stasis."[21] At the end of the nineteenth century, Allotment invited the Indian to assimilate with contemporary white society, and assimilationists such as John Rollin Ridge viewed this path as their only way to survival. Yet in the modern intellectual environment fostered by those like Boas, Austin, and Dodge, those mixed-bloods who had survived through the uneasy adoption of civilized manners now found themselves degraded by their own perseverance to live and cast out by their acceptance of the invitation to come in. Primitivists regarded the half-breed as the unfortunate but unremarkable by-product of a corrupt civilization, no longer degenerate for being half-Indian but now for being half-white.

Spurred by this new view, John Collier's Indian Reorganization Act provided for "retribalization," or the reintegration of more traditional forms of Indian life and self-governance on the reservation. Arriving in Taos at the invitation of Luhan, Collier observed that the small community of Pueblos "had survived repeated and immense historical shocks . . . amid a context of beauty which suffused all the life of the group," and

21. Ibid., 203.

he believed that the Indians possessed "the fundamental secret of human life—the secret of building great personality through the instrumentality of social institutions."[22] When Roosevelt appointed him Indian commissioner, he proposed to change the philosophy of the Bureau of Indian Affairs, which would no longer view the Indians as the troublesome wards of the nation but rather as utopian paradigms. In preparation for this change, Collier cited the "Meriam Report," or *The Problem of Indian Administration* (1928), prepared by the Institute of Government Research and directed by Lewis Meriam. This report presented an official acknowledgment and explanation for the failure of Allotment and, significantly, found the mixed-bloods complicit in the failure.

Contrary to the hope of earlier reformers that the mixed-blood might aid the full-blood in assimilating with American society, many legislators believed that the mixed-bloods habitually exploited the sweeping changes instituted by the privatization of Indian lands. Some had married Indian women to flee jurisdiction or appropriate Indian land. William Unrau explains that some allotment policies mandated "exclusive benefits for mixed-bloods," which were "justified on grounds of the 'civilizing' impact they would have on the tribes as a whole." Almost immediately, however, reports accused mixed-bloods of claiming the most valuable allotments in order to sell them and of using their interpretive skills to broker fraudulent deals between full-bloods and white investors. Legislative measures leading to Reorganization therefore prohibited white men and mixed-bloods who had married Indian women from acquiring property on the reservation. Those who opposed mixed-blood property rights invoked traditional arguments of hybrid degeneracy and criminality. Congressman Abraham Parker of New York, echoing the polygenist dogma, referred to such men as "degenerate progeny," and Congressman Samuel Peters of Kansas argued, "some of the worst characters, the vilest outlaws, men who violate every law known to humanity as well as to Christianity, are the children of white men who went among the Indians and intermarried with them. I would rather trust my life or my property today in the hands of a full-blood Indian than trust it in the hands of a half-breed who has been raised in

22. Vickers, *Native American Identities,* 85.

the midst of the barbarous influences that surround many of these tribes."[23]

A liberal policy that sought to undo the destructive effects of Allotment and halt such abuses, Reorganization stopped the siphoning of reservation land and resources and provided for the purchase of additional land with tribal funds, for social and economic services, for rehabilitation programs, for hiring preferences for Indians at the Bureau of Indian Affairs, and for the restoration of tribal authority. The Meriam Report anticipated this policy six years earlier, when it recommended the incorporation of the reservation as a profit-motivated enterprise. While individual Indians should hold stock in the reservation, the report warned that no individual should autonomously decide to strike a bargain that would diminish the holdings of the tribe, or corporation, as a whole. New policy should prohibit the sale of individual interest in communal lands unless the sale furthers the productive enterprise of the entire reservation and its people.

Collier's new policy did not, however, adopt Boas's most fundamental redefinition of the Indian as linguistic and cultural entity and not a biological entity. In the attempt to limit the benefits extended to mixed-bloods, the Indian New Deal ironically returned to a more traditional concept of race, establishing blood quantum as the criterion for determining Indian identity and economic status, further narrowing the legal definition of the Indian from one with one-quarter tribal descent to one with one-half. Although he knew that the distinction had become practically irrelevant, Collier, compromising with the more conservative segment of Congress, sought to ensure that mixed-bloods, "false Indians," could not reap the benefits properly offered to full-bloods, "true Indians."

This uncertain distinction in Reorganization policy preceded current debates about discursive authenticity in Native texts. Today, for more rigorous scholars, hybrid texts may not be properly classed as Native texts, as for Congress hybrid Indians could not be classed real Indians. In spite of its radical reconceptualization of race, then, Reorganization stalled the progress toward the understanding of hybridity as a condition

23. Quoted in William E. Unrau, *Mixed-Bloods and Tribal Dissolution: Charles Curtis and the Quest for Indian Identity,* ix, 105–6.

of racial and discursive simultaneity, reevaluating but not abandoning the nineteenth-century dialectical view of race. For the half-breeds lingering somewhere between the primitivist utopia of the reservation and the wasteland of modern civilization, the politics of the New Deal only offered more of the same old deal. Progressive writers such as Mary Austin and Oliver La Farge dramatized both the problems and the promises presented by existence in this invisible borderland.

Oliver La Farge's Navajo Stories

La Farge was a Harvard-educated anthropologist who did field work in the American Southwest and later served as president of the Association for American Indian Affairs, helping to guide Collier's efforts of Reorganization. His Pulitzer Prize–winning novel, *Laughing Boy* (1929), told the story of a tragic romance between two young Navajos, a man deeply immersed in the tribal traditions and an educated woman torn between white and Native cultures. The novel most dramatically represents the contradictions of the primitivist aesthetic of the Taos Society of Artists and the impending Reorganization policy, the view of racial blending as an unfortunate corruption of the inherent wholeness of traditional Native culture. For Scott Vickers, La Farge's genius lies in his strategy, like that of Apess, Ridge, or Jackson, of posing a "countermyth" against the "master myth" of Anglo-Saxon ascendance: "By personifying his Indian Others and grounding them in a meaningful cosmology separate from that of Christian culture, La Farge creates a powerful antidote to the 'alien' nature of the Other—he makes his a deeply human hero . . . by filling Indianness with its own substantial mythos, enforced by 'real,' active gods."[24] But Vickers's assessment does not account for the conflict manifested in La Farge's writing between the traditional biological definition of the Indian and the more progressive cultural definition. Although inspired by the spirit of cultural pluralism that had by 1929 almost completely changed the orthodox understanding of race, La Farge's countermyth of an integrated, autonomous Indian cosmology provides not an antidote to otherness but, like Reorganization, a revaluation of otherness. It envisions a society as

24. Vickers, *Native American Identities,* 55.

segregated as any in nationalist romance, but instead of advising white maids to shun dark chieftains, it cautions Indians to maintain their distance from the chaos and moral malaise that characterized modern white civilization.

La Farge models his hero, Laughing Boy, on "Slayer of Alien Gods," the young demigod of Navajo creation myth, to signify the ideological challenge he represents. Slim Girl, Laughing Boy's romantic interest, is not so idealized. Recently returned to the reservation from California, she represents the taint of white society that the primitivists perceived in mixed-bloods and assimilated full-bloods. Coming from the "bustle and comfort" of civilization, she remains insensible to the mythic, luminous landscape and to Laughing Boy's "path of beauty," sensing instead "hostile fury" in the "empty desert," as would any white person who has become alienated from nature.[25] This taint most dramatically manifests itself as Slim Girl's sexual liaisons with white men, which La Farge portrays as misguided and horribly tragic. While living an assimilated life in California, she becomes pregnant by a white man who abandons her to a life of prostitution. When she returns to the reservation, she relapses and offers sexual favors to a white rancher. Just as she resolves to return to Laughing Boy and the "path of beauty," she is murdered, becoming, like Jackson's Alessandro or Neihardt's Antoine, a victim of white society.

While venturing, as Vickers suggests, an Indian cosmology completely autonomous of Christianity, La Farge's novel nonetheless idealizes the myth of Indianness as the members of the Taos Society did in their painting. La Farge and the primitivists suggest that racial and cultural blending results in a perverse corruption of a more pure Native ideal, espousing a form of racialism opposite those of Buffon, Knox, and Lombroso, but equally detached from social reality in its privileging of one over another and equally incapable of imagining hybridity as a cultural synthesis. Nevertheless, a number of stories that La Farge published in the *Saturday Evening Post* in the decade following *Laughing Boy* and concurrently with the magazine's publication of Walter Edmonds's work suggest a movement away from the romantic racialism toward the linguistic formulations of race that characterize the writing

25. Oliver La Farge, *Laughing Boy*, 99.

of La Farge's mixed-blood contemporaries, Mourning Dove and John Joseph Mathews, as well as the Native fiction appearing in the later twentieth century. Although suspicious of racial mixing as both a sexual and ideological violation of Native cultures, these stories, unlike the magazine's more nostalgic tales, suggest that the differences between whites and Indians are learned and cultural, not biological and essential. They demonstrate La Farge's gradual abandonment of the impulse, common to both romantic racialists and modern primitivists, to value one sort of blood over another and his recognition of the synthesis inherent in modern Indian life where the mixed-blood becomes an agent of hopeful intercultural exchange rather than of debasement and alienation. La Farge's eventual acceptance that cultures must inevitably blend, that valuable lessons might indeed be gained in the process, is reflected in his increasing interest, apparent in the later stories, in the translation of Navajo words and practices for whites and, conversely, of white practices for Indians.

La Farge's characters are not mixed-bloods in the biological sense, a circumstance that itself suggests that American fiction had begun to abandon the racialist understanding of hybridity. Mary Austin had published stories in magazines such as *Outing, Sunset,* and the *Atlantic Monthly* since the turn of the twentieth century, but her 1934 collection, *One-Smoke Stories,* represents her most self-conscious intervention into the issues surrounding Allotment and hybridity. On one hand, the collection romanticizes primitive ways like *Laughing Boy,* showing the dangers of mixed-bloods who too readily embrace civilization. In "The Man Who Lied about a Woman," the conflict arises from an Apache tradition that reserves a special punishment for a man who slanders a woman. Nataldin, a proud and prosperous young Apache, falls in love with Tall Flower, a Navajo girl, who leaves the reservation and later returns, to Nataldin's shame, pregnant. To save face with the men of his tribe, Nataldin boasts of his paternity, but he is exposed as a liar when Tall Flower gives birth to a white baby. In "Mixed Blood," the Pueblo-Spanish Venustiano attends a boarding school. When he returns to the reservation, he scorns Indian ways but seeks to marry a Pueblo girl. She rejects him because he is stained by both white blood and white civilization, but through the efforts of the reservation community, Venustiano abandons white ways and becomes again a true Pueblo. Both plots, that of an Indian girl despoiled by a white man, and that of an Indian who must unlearn civilized ways, are common in primitivist writing including La Farge's. But *One-Smoke Stories* also demonstrates the flaws in the biological interpretation of race that had characterized earlier magazine fiction. In "White Wisdom," the half-breed Dan Kearny is raised by his father, a white rancher, but goes to live with his Indian relatives when his father dies. To prove his superiority to the backward Indians, Dan courts a white girl, who finally rejects him. Utterly discouraged, Dan settles for an Indian wife and returns to the old ways. The story appears to be another nondescript expression of biological determinism but for Austin's surprise ending, when the narrator reveals that Dan was pure white all along, the son of the white rancher and his deceased white wife. He fails to assimilate into white society not because he is part Indian, but because whites and indeed Dan himself perceive that he is part Indian. As we will see in *Cogewea,* Austin suggests that race is determined by perception, which is changeable, rather than blood, which is not.

La Farge and Austin move toward an abandonment of not only the racialist view of the mixed-blood as a biological experiment but also the primitivist ideal of untainted cultural purity, embracing the mixed-blood as cultural translator and the understanding of hybridity as discursive simultaneity. We find in Arthur Train's "And Lesser Breeds without the Law" (*Mr. Tutt Comes Home,* 1941) a more vivid illustration of the contrast between romantic primitivism and the more progressive idea of hybridity evolving in the fiction of La Farge and Austin. Train's mixed-blood villain Spotted Dog embodies a form of primitivism so extreme that he seems a mirror image of the half-breed grotesques in antebellum fiction. Like Whitman's Boddo, he is stout, ugly, and depraved. What sets him apart from Boddo is that his evil nature derives from his white blood rather than his Indian blood, his Caucasian stain most evident in his contrast with the lovely pure-Indian maiden Dawn Flower. When Spotted Dog attempts to bribe Dawn Flower's mother into consenting to a marriage between himself and her daughter, the Pueblo gods warn a local medicine man that Spotted Dog, stained with white blood, must not marry Dawn Flower. The story later reveals that the old seer spoke wisely, for Spotted Dog, worse than merely a crass opportunist, had killed his previous wife. Train's representation of the mixed-blood is bound to a new form of racialism that inverts but does not abandon nineteenth-century stereotypes. The stain in the blood is now white; the pure-hearted, pure-blooded virgin is now Indian. Still, hybridity remains a formula for degeneracy. For La Farge and Austin, for Mourning Dove and Mathews, and, later, for N. Scott Momaday and Gerald Vizenor, a "mixed-blood" might be an Indian pedigree whose mixture derives not from a white ancestor but rather from a white education or a white language. In this newly conceived understanding of hybridity, La Farge's Navajo protagonists are indeed half-breeds in the sense that they must reconcile a white self with an Indian self. La Farge's conscious decision, in all of his fiction, to ignore the question of blood quantum in his characters, to abandon the racialist stereotypes rife in both nationalist and primitivist fiction, to call his characters neither "mixed-blood" nor "full-blood," signals his break from the biological definition of race and his articulation of hybridity as a category of language, acculturation, and, as Vizenor writes, of "consciousness" rather than heredity.

In La Farge's "Hard Winter" (1933), an Apache fiesta in New Mexico attracts both local Indians and white tourists to watch the Apaches dance. Old chiefs, whose primitive faces speak of a "culture and a way of thought far removed from reservations and Government officials," impress the younger Indians, who are temporarily liberated from the government schools and their "Christian influences." During the celebration, Tall Walker, a Jicarilla Apache, meets Juan Sota, a Taos Pueblo friend from his school days. Tall Walker notices that his friend has prospered, and Juan explains that a wealthy white woman "interested" in Indian culture has hired him to be her "guide." Several weeks later, Tall Walker remains curious about Juan's white benefactress. Leaving his Apache wife and his two young children behind to tend the sheep, he accepts Juan's invitation to the Taos fiesta, where he is introduced to a "tribe" of white intellectuals, artists, and dilettantes who, like Juan's woman, are "interested" in Indian culture. Tall Walker, whose features resemble those of a classic Indian warrior, is flattered by the attention he is given. He poses for painters, gets drunk on fine whiskey, and soon succumbs to the seductions of a particularly wealthy white woman. He remains in Taos weeks after the fiesta ends, wallowing in luxury and gradually forgetting his wearisome existence in Jicarilla, before a letter from his wife begs him to come home and move his livestock to the winter range. He is also concerned for his infant son, who had fallen ill, but he promises the white woman he will return as soon as he can. Upon his arrival at his village, early blizzards kill the Apaches' livestock, and by the time Tall Walker, his wife, and his daughter reach the snowbound winter camp, the infant has died. The white woman arrives then in her heated car and offers to pay Tall Walker if he will leave his wife and return with her. Looking back on his haggard wife, who fights her grief over their dead child as she wearily raises the tepee, Tall Walker reflects, "That is how Apache women are . . . that is why we were great warriors once." With silent anger, he turns his back on the white woman to help his wife.[26]

In this white woman and her circle of friends, La Farge presents an unflattering portrait of the community of enlightened artists and intellectuals who, over the last two decades, had gathered in New Mexico and become "interested" in Indian culture. La Farge depicts this artistic interest as a polite veneer for sexual predation and the willful destruction of natural Indian familial bonds. La Farge, once a part of this community himself, had seemingly become disillusioned with the idealization of primitive purity held by the Taos Society. Unlike previous narratives of separation, the story does not suggest that the danger of interracial union is biological. Although Tall Walker, as he finally realizes, is ideally matched with his enduring Apache wife, his sexual dalliance with the white woman is not depicted as revolting or unnatural, from either race's point of view. As La Farge views it, Indian-white sexual contact is rather a secondary function of the more general and more pervasive rape of primitive cultures by self-serving white "benefactors" through education, tourism, and commercialized artistic appropriation. Whereas positivist anthropologists such as Lombroso viewed social transgression as the consequence of biological transgression, La Farge, like Boas, takes the opposite view, suggesting that cultural corruption precedes both Juan Soto's and Tall Walker's sexual indulgences.

La Farge's "Higher Education" (1934) more directly examines this process of cultural violation, the root, in Boas's view, of the ethnocentric flaws of traditional anthropological inquiry. Lucille Niltsi, a sixteen-

26. Oliver La Farge, "Hard Winter," 5, 47.

year-old Navajo girl, returns to the reservation after spending five years in a government school. Fayerweather, a white archaeologist who has befriended the Indians, senses Lucille's misery and confusion at having to return to her Indian life after spending five years learning to be white. Thinking of the thousands of Indian youths who are stripped of their tribal names, their culture, and, most importantly, of their language, Fayerweather reflects, "How many times can the substance be shattered and yet recreate itself?" Wind Singer, Lucille's father, is discouraged when he finds that Lucille has forgotten the Navajo tongue and can no longer converse with her own family. After several days, Lucille seems happier. Fayerweather, however, becomes worried when the girl hints that she has fallen in love with "Show-Off" McClellan, the obnoxious white proprietor of a reservation trading post. Fayerweather, knowing that Wind Singer wishes his daughter to marry Strong Hand, a traditional Navajo man, warns Lucille that Show-Off is a "bad man" and advises that she could use her education to help her people, that she need not think of Indians as "savages," and that the Navajos possess "strength, intelligence, pride, skill, beauty, character, and a magnificent religion" that cannot be taught in white schools. Believing that he has made a positive impression on the girl, Fayerweather is mortified when he finds Lucille whoring in a back room of Show-Off's store. A few days later, faced with this shame and the prospect of a long dismal life on the reservation, Lucille throws herself into a deep canyon. Fayerweather is left saddened and frustrated by the entire affair, concluding, "I feel sort of sick of being white."[27]

"Higher Education" echoes *Laughing Boy* in its depiction of the tragedy of a Navajo girl alienated from her culture and ultimately destroyed by the influence of civilized education. The story also manifests Boasian pluralism in Fayerweather's enlightened affirmation of the "beauty, character" and "magnificent religion" of Navajo culture. More significantly, however, La Farge represents Lucille's alienation as a linguistic rather than a biological dilemma, reflected in her inability to speak to her family after she has forgotten the Navajo language. Lucille's father confides to Fayerweather, who speaks the Navajo language, "I can talk to you, but I cannot speak to my own daughter." In order

27. Oliver La Farge, "Higher Education," 9, 69, 71.

to represent his connection to the Navajo, Fayerweather, like Mourning Dove, punctuates his narrative with Native words and names, offering the reader subtle translations that add thematic nuance to the story. When Strong Hand, for example, thanks Fayerweather for his attempt to intervene with Lucille, he says, *"kehey,"* not simply, "thank you," but a "humble word, implying deep gratitude and the laying aside of pride."[28] With such translations, La Farge portrays racial identification in linguistic terms, demonstrating the tenuousness of Lucille's blood tie to the tribe, the destruction of this tie through the forgetting of her Native tongue, and the strong bond of empathy formed by both Fayerweather and the Navajo through linguistic understanding. As in "Hard Winter," La Farge portrays Lucille's physical debasement with Show-Off as a consequence rather than a cause of her cultural and linguistic alienation, constructing a Boasian model of intercultural exchange based on language and moderating the primitivist view that any such exchange corrupts Indian life. Ultimately, La Farge finds value in mediation, not in the sexual interference represented by Show-Off, the white woman in "Hard Winter," or Lynn Graves in "Scarlet Ibis," but rather the linguistic negotiation represented by Fayerweather. While Lucille may perish in her foolish pursuit of the gaudy accoutrements of civilization, Fayerweather himself remains to give meaning to the tragedy for white readers, to translate the experience of the Navajo, and to receive their humblest thanks. Published in the same year that Collier's efforts to retribalize Native cultures were realized, the story imagines a new form of hybridity, perhaps embodied more by the multilingual ethnologist than by the overassimilated Navajo girl, that establishes translation as the means to the discursive simultaneity cultivated in the work of later Native writers.

La Farge's "Horse Tamer" (1938) returns to the theme of failed assimilation but without the ominous tragedy depicted in *Laughing Boy,* "Hard Winter," and "Higher Education." Like Slim Girl and Lucille, Bill Taft is a young Navajo recently returned to the reservation after being educated in Los Angeles. Bill is proud of his worldly experience, but he cannot find a job, and his parents tell him to "forget it all and learn to be an Indian again." Former friends now see him as a spoiled

28. Ibid., 66, 71.

schoolboy, and even Jenny, a Navajo girl whom he befriended in the city and who has also returned to the reservation, has reverted from a bright "schoolgirl" to a "plain Navajo."[29] Bill secretly wants to marry Jenny, believing that their education makes them especially compatible, but his lack of money prevents him from seeking the consent of Naslini Nez, Jenny's father. Fortunately, Bill wins Jenny's heart, Naslini's approval, and the acceptance and admiration of the entire Navajo community when he miraculously tames a killer bronco at a reservation rodeo.

While the story offers no explicit meditation on either biological or linguistic blending, it anticipates the hope of mixed-blood novelists such as Mourning Dove and Mathews who endeavor to synthesize the experience of the purely white and the purely Indian in a third, independent "consciousness of coexistence," in Vizenor's terms. Published nearly a decade after *Laughing Boy,* the story suggests La Farge's abandonment of primitivist idealism and his acceptance of the value of intercultural exchange and the mixed-blood as an agent of this exchange. Bill Taft does not repudiate his experiences in the white world as his parents and Jenny do. Neither does he compulsively abandon his Native identity as does Lucille in "Higher Education." Combining his formal knowledge of horses gained in school with traditional Indian riding skill, Bill wins the reputation as "horse tamer," finding his place among his people through the fortunate synthesis of two conflicting traditions.

La Farge's comic story represents an inconspicuous but significant movement toward an understanding of hybridity as simultaneity rather than as alternation. Bill does not vacillate between his Indian and white identities, though he is pushed first to be white by his teachers and later to be Indian by his parents. He does not forget his education and "go back to the blanket" as Jenny does, nor become corroded in spirit like Lucille in "Higher Education" and Slim Girl in *Laughing Boy.* Against the advice of both whites and Indians, Bill jauntily attempts to put his education to use among his own people, integrating his experience without the paralyzing disorientation and moral malaise endemic in earlier fictional mixed-bloods. The story is unique among La Farge's work, and also among other progressive narratives since *Ramona,* in

---

29. Oliver La Farge, "Horse Tamer," 11.

that it does not conclude with the tragic downfall of an Indian infected and destroyed by civilization. Bill's hybridity, in fact, saves him rather than dooms him. He tames the horse using a technique of stroking and whispering that combines zoological principles learned among the whites with riding rituals remembered from tribal tradition. Bill prevails not because of his whiteness and in spite of his Indianness like the Aryanized half-breeds of romantic magazine fiction, or because of his Indianness and in spite of his whiteness like the overeducated Natives in primitivist stories, but because of both. "Horse Tamer" ventures the radical idea, hitherto untried in American fiction, that hybridity indeed might be an advantage, both philosophically and practically. No Indian, no white man, only a cultural half-breed, La Farge suggests, could tame the killer bronco. The story demonstrates La Farge's shift from the romantic primitivism of *Laughing Boy* to the more pragmatic appreciation of the synthesis of traditional culture with modern American experience that twentieth-century Native writers have come to recognize as a necessary and sometimes advantageous condition of their life and their art. It also implies a flaw in the critical impulse to seek authenticity in hybrid texts. It implies that by finding value only in untainted Native discourse, scholars, like the primitivist writers, blind themselves to the independent possibilities contained in hybrid subjectivity.

Hybrid Subjectivity in *Cogewea*

The daughter of Joseph Quintasket, a mixed-Okanogan, and Lucy Stukin, a full-blood Colville, she had, like Mary Jemison, two names: the English Christal Quintasket and the Salish Hum-Ishu-Ma, or Mourning Dove. Like La Farge and the new generation of anthropologists, Mourning Dove saw language as the means to reconcile racial difference. She dedicated her hybrid education to the translation of Native oral tradition to a non-Indian audience, but unlike other folklorists or anthropologists, she aspired to do so in the form of the Western romance novels that had inspired her imagination as a child. Her work attracted the attention of the gentleman historian and Indian advocate Lucullus Virgil McWhorter, who enthusiastically volunteered to help her edit and publish her work. The following decade of collaboration between the two produced *Cogewea* and has since become the central problem for scholars of the novel, complicating conventional assumptions of authorship and authenticity but also revealing a discursive synthesis that has shaped the work of Momaday, Silko, Erdrich, and other current Native writers.

Cogewea dramatizes a love triangle on the Horseshoe Bend ranch on the Flathead reservation. Cogewea, or Little Chipmunk, entertains the affections of Jim LaGrinder, the mixed-blood foreman of the Horseshoe Bend, and the white greenhorn Alfred Densmore, recently arrived from the East in search of his fortune. Like the dime novel, *Cogewea* sketches its characters in bold strokes. The romantic heroine, like Ramona, is tomboyish, beautiful, and conflicted: "Her eyes of the deepest jet, sparkled, when under excitement, like the ruby's fire. Hair of the same hue was as lustrous as the raven's wing, falling when loose, in great billowy folds, enveloping her entire form."[30] Racially and temperamentally, the reader immediately recognizes her suitability to the cocksure but true-hearted Jim, the self-proclaimed greatest rider on the Flathead, who embraces his Indian identity and patiently courts Cogewea in spite of her protests that she loves him only as she would a brother. Densmore immediately emerges as the story's villain, announcing in soliloquies his intentions to seize Cogewea's fortune by marriage, dispatch her in a phony hunting accident, and return to his white sweetheart in the East. Through his false charm, his vague promises to introduce Cogewea to the world beyond the Flathead, and his feigned interest in Indian custom, he manages to lure his reluctant prey away from the ever-faithful Jim, who, like Stemteemä, Cogewea's full-blood grandmother, instinctively senses something dangerous in the *shoyahpee,* or white man.

Cogewea's difficulty in choosing between her suitors represents the problem of assimilation central to the novel. Although she professes her devotion to Stemteemä and the tradition she represents, Cogewea, like Hergesheimer's Margaret, initially imagines marriage to a white man as the surest route to assimilation. She craves the material comfort of white society and, in the moment when she decides to defy her grandmother and elope with Densmore, she confesses, "my white blood calls me to

---

30. Mourning Dove, *Cogewea, the Half-Blood: A Depiction of the Great Montana Cattle Range,* 15. Further citations will be made parenthetically with the abbreviation *C.*

see the world ... to live" (C, 253). She appeals here to the old biological ideal, but her error in making this decision demonstrates Mourning Dove's dissatisfaction with racial identification based on blood. The elopement, of course, proves disastrous. When Densmore discovers that Cogewea's fortune is much smaller than he believed, he beats her in frustration, robs her of the money she withdrew from the bank for their honeymoon, and escapes to perpetrate new schemes elsewhere. Jim rescues her and vows revenge on Densmore, but Cogewea, humiliated, forbids it, having learned the hard lesson that Stemteemä has always preached: "Let the maidens of my tribe shun the Shoyahpee" (C, 176). A happy ending, however, quickly follows this tragedy. After time has healed Cogewea's wounds, she finally agrees to marry Jim. Love, wisdom, and good fortune validate the match as Cogewea discovers in the novel's closing pages that she has inherited a real fortune from her long-lost white father.

This seemingly conventional Western romance manifests, like *A Narrative of the Life of Mrs. Mary Jemison,* a number of structural, stylistic, and thematic inconsistencies that form the basis of subsequent evaluations of the text. Charles Larson summarizes what critics find most problematic in the novel:

> The narrative voice in the novel has been split in two. Just as Cogewea cannot decide whether she wants to be Indian or white, so Mourning Dove obfuscates the ending by trying to have it both ways.... White people cannot be trusted, Mourning Dove tells us, yet there is apparently nothing wrong with her ... inheriting ... [her] father's tainted money.... Further obfuscation within the narrative voice is suggested by the author's strange blend of the comic and the serious. A number of the comic chapters in the book, describing the high jinks on the range, are oddly juxtaposed with the more serious "protest" sections ... [a] didacticism which often includes ethnographic comments on her people.... The criticisms of the white man's world, so inconsistent with the novel's romantic theme, suggests that the text of the novel may have been altered by an editor. Besides the rather manic-depressive plot, the author's use of language is often artificial; there is a superabundance of clichés, as well as stilted dialogues that are foreign to the characters involved.[31]

31. Charles R. Larson, *American Indian Fiction,* 176–77.

Scholars almost universally attribute such inconsistencies to the collaborative influence of McWhorter. McWhorter's influence has confused Mourning Dove's public persona as well as her writing. Most current knowledge of her background derives from McWhorter's introduction to the novel, where he mythologizes her participation in the "last grand roundup of the buffaloes" in Montana, her "sympathies" with the buffaloes as "the one remaining link with an era past," and her "deep" identification with the "mixed-blood, the socially ostracized of two races" (*C*, 9, 11). Casting his protégé as both vanishing Indian and racial pariah, McWhorter immediately evokes two of the nineteenth-century stereotypes of the Indian that the novel itself works to resist. In his effort to generate advance publicity for *Cogewea* and court the interest of potential publishers, McWhorter introduced Mourning Dove to the Spokane press in 1916 as "the first American Indian novelist" eleven years before she actually published a novel. Although their collaborative work had mostly concluded by 1916, financial setbacks, a paper shortage during the First World War, and a generally cautious attitude among publishers despite the proven public interest in Native writing, delayed publication until 1927, when the Four Seas Company of Boston eventually agreed to divide printing costs with McWhorter and Mourning Dove.

Mourning Dove herself seemingly credited Sho-Pow-Tan, or "Big Foot," the name the Okanogan tribe endearingly gave the white anthropologist, with the publication of the novel. In 1928, she writes in a letter to McWhorter: "I have just got through going over the book *Cogeawea* [*sic*], and am surprised at the changes you made. I think they are fine. . . . I sure was interested in the book. . . . I felt like it was someone elses [*sic*] book and not mine at all. In fact the finishing touches are put there by you, and I have never seen it." Offended by a local Indian agent's accusation that he had written *Cogewea* in its entirety, McWhorter publicly insisted that Mourning Dove was the sole author, yet Martha McKelvie, a friend of McWhorter, confided to him in a letter, "There is no chance that any thing bad would come of the world knowing that you practically wrote *Cogewea*. . . . In the field of all arts, interpreters are necessary."[32]

32. Quoted in Dexter Fisher, introduction to *Cogewea, the Half-Blood: A Depiction of the Great Montana Cattle Range*, xv, xxv.

Such clues of McWhorter's editorial influence invite scholars to play the game of guessing which parts of the novel belong to the editor and which to the author, the same game they continue to play with Jemison's story. The perceived inconsistencies also have caused scholars such as Larson to treat *Cogewea* as inauthentically Native. Although, as Larson finally concedes, there is no documentary evidence to suggest which parts of *Cogewea* have been inserted or "interpreted" by McWhorter and which parts are authentically Mourning Dove's, Fisher proposes that the novel's two contrasting languages serve as scholars' most reliable clue: "It is in the language of the novel that McWhorter's influence is most obvious because some of the passages are totally unlike Mourning Dove's own direct and simple style as reflected in her original drafts. . . . Language was for her a constant challenge as she struggled to translate into English what she knew in Okanogan. . . . [S]uch passages are particularly obtrusive in contrast to the Okanogan tales told by Cogewea's grandmother, which seem to reflect Mourning Dove's own unadorned style." Citing McWhorter's insertion of chapter epigraphs from *Hiawatha* and other Western romances, historical and ethnographic endnotes of only marginal relevance, didactic passages within the narrative itself condemning governmental mistreatment of Indians, and his own advertisement on the title page that the novel is "told through him," Fisher similarly concludes, "McWhorter unquestionably had a tremendous amount of control over Mourning Dove's manuscript. . . . The result is that the narrative . . . sags at times under the weight of vituperation."[33]

One obvious example of such stilted and obtrusive language details the Indian custom of smoking. Although the lecture appears as spoken by Cogewea, the language rings of an ethnographic lecture:

> Smoking is an exclusive characteristic of our race. . . . Its origin is scarce preserved in the dim legends of the past. The oldest pipes were straight, tapering trumpet-like tubes, made of clay or stone. Perhaps these were closely contemporaneous with the non-angular variety, showing the funnel-like orifice for both the stem and tobacco. Oftentimes these later pipes assumed fantastic forms, representing animals, birds, human and mythical beings; many of them evidently of a sacred nature. . . .

33. Ibid., xvi–xvii, xiii–xiv.

There always have been, and are still some individual men who do not smoke; but in our tribe, as in many others, even the women indulge, but not universally. It is not uncommon to see a young woman draw- ing on a cigarette in just the same manner as a white society lady. . . . Smoking is the only ideal of our race that the Caucasian has deemed worthy of perpetuation. . . . We did not use strong, straight tobacco and virus-infected wrappers. We employed a very mild and almost, if not entirely harmless mixture of bark and leaves, and among some of the tribes, a minute amount of tobacco. . . . Southern Indians used more of this narcotic plant than did their northern cousins, and here in the far northwest, we had none of it. Often the smoking material was slightly oiled by rubbing it with buffalo, or other melted fats. This was especially true of the plains Indians. The process improved the flavor and also augmented the fire-holding qualities. (*C,* 120–21)

Although Cogewea makes nominal reference to "our race" and "our tribe," the objectifying tone, according to Larson's and Fisher's readings, places the speaker at a much greater distance from Native culture than Cogewea usually assumes in the narrative. Even if Mourning Dove had sufficient education to write such passages, she uncharacteristically speaks of her tradition and of "mythical beings" from a professional distance, and she deploys jargon—"contemporaneous," "non-angular," "perpet- uation," and "augmented"—more familiar to a trained ethnologist than to Mourning Dove or especially to her character. Even early critics sym- pathetic to McWhorter's goals such as Granville Lowther criticized the "unnatural language" of the novel and advised Mourning Dove to "confine her writing to the life she knows and the people she knows and understands" such as the old storyteller Stemteemä.[34]

Cogewea's centenarian grandmother, the thematic center of the novel for readers like Lowther, speaks in the simple language that stands in contrast to the obtrusive ethnographic passages. She also embodies the Okanogan oral tradition Mourning Dove seeks to translate for her white audience, introducing tales meant to emphasize the historic abuse of Indian woman by white men in words that, for many readers, seem more authentically Indian: "The story I am telling you is true. It was given me by my father. . . . He told me the tales that were sacred to his tribe; honored me with them, trusted me. Treasured by my forefathers,

34. Ibid., xvi.

I value them, I know that they would want them kept only to their own people, if they were here. But they are gone and for me the sunset of the last evening is approaching and I must not carry with me this history" (*C*, 122). Both in these stories and in other dialogue, Mourning Dove integrates Native language into her text, a rhetorical innovation that arose from the new importance anthropology placed on language. When a rattlesnake crosses her trail, Cogewea declares to it, "My uncle has told me of your *tahmahnawis* power for doing secret evil to people. Your 'medicine' is strong and my grandmother would not hurt you. But I am *not* my grandmother! I am not a full-blood—only a *breed*—a *sitkum* Injun and that breaks the charm of your magic with me" (*C*, 26). Yet, even as Mourning Dove introduces the reader to such tribal words and concepts, the novel maintains the same sense of untranslatability recognized by Boasian relativism, of a tribal reality that Western inquiry, barred by language, can never fully contain. She writes, "The Stemteemä knew many interesting tales of the past; legends finer than the myths of the old world; but few of them known to the reading public and none of them understood. . . . Ever suspicious of the whites and guardedly zealous in the secrecy of their ancient lore, seldom do the older tribesmen disclose ancestral erudition, and when they do their mysteries are not comprehended" (*C*, 40–41).

Given this impossibility to convey the full understanding of one culture to another, the mixed-blood, as Mourning Dove sees herself, plays a critical role in her unique ability to mediate an interpretive rather than an authentic understanding of the Native language and worldview. For her, as for Momaday, Silko, and Erdrich later, the hybrid subject occupies a unique position as the only one capable of performing this mediation and in this sense assumes a significance independent of the white or the Indian, becomes something more than a half-person. In this role as interpreter, Mourning Dove assumes a greater potential than that of an Okanogan apple-picker whose awkward fusion of romance and Indian lore has been totally circumscribed by the professional ethnologist. Like La Farge in his later stories, Mourning Dove represents hybridity as a necessary condition for intercultural exchange and the half-breed as the necessary agent of this exchange. In all its rhetorical inconsistency and linguistic variation, she presents her novel as the conduit by which Indian culture may be interpreted or translated

in the language of Euro-American culture, if not authentically represented. On the modern frontier, where race lines have been irrevocably
blurred by the effects of assimilationist policies, Mourning Dove suggests that such hybrid languages provide the only available means for
intercultural understanding and the preservation of an oral tradition
irreversibly altered by the effects of colonization.

This basic acceptance that a purely authentic understanding of Native
culture is impossible within the perceptual frame of a white reader represents the genesis of the postcolonial understanding of hybridity as a
condition of discursive flux. But Bhabha's and especially Spivak's formulations of hybridity tend to neglect that this process of flux often reveals
more about the subaltern subject than it obscures. On its surface, for
instance, *Cogewea* seems a highly compromised text, a conventional
Western romance inexpertly written by a mixed-blood woman working
with a condescending and obtrusive editor. But the overt romantic
influence and editorial tampering distract from what is more subtly
hybrid and revealing of the Native in the novel. Mourning Dove conceived her romantic plot as a retelling of an Okanogan folktale in which
Cogewea's mythical namesake, Little Chipmunk, a sprightly but careless girl, ignores her wise grandmother's warnings to stay out of trouble. While picking berries, Little Chipmunk meets Owl Woman, a de-
vourer of children, who captures the girl and tears out her heart. When
Meadow Lark brings her back to life, she learns to respect the wisdom
of her grandmother. Similarly, Cogewea's failure to heed her grandmother's advice to stay away from the wicked Densmore drives the
plot of the novel to its own painful conclusion, while Jim's loving attention eventually heals her and brings new wisdom. Mourning Dove's
interpretation of a tribal story as a contemporary romance is itself an
unprecedented discursive strategy, a stunt, like Bill Taft's taming the
killer bronco, capable only by one with a familiarity with both traditions. In much of their work, we will see, Silko and Erdrich elaborate
Mourning Dove's invention, emphasizing mythical resonances in contemporary life as a defining characteristic of hybrid consciousness.

This new understanding of the mixed-blood writer's interpretive
role liberates readings of *Cogewea* from the traditional assumption of
McWhorter's dominance of the narrative voice. While the correspondence between McWhorter and Mourning Dove obviously reveals an

indefinite degree of collaboration between editor and author, it does not preclude Mourning Dove's negotiation with herself, nor should it distract scholars from the importance of this negotiation. In fact, it permits us to acknowledge her collaboration with McWhorter without dismissing her text as corrupted and inauthentic. Even more so than recent readings, such as Martha Viehmann's, that account for the relationship between McWhorter and Mourning Dove as a creative collaboration rather than a contest, a synthesis rather than a dialectic, it also allows a possibility that no scholar has considered: that Mourning Dove herself, not McWhorter, controls the narrative, that the stylistic inconsistencies demonstrate both the negotiation between Mourning Dove and McWhorter and the negotiation of Mourning Dove with herself. Synthesizing the formerly incompatible discourses of romance, ethnography, and Indian protest, Mourning Dove herself inevitably generates variations that scholars have attributed to McWhorter. Since McWhorter protested to the accusing Indian agent that Mourning Dove had indeed written *Cogewea* in its entirety, critics have regarded the statement as a plain lie, with no justification other than vague personal correspondences and their own assumption that Mourning Dove was simply incapable of writing in more than one voice. Although the influence of Sho-Pow-Tan cannot be discounted, neither can we discount that Mourning Dove, contrary to critical common sense, actually wrote the novel that bears her name.

As the concept of hybridity as translation allows readers to see Mourning Dove's text as synthetic rather than dialectical, it also opens new possibilities for literary criticism, which remains bound to dialectic terms: white or Indian, self or other, dominant or subversive. Scholars generally assume that Mourning Dove did not have complete control over the composition of her novel, positing the standard of a unitary authorial identity, a clear correspondence between an individual subject and a textual product that has traditionally formed the foundation of literary criticism. The perception of inconsistency, unnatural language, and a confusing voice assumes that rhetorical consistency, organic language, and a clear voice indicate the predominance of a singular authorial persona within a text. But, as Mourning Dove suggests in her role as translator, the hybrid writer is herself inconsistent or unnaturally conflicted between an Indian language and a white language, which she must struggle to reconcile. The traditional critical impulse, evident even in the most recent scholarship, to divide the authentic from the inauthentic replicates the polygenist impulse to divide the races of men and the political impulse of Reorganization to divide true Indians from false Indians. When such racial or rhetorical demarcations blur, when an "unnatural" hybridity emerges, critics likewise seek to impose a false unity or to deny signs of difference. Attempting to differentiate McWhorter's voice from Mourning Dove's voice similarly seeks to efface the hybrid characteristics of Mourning Dove's writing and to deny, like the primitivists who idealized a static traditional culture, at least part of the book as inauthentic. As in the case of Jemison's narrative, the attempt to determine who wrote what denies the cultural hybrid's unique ability to render such fundamental questions irrelevant. To dismiss its language as inconsistent or unnatural denies its ability to reflect the racial and cultural simultaneity so felt by mixed-blood writers since Apess and reflexively rejected by national culture as a perversion of the natural order. While the text might support the view that McWhorter exerted great influence on such passages as the lecture on smoking, it also suggests that Mourning Dove, as interpreter, was equally capable of exchanging the language of the Okanogan apple-picker for that of the professional ethnologist. As McWhorter might have circumscribed Mourning Dove, Mourning Dove might have circumscribed McWhorter.

As the presence of the half-breed upset the sacred assumptions of biology, the law, and national identity in the nineteenth century, the mixed voice that emerges in twentieth-century novels such as *Cogewea* and, later, in the work of Momaday, Silko, and Erdrich, upsets the modern critical assumption of a unitary authorial presence. Postmodern critique that abandons or expands the authorial function has therefore given contemporary readers, such as Gerald Vizenor and Martha Viehmann, a way of understanding hybrid texts (such as *Cogewea*) that elude Larson and Fisher and suggests synthetic understanding of hybridity. Viehmann, inspired by Vizenor's definition of the term "mixed descent" as "a symbolic category, moving beyond heredity to describe a strategy of discourse that promotes transformation," claims, "bringing mixed descent to discourse undermines the modes of speech and thought . . . that do not allow for ambiguity or change." Narratives of mixed descent, Vizenor and Viehmann argue, explode such dogmatic beliefs as biological or rhetorical purity. As the half-breed outlaws of the dime novel "challenge boundaries, overturn expectations, and commit social offenses," hybrid texts like *Cogewea* "break down genres and commit literary offenses." From this new perspective, the language of the novel does not appear confusing, inconsistent, or unnatural but rather enables the revolutionary transformation in fiction that Franz Boas envisioned in anthropology: the shift from biologically determined language to a linguistically determined biology. In introducing the concepts of cultural relativism, the untranslatability of certain beliefs, and the insistence that anthropologists learn the language of their subjects, Boas denied that culture could be fully contained by science and revealed the linguistic limits and potentialities of science. *Cogewea* similarly resists containment by traditional criticism and reveals the linguistic limitations of a monologic perspective, of the traditional assumption that an author, a character, a text, or a human being, must be either one thing or another, and not two things at once. Viehmann calls the novel "multivoiced" rather than "obfuscated," concluding that such an "expanded conceptualization of mixed descent . . . enriches interpretation of *Cogewea* by creating a central place for the collaboration between Mourning Dove and McWhorter within the analysis" and enables readers to "rethink the divisions between the two cultures and between 'pure' and 'amalgamated' individuals." It also opens an additional possibility that Viehmann does not consider: that in addition to that between author and editor, collaboration occurs even within Mourning Dove's own writing, that the mixed-blood writer exercises conscious control over these linguistic inconsistencies in her effort as translator to synthesize competing discourses.[35]

Throughout the narrative, Mourning Dove demonstrates this consciousness of rhetorical variation that calls into question the critical assumption of her lack of control over the composition. Her heroine, with whom she closely identifies, is infamous on the Horseshoe Bend for her "independence of speech" (*C*, 43) and her ability to switch effortlessly between the Okanogan tongue of Stemteemä, the abbreviated and figu-

35. Martha L. Viehmann, "'My People . . . My Kind': Mourning Dove's *Cogewea, the Half-Blood* as a Narrative of Mixed Descent," in Harold Bloom, ed., *Native American Writers: Modern Critical Views*, 227–28.

rative dialect of the cowpuncher, the formal business language necessary to assist her brother-in-law in the administration of the ranch, and the flirtatious banter peppered with puns and double entendres. Possessed of a linguistic ability superior to that of white people or older full-bloods, she relies on words as a form of resistance, anticipating Vizenor's conception of hybridity as a form of "survivance," or a form of survival that is not merely passive but active and resistive. The narrative recalls an incident from Cogewea's childhood, when two white ice-fishermen came to Stemteemä's teepee to inquire whether a nearby lake, covered only with a thin sheet of ice, was safe to traverse. Motivated both by girlish mischief and by a resentment of the presence of the white men on the lake, Cogewea proposes that she and her sisters "pretend not to understand English" and respond to the white men's question with only blank stares of feigned ignorance (*C,* 119). The fishermen, who decide to test the ice, are saved from drowning only by Stemteemä's last-minute warning. The grandmother, appalled that her girls would lead the men to their deaths, scolds, "what did you learn the language . . . of the pale face for? [The words] do no good unless you make use of them when needed" (*C,* 119). Less wise in some ways than her mixed-blood, bilingual granddaughters, she does not think that they might use their unique intelligence not to help the shoyahpee but to impair or injure them.

Cogewea employs similar tactics to exert a degree of control over her suitors. When Densmore, romancing her in the twilight, presses her for an answer to his marriage proposal, she abruptly interrupts his wooing by lapsing into the halting language of the range, "Aw! let up! This love makin' is hell! Let's ride!" (*C,* 95), placing Densmore, inept at both Western dialect and riding, at a disadvantage. Conversely, when Jim presses his suit by boasting, in the manner of a courting cowboy, of his unsurpassed skills in riding and shooting, she adopts a superior tone, speaking with a vocabulary and allusiveness that she knows confuses the unsubtle foreman. Similarly, when she wants to gain the favor or confidence of either man, she speaks to each in his own language. When Jim, infuriated by Cogewea's persistent blindness to Densmore's evil intentions, threatens to kill the easterner, she successfully placates him with "something of her old-time banter . . . falling into the easy range vernacular: 'I b'lieve yo' would! Some time, if yo' don't look out, maybe I'll disown yo' as a brother. Do yo' savey? Now run 'long an' hit th' hay! I'm a goin' tumble in an' harvest a good crop of sleep'" (*C*, 202–3). Often exasperated by his sweetheart's verbal gymnastics, he tells her, "Sometimes you talk nice and fine, then next time maybe you go ramblin' like some preacher-woman or schoolmarm. Can't always savey you" (*C*, 33), anticipating the frustration the novel's critics, who would also be unable to savey the multivoiced *Cogewea*.

Viehmann offers a more negative reading of Cogewea's multilingualism: "Cogewea's command of Salish, range slang, and proper English brings to life her indeterminate status. Her tendency to switch rapidly from one form of speech to another shows . . . her inability to choose between two different ways of life."[36] Viehmann assumes a traditional view of hybridity as alternation, assuming that Cogewea must choose one, not two, identities, as she does in the Fourth of July races. When, arriving at the fairgrounds, Cogewea discovers that the event is segregated into a race for "ladies" and a race for "squaws," she boldly declares her intention to ride in both races: "If there's any difference between a *squaw* and a *lady*, I want to know it. I am going to pose as both for this day" (*C*, 58–59; emphasis in original). She takes her position among the ladies gaily decked in a "riding habit of blue corduroy" and "red white and blue ribbons fastened in her hair" (*C*, 62). The costume, however, is not a disguise; she is unabashed among the white riders even as Verona Webster, a skilled white rider, sneers, "Why is this *squaw* permitted to ride? This is a *ladies* race!" (*C*, 63). After beating Verona by a nose, Cogewea rushes to the Kootenai Indian camp, where she dons tribal dress and varicolored face paints in preparation for the squaw race. Mimicking Verona's slur, a Kootenai girl objects, "You have no right to be here! You are half white! This race is for Indians and not for *breeds!*" (*C*, 66). Cogewea wins another close race with the Indian women, but when the judge discovers her subterfuge, he refuses to pay her the prize money for the white women's race, arguing, "she is a *squaw* and had no right to ride in the *ladies* race" (*C*, 68). Although the judge, fuming, will not openly admit to racism, Cogewea says it for

36. Ibid., 236.

him, refusing to accept both "*racial* prizes" awarded "regardless of merit or justice" (*C,* 70).

Beyond the obvious sympathy evoked in the scene for the "maligned outcast half-blood" for whom "there seemed no welcome on the face of God's creation" (*C,* 65), Mourning Dove more subtly asserts that race is not determined by inherent biological character but rather rests arbitrarily on social context. Viehmann observes, "Throughout the chapter, Mourning Dove uses quotation marks and italics to bracket the words 'breed,' 'squaw,' and 'lady' . . . [and therefore] makes clear that the social distinctions implied by the terms are the product of white society that defines itself against the Other."[37] This typographic variation thus marks a quiet revolution in the way American fiction represents race. As Boas, for the first time in science, represented the words "savagery" and "civilization" within quotation marks to emphasize the contested significance of these categories, Mourning Dove similarly becomes the first novelist to use these racialist terms in quotation marks with a consciousness of their relativity, irony, and inadequacy. In the same way that Cogewea mischievously shows that racial identity is as arbitrary and superficial as changeable holiday costumery, Mourning Dove demonstrates that racialized terms such as "breed," "squaw," and "lady," that traditionally appeal to biology for their legitimacy, are founded instead on the similarly uncertain grounds of language. Finally, the scene most vividly represents hybridity as simultaneity rather than alternation. In confronting the decision to enter the squaws' race or the ladies' race, Cogewea confronts the fundamental dilemma in American fiction of the white captive facing her redemption and the half-breed facing his origin: to be white or Indian. By entering both races, however, she chooses as none had chosen before her: She chooses not to choose and chooses to be both.

Even those texts that resisted romantic racialism implicitly accepted its biological terms, countering images of hybrid degeneracy in the historical romance and the dime novel with images of hybrid vigor, such as those in *A Narrative of the Life of Mrs. Mary Jemison* and *Ramona*. Although Jackson suggested that Indian degeneracy and outlawry arise

37. Ibid., 241.

from unjust policy rather than from tainted blood and anticipates Mourning Dove's and Mathews' fiction, she makes consistent appeals to biology, repeatedly referring to her heroine's raven hair, brown eyes, and olive skin as the outward signs of her natural robustness. *Cogewea* breaks from even the most sympathetic nineteenth-century representations of the mixed-blood in its refusal to accept race as a physically determined category. Although the novel appears conservative in its lesson, repeated many times in the authoritative and compelling voice of Stemteemä, that Indian women should stay away from white men and also in its resolution that finally pairs Cogewea with Jim, her "own blood," Mourning Dove, like Oliver La Farge, never suggests that the failures of miscegenation and, more generally, of assimilation, are biological. Echoing the ideals of the Taos primitivists, Mourning Dove portrays the taint of Indian-white contact as cultural rather than biological and attributes the precipitous collapse of Native languages and customs not to Indians' and mixed-bloods' genetic incapacity to adapt to civilization but to white vice and, as Collier and proponents of Reorganization argued, to flaws in the conception and implementation of previous Indian policy.

The mixed-blood, envisioned by Allotment as the key component in the integration of the white and Indian races, drifted instead, as both *Cogewea* and *Sundown* show, to the margins of the economy. Suggesting the error of such policy, Mourning Dove uses the villain Densmore as the mouthpiece for the old arguments for Allotment: "It may appear harsh, but the day has come when the Indian must desist from his wild, savage life. The Government is working hard for his betterment, and he should respond with a willingness to advance by adjusting himself to the new order of things. The opening of the reservation to settlement, tends to mingle him with his white brother, leading to an inter marriage [*sic*] of the two races. The tribesman will learn wisdom from his new neighbors, who will teach him how best to wrest his food supplies from the soil" (*C*, 143–44). When Cogewea forces him to admit the present failure of this policy, Densmore relies on the familiar deterministic explanation: "does not the Indian's solitary and taciturn nature stand in the way of his assimilating the highest standards of life?" (*C*, 144). Cogewea, however, offers a more sophisticated explanation that appeals not to nature but to culture:

The unalterable edict had gone forth: "Civilize or go under!" but where had there ever been a primitive hunter-race, able, ultimately to survive a sudden and violent contact with a highly developed agricultural civilization.... Development along any line, like the growth of the sturdiest tree must be methodically slow; coordinate with an Intelligence beyond the most vivid comprehension.... They purpose right, but they do not understand the Indian mind; never will, it would seem. Had a tribesman gone to your European homes with the ultimatum: "Desert your heavy houses; come into the open and adopt our mode of life," I am sure you Caucasians would have regarded him as an unreasonably brainless arrogant. (*C,* 139, 144)

Like Boas, Cogewea abandons hierarchical assumptions, expressed by earlier anthropologists, that higher culture would naturally elevate lower culture, and she also abandons the more fundamental objectification of more primitive cultures. Inverting the hierarchies of both nature and history, she imagines the European in the role of a colonized people, illustrating with Boasian relativism the fundamental flaw in the deterministic vision of race and history, effecting on an intimate level that which Reorganization sought to accomplish on a national level. Through the process of translation and discursive synthesis, Mourning Dove creates a frontier where traditional Indian culture is valued as highly as the progress of civilization, where the formally educated ethnologist must give way to the half-blood, who is no longer just an object of study but an independent subject in her own right, free to simultaneously appropriate any language, any identity she chooses.

Problems of Assimilation and Authenticity in *Sundown*

John Joseph Mathews only claimed a quantum of one-eighth Osage blood; under laws enacted by both Allotment and Reorganization, he was a white man. Like other mixed-blood writers such as Apess and Ridge, he took advantage of educational, economic, and political privileges unavailable to most Indians, which allowed him to produce his writing. Mathews was a big man on campus at the University of Oklahoma, a frat boy popular for his good looks and football skill. After graduating with a degree in geology, he served in the U.S. Signal Corps during the First World War, received degrees from Oxford and the University of Geneva, and he lived the life of an international playboy, bumming around Europe and hunting big game in Africa. He returned to Oklahoma in 1932 in order to reconnect with Osage culture and launched his literary career with the publication of *Wah'Kon-Tah: The Osage and the White Man's Road* (1932), a historical novel based on the journal of the first Indian agent sent to the Osage following Allotment. Although his meteoric and varied career seemed to make him a model of assimilation, he consistently felt like an outsider, according to his daughter, Virginia Mathews, and drew from this sense of alienation in his semiautobiographical portrayal of Chal Windzer, the mixed-blood antihero in his only novel, *Sundown*. While writer and character share many incidental experiences, perhaps the most significant identification between Chal and Mathews himself is the conflict embodied by "young Indians of mixed blood who return from encounters with the white world bruised, uncertain of their identity, and alienated from both worlds, white and Indian," a conflict that Louis Owens calls the genesis of "the modern American Indian novel."[38]

Sundown opens with an obvious metaphor to reflect Chal's mixed birth, a "dim" combination of the red light shining faintly from the cabin where his mother labors and the faint white moonlight shining from above, a blended glow that represents "a symbol of the new order" of the assimilated reservation yet remains "diffident in the vivid, full-blooded paganism of the old."[39] The novel soon orients itself more politically, depicting in early chapters the debate between Osage mixed-bloods and full-bloods concerning ways to implement the newly instituted allotment policy. Chal's father, John Windzer, vigorously leads the assimilationist or "progressive" mixed-blood faction that successfully lobbies for the allotment of the reservation and the distribution of oil leases to non-Indian companies. As many full-bloods warn, however, the progressives' vision of a golden age of Indian prosperity is quickly corrupted. While the mixed-bloods take pride in the accelerated economic development of the reservation and in the growth of Kihekah

38. Virginia H. Mathews, introduction to *Sundown,* vi; Louis Owens, "'He Had Never Danced with His People': Cultural Survival in John Joseph Mathews's *Sundown,*" in Bloom, *Native American Writers,* 45.

39. John Joseph Mathews, *Sundown,* 1–2. Further citations will be made parenthetically with the abbreviation *S.*

from a reservation hamlet to a bustling commercial town, Chal, following the dismissal of the tribal council by the federal government, sees the black derricks rising above his beloved blackjack trees as "some unnatural growth from the diseased tissues of the earth" (*S*, 78).

Mathews depicts John Windzer and the other reservation mixed-bloods with a complexity that demonstrates his simultaneous consciousness of the promises and problems of assimilation. Motivated both by Indian pride and white commercial ambition, the mixed-bloods become the unwitting agents of Osage decline, duped by the federal government into enacting policies they do not realize will destroy the reservation. Mathews interjects:

> In reality the allotment was forced upon the tribe by people outside the reservation who had no particular interest in the welfare of the tribe. John and the other councilmen took much pride in their progressive principles and were pleased when government officials patted them on the back and approved of their work. . . . In the breasts of the Progressives was the desire for riches and prosperity, but they did not have the white man's artfulness in reaching the objective, and their ideals were more sincere because their source was the pride of seeing their native country developed. (*S*, 49–50)

When Chal's father realizes his mistake in supporting Allotment and the government seizes the economic destiny of the Osages from the tribal council, he is betrayed by the whites and disgraced among the Indians. His mysterious death, which might have been suicide or, like the death of John Rollin Ridge's own assimilationist father, a political vendetta, represents a crucial turning point in Chal's education, causing the young mixed-blood to change his image of the government from a "beneficent patriarch" to a "sinister" giant (*S*, 60).

As Chal grows, attends college, and begins a promising career as an aviator in the Army Air Corps, he becomes increasingly frustrated with the frenzied activity of the town, the superficiality of college life, and his own tentative attempts to conform to the new order created by Allotment. He often runs wildly across the prairie to satisfy his intense urges for action and open spaces, but he later feels guilty for indulging such "primitive" impulses (*S*, 73, 78). Even the glamorous life of a flyer becomes boring for him. When he receives word of his father's death, he returns to the reservation for the funeral and, a short while later, resigns his commission and comes home for good. He becomes shiftless, living on oil royalties inherited from his father and abandoning himself to drinking binges. Mathews closes the novel ambiguously. Although sober, Chal stares vacantly at a robin outside the window of his mother's house and promises his ever silent, ever loving mother abruptly and somewhat pathetically, "I'm goin' to Harvard law school, and take law— I'm gonna be a great orator" (*S*, 311). Yet Mathews offers no reason to believe him. Like the reservation itself at the end of the era of Allotment and forced assimilation, Chal is left empty and uncertain of any future, drained of resources, sapped by decadence, impoverished, beyond hope or even despair in the numbness of plain existence.

Charles Larson, one of the first scholars to formally assess Mathews's work in 1978, offers a bleak evaluation of *Sundown*, a novel, he argues, that reveals "only a limited concern with the social issues confronting Native Americans of the time," that betrays a "sense of artificiality," and that remains "basically assimilationist" in its portrayal of a mixed-blood character who, warped by the "horrors of the recent past" and the "destruction of tribal life" enacted by Allotment, finds it impossible to negotiate his existence between the white and Indian worlds. Larson refers to Chal as a "cultural half-caste, no longer seeing much value in his Indian origins, while aping the worst in the white man's object-oriented world . . . a man with no identity at all . . . a weak character . . . reduced to a life of frustration and existential loneliness" in his abject failure to accept either culture. Although he recognizes *Sundown* as a thematic precursor of contemporary Native fiction, Larson ultimately finds Mathews's work "far less rewarding than . . . any of the subsequent novels by Native American writers."[40]

More recent critics, however, have revised Larson's initially negative interpretation. According to Scott Vickers, the ambiguous ending of *Sundown* reflects a "social realism [that] has come to set modern Native writing apart from the romanticized versions of Indian life that dominated earlier works by both Indians and non-Indians." Echoing Viehmann's reading of *Cogewea*, Louis Owens interprets *Sundown* as a

40. Larson, *American Indian Fiction*, 36, 37, 56, 58, 35.

"complex narrative of cultural survival" that documents "an awakening to a renewed sense of self...for Native Americans." The novel, Owens concludes, "does not end on a fatalistic note" but rather on an "ambivalent note." He interprets the bathing robin as a "purifying image" and argues that Mathews intentionally denies closure to the reader: "Mathews leaves open the possibility of 'another destiny, another plot' for the American Indian, refusing any romantic closure that would deny the immense difficulties confronting the displaced Native American, but simultaneously rejecting the cliché of the Vanishing American as epic, tragic hero."[41] Mathews thus represents Chal not as a weak character but as the model for later mixed-blood protagonists like Momaday's Abel who would use language as a way to find meaning in their seemingly unshakable sense of displacement.

Mathews evokes this new "crossblood consciousness" central to Vizenor's understanding of contemporary Native identity through an examination and evaluation of the competing models of assimilation and hybridity proposed by Allotment and Reorganization, the policies that form the historical frame of Mathews's narrative. In his continual efforts to conform to what he recognizes as a superior society, Chal alternately employs two different strategies: sex and speech. Chal's attempt to become civilized through courtship and sex with white women assumes a traditional biological basis of racial character. Just as some nineteenth-century racialists proposed and Allotment hoped to effect, Chal, the mixed-blood, seeks to elevate his innate savagery through intercourse with pure white women. These attempts, however, prove frustrating, and Mathews proposes a second model based on Boas's linguistic reorientation of race and Reorganization's revaluation of tribal culture. Although not wholly successful, Chal's metalinguistic analysis of his experiences reflect his attempt to blend the Osage and English languages and to articulate his consciousness of racial and discursive simultaneity. It also reflects Mathews's own movement between conflicting styles and narrative modes, and his creation, like Mourning Dove's, of a new model of hybrid identity that provides later Native writers with the means

41. Vickers, *Native American Identities,* 132; Owens, "'He Had Never Danced,'" 49, 54, 55.

finally to liberate the mixed-blood from the old chains of blood and to express hybridity as synthesis rather than conflict, as simultaneity rather than alternation.

From his childhood, Chal associates whiteness and civilization with femininity. On his first day of school, the Big Hills Boys, the children of traditional full-blood Indians, jibe Chal for his effeminate white looks, calling him a "little white gurl" (S, 28). Later, he reflects: "Somehow he got the idea that civilization was feminine; someone must have said 'her civilization' in referring to the Nation, and he henceforth associated the two.... In any case, he thought of civilization as a woman.... At such times he fancied the lady, Civilization, pale and beautiful, lying on her bed and people standing around her. Curiously, he didn't see the fullbloods standing around the bed of the lady, but sad-faced mixed-bloods, the traders and the new white people who had come into the town" (S, 66). This vision of the woman civilization as the sexual prize of the mixed-bloods and whites provides insight to Chal's relationships with the white women he uses as means to assimilate more effectively to his white surroundings and to relieve the constant awkwardness and inferiority he feels for having dark skin. When he scores a date with Blossom Daubeny, a beautiful and popular student at the university, the woman herself seems important to Chal only in her whiteness. Although he takes pleasure in holding her while they dance (S, 124), his real moment of triumph comes as he strides into the campus soda shop with Blo on his arm before the admiring glances of his white fraternity brothers. During his brief affair with Lou Kerry, a married white woman he meets during his flight training in California, he plays the role of a Spanish Don Juan, constructing elaborate and unnecessary lies and undertaking romantic stunts to facilitate their trysts. Chal's relationship with her is brief and highly charged with desire. Upon meeting her for the first time and catching an intimate glimpse of lace beneath her irresistibly pink skirt, he decides, "the most important thing in the world was to have this woman. He was ashamed of his thoughts and he wanted sincerely to hide them from himself. He believed he was being very primitive, but the feeling persisted, and he couldn't do anything about it" (S, 206). Sex with her, like his attraction to Blo, is racialized, inflating Chal with a sense of confidence and conquest. His shame for his bronze skin and black hair quickly disappear as he begins to believe in

his own lie about being Spanish and develops a more acute "contempt...for the people of Kihekah," a feeling of "being separated by a
great abyss...from the village with his people moving among the
lodges" (*S*, 208).

The satisfaction he derives from Lou, from Blo, and from his string
of other white girlfriends later in the novel is both sexual and racial:
"The way the girls at the dances looked at him and the way they acted
when he danced with them, filled him with self-assurance and he felt
that he had begun to be gilded by that desirable thing which he called
civilization. He was becoming a man among civilized men. He realized
that his bronze complexion was one of the reasons why girls and women
seemed to be attracted to him and he appreciated it as an asset" (*S*,
230). Seemingly convinced, finally, of his successful assimilation, of his
winning of Lou Kerry and these other white prizes, he quickly tires of
them and feels no qualm at abruptly abandoning each of these meaningless relationships. In Chal's vanity and self-delusion, his ridiculous
appropriation of the Latin lothario persona, and his consequent frustration with these encounters, lies Mathews's critique of the promise of
assimilation through biology once expressed in Thomas Jefferson's
speech on the marriage of races; in nineteenth-century racialism, which
saw intermarriage as a means to accelerate the evolution of the Indian;
and in Allotment, which invited mixed-bloods like John Windzer to act
as buffers between civilization and the reservation. Mathews recognizes
the deep flaws in the idea of progress envisioned by these biological
mandates, symbolized by the prone, pale woman, and by nineteenth-
century reformers whose allotment policy proved ill-conceived and ill-
implemented. As these ideas fail, Chal seeks a new understanding of his
uncertain position through speech, and Mathews thus explores a new
model of Native hybridity independent of biology.

Throughout his education, Chal registers his difference from white
people and his unequal relationship to whites in conflicting modes of
speech. When his father sends him to a reservation school run by federal
authorities, Chal immediately senses differences in his father's speech
"when a white man was listening" (*S*, 24). During his first days in school
Chal learns to associate assimilation with a capability for talking, while
Indianness is betrayed by muteness. He observes, "white people seemed
so helpless when they couldn't talk" (*S*, 83), and although he feels con-

tempt for the insincere chatter of men from the university who come to the reservation to recruit Indian students and athletes, he simultaneously resents the stupid fear of change among full-bloods, the incapacity to recognize "the glorious opening of a new life," and enrolls in the university.

Language, again, seems to Chal the key that he must use to open this new life. Since his childhood, he has sensed in the sounds and meanings of certain words a talismanic power to unlock new worlds and to assist him in his internal negotiation between his white self and his Indian self. As he socializes with the white boys, he becomes highly sensitive to their "fascinating words"—"gee whiz," "the hell yu bawl out," and "judas priest" (*S*, 36)—and in college he meditates intensely on the varied intonations and significances of words that seem simultaneously common and alien: "varsity," "chicken," "borealis." He develops a special affection for "extravaganza": "He didn't know what it meant, but he didn't want to know—it was beautiful and satisfying and that was all he required of it" (*S*, 156). But Chal finds adjustment difficult. During his first weeks away from the reservation, he feels paralyzed by his inability to adopt the quick rhythms of speech among the white "representatives of civilization" (*S*, 98, 117). Unlike his full-blood friends Running Elk and Sun-on-His-Wings, who decide to leave college, however, he resolves to assimilate. He resorts to his innate sensitivity to words and signs, exhaustively analyzing and mimicking the relative firmness of handshakes among fraternity brothers, or the compulsive use of the formality, "I trust," by upperclassmen addressing freshmen (*S*, 119, 114). Eventually, Chal's efforts at projection of this assimilated self win him campus popularity, but sometimes he reverts, stripping off his varsity clothing "to play the role of coyote" (*S*, 152), fleeing to the rangeland beyond the edge of campus, and chanting traditional Osage songs. These experiences leave him conflicted: both comforted by the brief reconnection with his tribal childhood and ashamed by his continued difficulty in adjusting to civilized life and in learning to "talk as other people talked" (*S*, 149).

Like La Farge's Bill Taft, Chal represents the difficulty of the mixed-blood's position in Chal's strategy of mimicry, which impels him simultaneously to embrace and reject two seemingly exclusive identities and traditions. His father names him to be a "Challenge" to the white disinheritors of the Osage, yet John Windzer proudly takes his own name from British aristocracy, and he cannot clearly articulate "what he challenged" (*S,* 3, 5), manifesting his confusion as linguistic paralysis. He derives his status as a tribal leader from his "ringing words," yet as he struggles to articulate his principles on the night of Chal's birth, he feels annoyed that "his confused mind tonight could not formulate words" (*S,* 3). Chal also experiences this inarticulateness in his attempt to mimic the speech of his classmates and, more clearly, in a scene where Chal beholds the full moon and is moved to prayer: "He tried to think of all the beautiful words he had ever heard, both in Osage and English, and as he remembered them he spoke them aloud to the moon, but they would not suffice it seemed; they were not sufficient" (*S,* 71). Owens offers a perceptive reading of this passage that provides insight into Mathews's exploration of the possibilities and limits of linguistic adaptation: "In his desire to utter a polyphony of 'beautiful words,' Chal is attempting to create a prayer that would comprehend the potentially rich heteroglossia of his world, to fuse the 'internally persuasive' language of his Osage heritage with the 'authoritative' discourse of English in a syncretic utterance, and by speaking this hybridized utterance to the Osage moon, to put the parts of himself together in an identity that can comprehend both worlds."[42] Owens, however, remains skeptical of Chal's ability to successfully fuse his Osage and English identities and achieve this discursive synthesis. In fact, at other moments in the novel, Mathews suggests that Chal does indeed achieve a measure of liberation through language. His initial identification with Granville, the British flying ace who passes peacetime teaching geology at the university, occurs through language: "he fascinated Chal with his beautiful words; English that flowed softly and was almost lyrical. . . . Because of this . . . Chal had been drawn to him" (*S,* 172). Their kinship is confirmed when Chal learns that Granville, like him, is an outsider on campus. He notes subtle differences in Granville's pronunciation of certain words like "Elgin"—"he made the 'g' hard"—and admires the confidence that Granville displays in his "queerness," a security that Chal himself cannot achieve. One night during a drunken malaise, reduced to "talking nonsense" to himself, he fishes the single word from

42. Owens, "'He Had Never Danced,'" 49–50.

his memory, "extravaganza," which awakens "terrific emotion" and launches him into a wild dance on the roadside grass and a song of the old Osage: "The dance became wilder and suddenly, in his despair, he broke the rhythm of his singing and yelled. . . . He wanted to challenge somebody, to strut before an enemy. . . to declare to the whole silent world about him that he was a glorious male; to express to the silent forms of the blackjacks that he was a brother to the wind, the lightning and the forces that came out of the earth" (*S,* 297). This epiphany removes the word from any cultural context that might corrupt, diminish, or confuse its inherent power, and becomes, consequently, a magic word by which Chal can liberate himself, if only for a moment.

At other odd places in the narrative, Mathews, like Mourning Dove, conflates formal narrative with colloquial diction, seeming, as author, to adopt the speech of his characters. When Granville and Chal are lunching with the Carrolls, a folksy farm couple, Cal Carroll briefly becomes the narrator of the novel, assessing Granville's manner through uncharacteristic internal monologue: "Cal knowed he was right. He knowed that fellow was a furriner the minute he seen him—couldn't hardly fool him. . . . That feller had sat there and never opened his mouth—lettin' his pipe go out, listenin' " (*S,* 180, 185). Mathews similarly substitutes "guv'mint" for "government" during narrative moments representing Chal's father and uses "varsity" for "university" during chapters portraying Chal's college days. These rhetorical inconsistencies, similar to those that trouble scholars of *A Narrative of the Life of Mrs. Mary Jemison* and *Cogewea,* seem evidence of Mathews's fluid narrative consciousness that reflects the fluidity of Chal's consciousness as he attempts to blend linguistically with his surroundings at college, on the reservation, in conversation with Granville and Carroll, and to contain "both sides" impossibly and simultaneously within himself. While critics debate the success of Mathews's innovative strategies and the value of his novel within the tradition of Native writing, his introduction of language as a more useful way to define the mixed-blood distinguishes him from the long tradition in American culture of understanding hybridity in solely biological terms. In her introduction to *Sundown,* his daughter Virginia Mathews states the significance of this revolutionary reconception of racial identity in deceptively simple terms: "In response to a conjecture whether one looked or did not look Indian, he [Mathews] would reply: 'Being Indian isn't in looks, in features or color. Indian is inside you.'"[43] This deceptively simple assertion raises the fundamental questions of assimilation and authenticity that inevitably attend current readings of hybrid writers and hybrid texts.

As Larson claims, the ending of Mathews's novel does not represent the fulfillment of these dreams of interracial harmony and democratic assimilation. Chal, for all his clever adaptations, remains a "cultural half-caste" steeped in "existential loneliness." Similarly, Cogewea, though justly rewarded by a huge fortune at the end of the novel, is left scarred, forever wary of the shoyahpee, and tied to Jim, her own blood. While both of these novels argue for the artificiality of racial constructs, they do not deny that even the perception of racial difference exerts an oppressive influence, as Austin also suggests in "White Wisdom." While Cogewea may win both the ladies' and the squaws' races, she may not claim both purses. While Chal may strip off his varsity sweater and dash as a coyote across the prairie, he cannot shed his guilt for such savage behavior.

Critics have traditionally claimed that the attempt itself at assimilation necessarily prevents these characters or the novelists themselves from discovering a Native authenticity. Larson generally describes these early mixed-blood novelists as "assimilationists" for whom the representation of Indian consciousness was "confusing." Like Ridge, these writers "suggested that assimilation was the only means of survival." Only later writers, Larson argues, demonstrate an "ethnic consciousness ... moving from assimilation ... toward a separate reality ... [a] sense of Indianness" that D'Arcy McNickle defined in 1973 as "Native American tribalism."[44] But such insistence among critics on authentic Indianness now seems like a return to the romantic racialism or to the primitivist cryogenization of an unspoiled Native ideal. Gerald Vizenor adapts a linguistic paradigm in his development of a contemporary theory of Native expression that abandons traditional simulations of authenticity, an ideal no longer relevant to contemporary "post-Indian" experience. Vizenor's model of "trickster hermeneutics," the postmod-

---

43. Virginia Mathews, introduction, xiv.
44. Larson, *American Indian Fiction,* 10–11.

ern pastiche of genres, languages, and styles, expresses, like Mourning
Dove's inconsistent narrative, a discursive synthesis, a sense of opposing,
even mutually exclusive voices speaking simultaneously. While Vizenor
does not specifically consider the ways that Mourning Dove or Mathews express this consciousness, the mediations of these early Native
American writers exemplify his model of Native American hermeneutics, quintessentially postmodern, and arising from modernist tenden-
cies toward linguistic and narrative experimentation.

Revolutionary changes in the scientific and legislative conception of
the Indian in the era between 1887 and 1934, the prolonged effects of
Allotment, and the more widespread national crises of the 1930s prepared for this emergence of the mixed-blood as the symbol of Indian
persistence and resistance. During this time, the formation of a threatening fissure in the golden, but now seemingly fragile, image of American economic and political dominance, a fatal corruption of Manifest
Destiny, appeared in Walter D. Edmonds's revival of classic nationalist
narratives, which gained new relevance as the nation faced the threat of
global war, economic dissolution, and the erosion of the Anglo-Saxonist
ideal. As Bhabha argues, "Cultural difference is to be found where the
'loss' of meaning enters, as a cutting edge, into the fullness of the demands of culture."[45] In the ideological void created by the partial collapse of these nineteenth-century myths, hybrid voices emerge through
the waning confidence of nationalist narratives.

While these writers' adoption of the English language and popular
narrative forms can be viewed as yet another capitulation, as a corruption of an authentically Native identity, as many critics have argued,
postcolonial theorists like Bhabha have argued that an oppressed people can effect self-expression and even subversion by learning to use
tools, such as popular fiction, that had once been used against them.
But even Bhabha neglects the unique discursive synthesis created by
these early mixed-blood novelists, for whom hybridity is not a condition
of inner conflict but rather a new kind of blended subjectivity, of a Métis
consciousness. For cultural hybrids like Mourning Dove and Mathews,
translation constitutes self-expression and education involves a para-

45. Bhabha, "DessemiNation," in *Nation and Narration*, 313.

doxical sort of adaptation, constantly reminding them of their confine-
ment and segregation while at the same time dissolving those barriers
that have confined and segregated them, barriers between the reservation and the outside world, their past and their future, their decline
and resurgence. They occupy a central place in American literature and
have taken over the function of speaking for and about Indians that
publications like the historical romance, the dime novel, and the *Saturday Evening Post* once performed.

Mathews's simple statement, "Indian is inside you," attests to the
radical redefinition of race that takes place in the popular fiction of the
early twentieth century. Inspired by Franz Boas and his heirs to question the significance of hybridity, Mathews expresses a racial consciousness that does not derive from blood quantum or other physical tests
traditionally applied by anthropologists. In hybrid texts such as *Cogewea,
Sundown, Joaquín Murieta, A Son of the Forest,* and *A Narrative of the
Life of Mrs. Mary Jemison,* we witness the long, often halting process of
this transformation. For Mathews, the Indian in you resides in your
consciousness, in your language and custom, in your orientation toward life and history. Mathews speaks in the second person, blurring
the distinction between himself and his audience. "You" might be him
or you. This simple change from "her" or "him" to "you" not only
posits a more subjective, unquantifiable racial identification, but also
begs the audience—you—to question your own orientation, to wonder if there might be some Indian inside you. This hint of interracial
intimacy within the American self illuminates the half-breed ghost that
has haunted American culture from the beginning: in Apess's observation in "An Indian's Looking-Glass for the White Man" of the frequency of illegal Indian-white marriages in a commonwealth dedicated
to racial separation; in Child's subtle suggestion that Mary Conant's
half-Indian son, Harvard graduate and peer of New England, has sired
Narragansett children and grandchildren to Boston's proudest daughters; and in Rowson's alternative genealogy in *Reuben and Rachel,*
which imagines all our nation descended from the Edenic union of a
white man with an Indian woman. Such promises of Indian blood cours-
ing American veins, of the marriage of races only tentatively imagined
by Thomas Jefferson as the model for a New World republic, prompted
stiff denial or vitriolic protest from the architects of national culture

in the nineteenth century. In the twentieth century, in the words of Mourning Dove, Mathews, and Momaday, these alternative myths, liberated from biology as Lo Dorman and Jerry Jo have been liberated from the Yukon permafrost, assume new relevance. To the objective question that troubled legislators and anthropologists in the wake of Allotment, "What is an Indian?" these hybrid voices answer that "Indian" is not a person to be legislated or a blood to be claimed, not a *thing* at all, but rather a subjective, intangible consciousness, and they seem to ask, in turn, the question that continues to trouble Native American literature today: "What *is* Indian?"

Epilogue

Contemporary Reflections on Mixed Descent

> At one time, the ceremonies as they had been performed were
> enough for the way the world was then. But after the white
> people came, elements in the world began to shift; and it became
> necessary to create new ceremonies. I have made changes in the
> rituals. The people mistrust this greatly, but only this growth
> keeps the ceremonies strong.
>
> —Leslie Marmon Silko, *Ceremony*

What Is Indian?

Liberated from a strictly biological discourse, the literary and anthropological concept of Native hybridity has taken a more fluid form in
the twentieth century, one based on subjectivity rather than on objec-
tivity, on consciousness rather than on blood quantum, one reflected in
a blend of languages and narrative structures rather than in measurements of the cranium or "organs of generation." Yet even with these
profound changes in the culture's understanding of race, the older, evil
incarnations of the half-breed have not died out. In his Pulitzer Prize–
winning novel, *Lonesome Dove* (1986), Larry McMurtry casts as his lead
villain the half-breed Blue Duck. In the television version of McMurtry's
novel (1988), one of the highest-rated miniseries in history and winner
of seven Emmy Awards, Blue Duck, played with relish by Frederic For-
rest, spits venom at his old nemesis, former Texas Ranger Woodrow
Call, even as he awaits hanging in his jail cell: "I raped women and stole
children and burned houses and shot men and run off horses and killed

cattle and robbed who I pleased all over your territory, and you never even had a *good look* at me!" As marshals escort him to the scaffold, Blue Duck springs a final suicide attack, grabbing a deputy as he hurls both himself and the innocent lawman from an upper-story jailhouse window and follows the long line of sensational half-breeds to maniacal self-destruction.

But monsters like Blue Duck are no longer the only sort of mixed-blood to appear in American popular fiction, nor are they the most common, as they once had been. N. Scott Momaday's *House Made of Dawn,* the story of a mixed-blood army veteran lost between the reservation and modern Los Angeles, also won a Pulitzer, marking a popular and critical recognition of texts that challenge romantic racialist images such as Blue Duck and the profound changes the culture has undergone since the *North American Review* first judged Child's tentative portrayal of Hobomok, the half-Indian son of a Puritan mother, "revolting." The mixed-blood has arrived as the embodiment of intercultural negotiation and, in popular films like *Hombre* (1967), *Billy Jack* (1971), and *Chato's Land* (1972), countercultural allure. The grotesque has become the exotic; the outlaw has become the outlaw hero. The detachment of racial identity from biology has provided for the mixed-blood's acceptance as something other than an atavistic menace, but this change, developing over more than a century, also has raised new questions among the current generation of Native American writers, who continue to struggle with the consequences of this redefinition of the Indian and still find it difficult to answer the question posed by the first generation of Indian novelists: What is Indian?

Boas, Mourning Dove, and Mathews suggested that Native identity resides not in heredity but rather in culture, language, consciousness, and even will, as early mixed-blood heroes like Cogewea at the Fourth of July races freely and simultaneously claim Indianness and whiteness regardless of their quantum of blood. This liberation of the mixed-blood in American fiction has detached Indian hybridity from romantic racialism but it has also generated debates concerning authenticity. As Cogewea's full-blood rivals protest, "This race is for Indians and not for *breeds!*" current novelists and scholars speculate that being Indian has lost meaning now that anyone, in effect, can join the race. This epilogue briefly considers responses among some recent Native American novelists to the twentieth-century redefinition of hybridity and its attending problems. While some, like D'Arcy McNickle, express disorientation, others, like N. Scott Momaday, Leslie Silko, and Louise Erdrich, despite occasional attacks on their credibility as authentic Indian voices, have created new meanings of hybridity. Where the old definitions have failed, new meanings have arisen that abandon both biology and culture as signifiers of racial identity in favor of the individual will: a choice to define oneself as Indian according to one's own terms, reflecting the contemporary sense of Native self-determination and the refusal of substitute identities, as McNickle argues, mandated by the dominant culture.

But even as individual writers freely create these new meanings based on enlightened hybrid subjectivity, others find problems in the contemporary, indeterminate understanding of Indianness. In James Welch's bleak *The Death of Jim Loney* (1979), an alienated mixed-blood wanders the Blackfeet reservation in an alcoholic daze, growing more distant from the women who want to save him. Rhea, his white girlfriend, cavalierly tells him what the modern concept of hybridity also promises: "Oh, you're so lucky to have two sets of ancestors. Just think, you can be Indian one day and white the next. Whichever suits you." Loney, however, feels that she is hopelessly naive. As he follows his path toward suicide, he reflects on his anonymity, envying "real Indians" like the "Old Chiefs" or his reservation acquaintances who have maintained a more traditional life. Loney pathetically imagines himself a member of one of the large "reservation families, all living under one roof, the old ones passing down the wisdom of their years, of their family's years, of their tribe's years, and the young ones soaking up their history." In reality, he "had no family and he wasn't Indian or white. . . . [Rhea] had said he was lucky to have two sets of ancestors. In truth he had none."[1]

In his novel *Indian Killer* (1996), Sherman Alexie finds it similarly difficult to describe the contemporary urban Indian, those mixed-bloods uncertain of their parentage or even of their tribal origins, who do not "create a new consciousness of coexistence" like Vizenor's "crossblood culture heroes" but rather drift through dive bars and alleyways, invisible to whites who, blinded by images such as Blue Duck, will not see them. Like the insubstantial people Columbus mentioned on his first

---

1. James Welch, *The Death of Jim Loney,* 14, 102.

voyage to the New World, or Jane Tompkins's Indians who in popular Westerns were there but not there, or even the ghost of Injun Joe himself, John Smith, the fatally anonymous Indian in Alexie's novel, adopted and raised by an affluent white couple, wanders the crowded streets beneath detection: "No one even noticed John. That is to say a few people looked up from their books and a couple drivers looked away from the street long enough to notice John, then turned back to their novels and windshields. . . . John the Indian was walking and his audience was briefly interested, because Indians were briefly interesting. . . . Somehow, near the end of the twentieth century, Indians had become invisible." While some of these invisible Indians, such as Marie Polatkin, an outspoken college student and helper of the homeless, bond as outcasts to "create their own urban tribe," many others, like John, find unbearable despair in their isolation, a misery rooted in the confusing quest to discover what it means to be an Indian in postmodern America.[2]

Almost two centuries since Child, Cooper, and Sedgwick erased the mixed-blood from the national memory, Alexie's urban tribes continue to struggle against the barrage of simulations like Blue Duck that threaten utterly to disintegrate their already tenuous sense of tribal identity. Alexie cites not only these more obviously racist images but also "those pretend Indians" who "called themselves mixed-bloods and wrote books about the pain of living in both the Indian and white worlds." Alexie represents these phony Indians most insidiously in the characters of Jack Wilson, a white ex-cop and locally famous writer of Indian mystery novels who claims tribal descent, and Clarence Mather, a professor of Native American literature who has intermittently visited reservations and claims cultural kinship with Indians. Speaking for the hopelessly brown "real Indians" like Marie, Alexie writes, "Those mixed-blood Indians never admitted their pale skin was a luxury. After all, Marie couldn't dress up like a white woman when she went on job interviews. But a mixed-blood writer could put on a buckskin jacket, a few turquoise rings, braid his hair, and he'd suddenly be an Indian."[3] While some current scholars celebrate the semiotic ambiguity of "Indian" as liberation from the racist imagination of the past and from the con-

2. Sherman Alexie, *Indian Killer*, 30, 38.
3. Ibid., 232.

strictive critical insistence on authenticity, Alexie also recognizes that the indefiniteness of racial identity embodied in the late twentieth century by "pretend Indians" and "mixed-blood writers" like himself may also be opportunistically exploited.

Near the conclusion of Alexie's novel, Reggie Polatkin, Marie's cousin, meets Wilson at an Indian bar and confronts him about his claim of mixed-descent: "How much Indian blood you got anyways? Maybe a thimble's worth?" Wilson replies, "The blood don't matter. It's the heart that matters." While he seems to speak for all the progressive-minded scientists and writers of the nineteenth and twentieth centuries who struggled to disassociate race from biology, Reggie's mockery reveals the absurdity risked in carrying this position to its extreme: "I was reading a movie magazine last week and found out that Farrah Fawcett is one-eighth Choctaw Indian.... That means she's got more Indian blood than you do. If you get to be Indian, then Farrah gets to be Indian too.... You really think that's how it works, don't you? ... You think you can be Indian just by saying it, enit?" Stripped of his pretensions, Wilson leaves the bar followed by the derisive laughter of more authentic Indians, and in the gritty reality of an Indian barroom, contemporary race theory becomes ridiculous.[4]

Perhaps the epitome of the pretend Indian, Jamake Highwater, once a celebrated Indian spokesman and author of *This Song Remembers* (1980), was unmasked in 1984 by reporter Jack Anderson, who discovered that Highwater had faked his Indian ancestry. Vizenor explains that Highwater "simulated his tribal descent ... with such assurance that others feigned their own identities in his presence.... He was more answerable as a simulation than others were to their own real crossblood identities." Highwater defended his masquerade in the apologetic *Shadow Show: An Autobiographical Insinuation* (1986): "The greatest mystery of my life is my own identity.... To escape things that are painful we must reinvent ourselves. Either we reinvent ourselves or we choose not be anyone at all.... I begin to think that our borrowed lives are necessities in a world filled with hostility and pain, a confusing world largely devoid of credible social truths."[5] Although Vizenor ultimately rejects

4. Ibid., 367–68.
5. Gerald Vizenor, *Manifest Manners: Postindian Warriors of Survivance*, 1983; Jamake Highwater, *Shadow Show: An Autobiographical Insinuation*, 9, 11.

Highwater as a plain "culture consumer," this pretend Indian's reflection on the uncertainty of racial identity and the continual necessity of reinventing the self in postmodern life strikingly exemplifies the dilemma of mixed-blood writers who ambivalently view this collapse of objective definitions of race as both the liberation from obsolete racialist categories and the disintegration of tribal identity.

On one hand, Welch, Alexie, and the controversy surrounding Highwater suggest that two centuries of expanding the definition of the Indian has culminated in the necessity to limit it, and that the abandonment of the biological interpretation of race has resulted in the necessity to reaffirm it or at least reexamine it. In his recent essay "Autobiographies of the Ex-White Men: Why Race Is Not a Social Construction," Walter Benn Michaels writes, "Even if race is not a biological fact, many people have believed in it as a biological fact and some people, no doubt, continue to believe in it as a biological fact. And this belief, mistaken though it may be, has obviously had, and no doubt continues to have, significant consequences. . . . Indeed to say that because there are no races in nature, there are no races, must be in this view as much a non sequitur as it would be to say that because there are no classes in nature, there are no classes."[6] Michaels argues, in other words, that the acute social consciousness of race gives it a physical reality, as if it were a biological fact. To deny race, as Welch and Alexie also imply, does not make it disappear, nor does it diminish its effects on those like Jim Loney and John Smith, who live among those who "continue to believe in it as a biological fact." To deny race only makes its effects more acutely felt.

The critical furor generated by Highwater's masquerade attests to fact that many still consider race a physical category; because he does not possess Indian blood, he cannot claim such. If race really had ceased to be biologically relevant, no one would have noticed his fraud, since claiming to be Indian would indeed have made him such. The controversy renews the imperative to establish one's authenticity. In *Sending My Heart Back across the Years*, Hertha Dawn Wong writes:

6. Walter Benn Michaels, "Autobiographies of the Ex-White Men: Why Race Is Not a Social Construction," 236, 237.

Did my newly discovered part-Indian heritage now make me an "insider," someone who might speak with the authority of belonging? "Of course not," was my first response. Because my ancestry is German, Scotch-Irish, and French as well as Native American, because I do not believe that blood quantum alone determines Indian identity, and because we [her tribe] do not have a community to which to return, I felt that I could write only as dimly related to, but outside of, the indigenous communities of the United States. But over the years, I have met other displaced mixed-blood people, all of us wrestling with the various labels, the rankings of legitimacy and illegitimacy, imposed on us by others and accepted or resisted by ourselves.[7]

The anxiety of this literary scholar at the turn of the twenty-first century about establishing her authenticity and identifying her proper discourse echoes the anxiety among anthropologists and legislators at the turn of the twentieth century, who similarly struggled to reinforce the increasingly permeable borders between nation and reservation, Indian and white, in a world where once-stable scientific and political truths such as Anglo-Saxonism and Manifest Destiny began to crumble.

Today these borders are much more indistinct than they were a century ago. Momaday has publicly stated, "I don't know what an Indian is. The 'American Indian'—that term is meaningless; to me it means very little." Lawrence Towner, a friend of D'Arcy McNickle and a scholar of his work, similarly suggests that such designations have become untenable. McNickle, Towner writes, "was half Indian and half white, biologically. But in his essential self he was both totally Indian and totally 'European,' a contradiction I had no difficulty in resolving when listening to him, but which I was at a loss to explain when he was absent." Bound to a dialectical understanding of race, Towner's puzzlement reflects the confusion of critics who struggle to interpret the simultaneous discourses in hybrid texts like *A Narrative of the Life of Mrs. Mary Jemison, A Son of the Forest,* and *Cogewea.* This abandonment of racial categories, while apparently paradoxical to those like Towner who have been conditioned to see people either as one or the other, opens up new possibilities for existence, as writers like La Farge, Mourning Dove, and Mathews grasped during the era of the systematic de-

7. Wong, *Sending My Heart,* v.

struction of tribal life by Allotment policy. Vizenor suggests that the mixed-blood, "denied an absolute cultural corner" and granted the ability to "waver" between two worlds, is therefore "spared from extinction in word and phrase museums."[8] Despite his severe criticism of Highwater, Vizenor, like La Farge and Mourning Dove, senses not only the isolation inherent in hybridity but also its potential advantages. For better or worse, pretenders like Highwater provoke speculation on the meaning and relevance of essentialist racial categories. McNickle, Momaday, Silko, and Erdrich have taken advantage of the apparent loss of meaning to create their own, yet these writers represent distinct positions, illustrating a movement from a concept of hybridity of conflicted twoness, alternation, to one unitary oneness, simultaneity.

D'Arcy McNickle's Tribalism

According to Dorothy R. Parker, D'Arcy McNickle "found a new awareness of his mixed-blood heritage" in writing his novel *The Surrounded* (1936) and drew from the experience in his lifelong work of "interpreting Indians to whites, whites to Indians," a mission for which childhood had prepared him. McNickle was born to an Irish father and a mother from a clan of mixed French-Ojibwe. Although McNickle and his family found a home on the Flathead reservation in Montana and were listed as one-quarter Cree on the tribal roll, both parents sought a white education for their child. Yet McNickle devoted his career to the study and improvement of the Indian, working with John Collier and Oliver La Farge as an administrator at the Bureau of Indian Affairs during the Indian New Deal and later founding the Center for the History of the American Indian at the Newberry Library. Parker notes that the evolution of *The Surrounded*, McNickle's first novel, reflects not only "McNickle's growing awareness of the Salish traditions that had marked the periphery of his childhood" but also his ambivalence toward those traditions: "The earliest extant version of the novel, "The Hungry Generations" . . . is an affirmation of mainstream American ideals of justice

---

8. Momaday quoted in Larson, *American Indian Fiction*, 93; Lawrence W. Towner, afterword to *The Surrounded*, 302; Vizenor, *Earthdivers*, xvi–xvii.

and the Puritan work ethic. In this early version, Archilde [the mixed-blood protagonist] buys into the American dream. In the published work, however, he rejects that dream as he gradually discovers the traditional culture of his mother's people." James Ruppert similarly observes in the composition of *The Surrounded* a tension that belies McNickle's ambivalent attitude toward assimilation, a conflict between writing a faithful representation of the reservation experience and the demands of "what he perceived to be a publishable novel." Like *Cogewea, The Surrounded* presents, for Ruppert, "several channels of communication governed by different intentions, which create different perspectives." Parker observes that earlier in his career, with the publication of *The Surrounded* and his work implementing Reorganization, mediating between Washington and the scattered tribes, "McNickle assumed that assimilation was a natural, indeed, an inevitable process and that the pertinent questions to be asked were whether it could or should be accelerated in a particular direction."[9]

Although assimilation might be natural and inevitable, McNickle nonetheless insisted on Indians' rights to maintain their tribal identity, to adapt to the white world in their own time and in their own way. This seemingly conflicted political view has much in common with that of Mathews, his contemporary, regarding Allotment, and reflects his hybrid consciousness. In *Native American Tribalism* (1973), McNickle's seminal description of postassimilationist Indian identity, he regards Native cultures not in their disappearance but, as Vizenor would put it later, in their survival and resistance. McNickle writes, "the generalized picture today is of a people that has survived in numbers, in social organization, in custom and outlook, in retention of physical resources, and in its position before the law." Although his description of "a persistent core of psychological characteristics" of Indians vaguely echoes positivist anthropology, he remains wary of researchers' continued inability to define exactly what these characteristics are. He concludes, rather, "Indians remain Indians . . . by selecting out of available choices those alternatives that do not impose a substitute identity." McNickle

9. Dorothy R. Parker, "D'Arcy McNickle: Living a Broker's Life," 240; James Ruppert, "Textual Perspectives and the Reader in *The Surrounded*," in Bloom, *Native American Writers*, 73; Parker, "D'Arcy McNickle," 240, 241, 253.

neither views racial identification as biological nor even as cultural but rather as voluntary. "Indian" is not a state into which one is involuntarily born through heredity or circumstance but rather a "custom and outlook," a "position before the law" one chooses to assume regardless of blood or education. If Indians share any "common characteristic," McNickle concludes, it is simply that "they call themselves Indians." For McNickle as for Vizenor, hybridity represents not simply a consequence of survival through assimilation but rather a voluntary, more active form of resistance to the imposition of "substitute identities" that the nationalist, racialist imagination would impose on them.[10]

The Surrounded, in this sense of self-determination, shares more with the later narratives of the Native American renaissance than it does with its contemporary texts like *Cogewea* and *Sundown.* McNickle's novel, for example, introduces a theme more widely recognized in the work of Momaday and Silko, that of the young mixed-blood who chooses to return to his reservation after spending a period of education among the whites. When Archilde Leon returns to the Flathead, he finds that his father, a Mexican rancher, and his mother, a traditional Salish woman, have separated, the split between them reflecting the split within Archilde's own consciousness. Almost immediately, however, a series of brutal encounters with white reservation authorities urges him to identify more fully with his mother's tribal roots and also to repudiate his Christianity and education. Near the conclusion of the novel, Archilde is deeply moved by a dream that his mother has on her deathbed, a vision in which her lifelong embrace of Christianity causes both the corruption of her people in this life and their separation from their beloved pagan relatives in the next life:

> In this dream, I fell sick, I died and went to heaven in the sky. Since I had lived a holy life I went to heaven. . . . It was all strange. . . . I saw none of my friends or relatives there. There were no Indians there at all. . . . These white people had everything they wanted, big houses all painted, fine garments like they wear, rings on their fingers and gold in their teeth, they had it all; but there were no animals to hunt and when I looked in the rivers there were no fish there. . . . Pretty soon

10. D'Arcy McNickle, *Native American Tribalism: Indian Survivals and Renewals,* 15, 9, 11, 10, 13.

the people were saying I did not look happy, so the white God sent for me. He was a kind man. "Why is it you're not happy?" he asked me. So I told him and he said I could go away and go to the Indian heaven if I wished. Then I went to the Indian place and I could hear them singing. Their campfires burned and I could smell meat roasting. There were no white men there at all. I asked to come in but they told me no. I was baptized and I could not go there.[11]

The nightmare, dreamt on three successive nights, shakes the old woman so terribly that before her death she renounces her baptism and refuses the last rites. This vision represents the moral center of McNickle's novel and anticipates his claim in *Native American Tribalism* that Indians remain Indians by choice, not by birth or artificial religious rites that seek to impose a substitute identity on Indians like Archilde's mother. In her moment of enlightenment, she chooses to renounce Christianity, chooses to enter the Indian heaven, chooses to remain Indian.

Archilde's dying, proudly pagan mother inspires him similarly to reject the white world. Most scholars read Archilde's repudiation of white society pessimistically. Ruppert, for example, argues that Archilde's "hopeful outlook," his feeling that he is "free and strong" following the death of his mother, is simply a cruel illusion that prevents Archilde from recognizing "the powers-that-be . . . that will eventually destroy" him.[12] They consider Archilde's choice to embrace his tribal roots a regression rather than a liberation, despite McNickle's insistence that such a choice represents the first step toward self-determination and survival: Indians, after all, are those who call themselves Indians. For McNickle, hybridity, the awareness of a cultural synthesis in oneself, leads to an awareness of choice and the ability to choose. For McNickle, tribalism is not a retreat from a world to which Indians cannot conform but to which they will not conform. McNickle's embrace of tradition, like that of the troubled mixed-blood protagonists of the Native American renaissance, presupposes a knowledge of the white world, a hybrid consciousness that, through contrast, reveals tradition as a source of healing, a consciousness that Momaday and Silko would develop more fully.

11. D'Arcy McNickle, *The Surrounded*, 208–9.
12. Ruppert, "Textual Perspectives," 75.

N. Scott Momaday's Word of Creation

Like most other mixed-blood writers who came before him, N. Scott Momaday knew both the Indian and white worlds and used this knowledge to interpret them for each other. The son of a mixed-Cherokee mother and Kiowa father, both of whom worked as artists, writers, and teachers on and off reservations, Momaday took advantage of an unusual education. Over the last three decades he has compiled an impressive résumé that includes numerous awards, honorary degrees, endowments, and professorships at some of the most prestigious universities in the world. In 1969, he received the Pulitzer Prize for his first novel, *House Made of Dawn,* a book equally shaped by the abstruse narrative theories of English-department seminar rooms, the oral traditions gleaned from his father's Kiowa tales, and his childhood experiences at Jémez Pueblo in New Mexico. Like *Cogewea,* which preceded it, and numerous novels that would follow, the novel attempts to merge oral tradition with modern fictional modes.

Momaday represents the first of the current generation of Native writers who are stylistically adept, professionally savvy, politically aware, and dedicated to the honest description and creation of a contemporary Native consciousness. After more than two decades that saw the publication of virtually no novels by Native writers, this cultural rebirth arose from the Indian protest movement known as the Trail of Broken Treaties. McNickle, whose career spans these decades, accounts for the curious absence of Native American fiction by citing trends in U.S. Indian policy. During the 1930s, Reorganization fostered the protection of Native traditions and growth of Indian art forms. The activism of the 1960s similarly generated sympathy for the Indian perspective. In the interim, McNickle identifies the Termination Act (1953), a policy that once again limited federal subsidy to reservations, as the expression of a legislative and more widespread cultural denial of the presence of the Indian, a denial that, according to many critics, replicated the errors of Allotment. In *The Dispossessed,* attorney Parker M. Nielson chronicles his legal battles on behalf of mixed-blood Utes who, failing to meet the required one-half quantum of Indian blood, had been "terminated" as dependents of the government and exempt from annuities and benefits. The Republican policy, echoing Edmonds's earlier criticism of the New Deal as economically destructive and antithetical to the pioneer spirit, decided that Indian self-determination would be better served by weaning them from government assistance, which actually fostered their dependence. Following the Second World War, Nielson explains, "a new group of well-meaning non-Indians in Congress and the BIA [Bureau of Indian Affairs] decided that the American Indian must be 'freed' or 'emancipated,' as other disadvantaged groups in society had been ... [signaling] the change of U.S. Indian policy to 'termination' and the end of the Indian Reorganization Act." In *Native American Tribalism*, McNickle argues that Termination sought to "legislate Indians out of existence by destroying the guarantees [under Reorganization] that had protected their remaining lands and their tenuous hold on self-government."[13] In response, younger Indians initiated nationwide organization efforts and a protest movement, the Trail of Broken Treaties, which lasted more than a decade. This movement witnessed the forceful occupations of Alcatraz Island in 1969, the Bureau of Indian Affairs headquarters in 1972, and the village of Wounded Knee on the Pine Ridge Reservation in 1973. Dozens of less-publicized protest actions involving the forceful seizure of public property by Indians and the refusal to comply with laws that mandated integration accompanied these violent encounters.

During this time, when the most militant representatives of the Native community advocated self-determination through separation, Momaday's efforts to bridge the cultural gap between Indians and whites must have seemed to members of the American Indian Movement who skirmished with federal marshals at Wounded Knee unforgivably accommodating and academic. In this tense climate, cultural and political mediators were widely mistrusted in the Indian community, and this mistrust was manifested linguistically. McNickle explains that the hostility between mixed-blood tribal leaders and more progressive tribal councils was "often occasioned ... when tribal matters were discussed in a tribal language," a practice that some mixed-bloods, who "were in part assimilated to the white political system ... and were not at home in the [tribal] language," regarded as socially retrograde and out of

13. Parker M. Nielson, *The Dispossessed: The Cultural Genocide of the Mixed-Blood Utes*, 36; McNickle, *Tribalism*, xv.

step with "the intricacies of government and modern technology."[14] Conscious of these linguistic tensions and following earlier translators like Mourning Dove, Momaday's strategy to merge the white tradition and the Indian tradition depends, like *Cogewea* and *Sundown,* on linguistic variation and exchange.

House Made of Dawn depicts Abel, a mixed-blood World War II veteran traumatized by his military experience who returns to live with his grandfather, Francisco, on a New Mexico reservation. Abel has a sexual dalliance with a white woman vacationing on the reservation and later kills an albino whom he perceives as a supernatural threat. Following his seven-year prison term, Abel settles among the urban Indians of Los Angeles. Ben Benally, a friend from near Abel's reservation, provides work and a place to live. Milly, a white social worker, provides bureaucratic assistance and sexual diversion. Tosamah, the self-styled "Priest of the Sun"—who runs a storefront peyote church, administers the drug to his small congregation, and delivers impassioned sermons integrating tribal and Christian beliefs—provides some insight into Abel's sense of dislocation. Despite these positive interventions, Abel cannot hold a job or avoid drunken confrontations. One such encounter with a brutal policeman leaves him badly beaten. Defeated, he returns to New Mexico, where he attends to the death of his grandfather and, in some measure, finds healing by running the traditional death race in the cold dawn.

Abel's alienation manifests itself in his inability to speak, a silence that some, like his lawyer and judge, perceive as stupidity and others, like Tosamah and Father Olguin, the withered reservation priest, perceive as psychosis. Abel himself perceives his detachment from both whites and Indians as linguistic confusion; like Chal, who cannot remember Osage songs in *Sundown,* Abel simply cannot find the right words: "He had tried . . . to speak to his grandfather, but he could not say the things he wanted; he had tried to pray, to sing, to enter into the old rhythm of the tongue, but he was no longer attuned to it. . . . Had he been able to say it, anything of his own language—even the commonplace formula of greeting "Where are you going"—which had no meaning beyond sound, no visible substance, would once again have shown him whole

14. McNickle, *Tribalism,* vi, x.

to himself; but he was dumb. Not dumb—silence was the older and better part of custom still—but *inarticulate*."[15] Although Momaday's stream-of-consciousness narrative sometimes reflects Abel's thoughts, the character ultimately remains a cipher that the reader only imperfectly glimpses from the reactions he provokes in others. Throughout the novel, he utters barely four lines of dialogue. Just as he cannot recall the language of his grandfather, the language of the city proves equally perplexing. Only through Ben does Momaday articulate Abel's inarticulateness: "And they [whites] can't help you because you don't know how to talk to them. They have a lot of *words*, and you know they mean something, but you don't know what, and your own words are no good because they're not the same; they're different, and they're the only words you've got" (*HD*, 139).

Tosamah's sermon on the Gospel of John, which begins famously, "In the beginning was the Word," contrasts Native oral tradition of storytelling, which he regards as a purified use of the Word, to the corruption of the Word in the white man's written language:

> In the white man's world, language, too—and the way in which the white man thinks of it—has undergone a process of change. The white man takes such things as words and literatures for granted, as indeed he must, for nothing in his world is so commonplace. On every side of him there are words by the millions, an unending succession of pamphlets and papers, letters and books, bills and bulletins, commentaries and conversations. He has diluted and multiplied the Word, and words have begun to close in upon him. He is sated and insensitive; his regard for language—for the Word itself—as an instrument of creation has diminished nearly to the point of no return. It may be that he will perish by the Word. (*HD*, 84–85)

Tosamah describes Abel's own condition in which the white world, with its linguistic dilutions and multiplications, has rendered him, like Lucille in Oliver La Farge's "Higher Education," unable to converse with his grandfather in the old tongue. Because Abel's problem is linguistic, the solution that Momaday proposes is also linguistic. At the bedside of his grandfather, Abel wonders at the old man's dying utter-

15. N. Scott Momaday, *House Made of Dawn*, 53. Further citations will be made parenthetically with the abbreviation *HD*.

ances, Spanish and tribal words tumbling together in his dying remembrance: *"Abelito . . . kethá ahme . . . Mariano . . . frío . . . se dió por . . . mucho, mucho frío . . . vencido . . . aye, Porcingula . . . que blanco, Abelito . . . diablo blanco . . . Sawish . . . Sawish . . . y el hombre negro . . . sí . . . muchos hombres negros . . . corriendo, corriendo . . . frío . . . rápidamente . . . Abelito, Vidalito . . . ayempah? Ayempah!"* (*HD*, 171). Although Abel characteristically can think of nothing to say to him, the words, recalling a ceremonial race that Francisco had won as a young man, resonate in his mind. After he dispatches his grandfather's body according to both traditional and Christian rites, Abel smears his face with ash like the runners, the *hombres negros* of Francisco's memory, and begins his own death race, *corriendo, corriendo,* running like his grandfather into the cold morning. As he runs, his grandfather's words in his mind, he finally recalls the words of the creation song that have always eluded him: *"House made of pollen, house made of dawn"* (*HD*, 185).

Momaday's notion of translation seems more compromising than McNickle's idea of being Indian by choice, in that Abel, Ben, Tosamah, and the other relocated Indians, in order to survive, must somehow merge their traditional words, practices, and beliefs with those of the dominant culture in order to survive. Ben and Tosamah persist and even prosper in Los Angeles because they achieve this compromise; Abel, broken, returns to the reservation because he cannot. None of them may simply choose to be Indian, nor may they freely define themselves in their own terms, because, as Ben knows, "your own words are no good."

But within this merging lies the possibility of existence beyond the more reactionary tribalism. McNickle defines the choice to be Indian as an act of nonconformism, a willful rejection of substitute identities. McNickle readopts the racial dialectic in his description of Indianness. To be Indian is to be different—separate—as Archilde's mother, who renounces her baptism so that she may join the spirits of her pagan ancestors in death, and as Archilde himself, who, inspired by his mother's example, escapes into the hills of the Flathead, choosing to be Indian but nonetheless isolating himself from the hostile world beyond those hills. Momaday chooses not to retreat but to merge, and in doing so he sets out to change the dominant culture as it changes him. Momaday makes compromises, but he also makes others compromise, anticipating

Homi Bhabha's argument that the nation is *"internally* marked by cultural difference and the heterogeneous histories of contending peoples."[16] For Momaday as for Mourning Dove, finding a contemporary Indian voice depends on such a blending of languages and traditions, as the feast of Santiago described early in the novel blends Christian hagiography with Native ritual (*HD*, 34–35). Like those Indians at the festival who "after four centuries of Christianity...still pray in Tanoan to the old deities of the earth and sky," Momaday and other mixed-blood writers "have assumed the names and gestures of their enemies, but have held on to their own, secret souls; and in this there is a resistance and an overcoming" (*HD*, 52–53). From this perspective, Momaday's translation of Native experience into the forms of contemporary secular, even academic fiction seems less like an exercise of accommodation than one of survivance and synthesis.

Interwoven Beadwork in Erdrich's *The Antelope Wife*

Some scholars insist that the syncretism manifested in narratives of mixed descent such as *House Made of Dawn* does not represent "resistance and overcoming" but rather the continuing fraudulence of what it means to be Native, recalling Spivak's axiom that the subaltern cannot speak in terms other than those circumscribed by the dominant discourse. Erdrich, however, rejects this prohibitive view. Although all of Erdrich's novels explore mixed-blood identity, *The Antelope Wife* does so with the greatest self-consciousness. A conspicuously idiosyncratic work that stands apart from her celebrated Matchimanito cycle of novels, it represents the search for parentage and for self, describing the search with the elaborate metaphor of Ojibwe beadwork, an intricate interweaving of color and design, communal histories, and individual personalities. Peter G. Beidler and Gay Barton, who have presented genealogical charts for all of the families portrayed in Erdrich's work, describe those in *The Antelope Wife* as "more problematic than those in earlier novels...partly because Erdrich leaves out many connections."[17] These lapses do not reflect authorial carelessness. On the contrary, they indicate

16. Bhabha, "DessemiNation," in *Nation and Narration*, 297.
17. Peter G. Beidler and Gay Barton, *A Reader's Guide to the Novels of Louise Erdrich*, 39.

one of the novel's primary thematic concerns: the attempt to rediscover lost connections to ancestors and the past.

Because the novel adopts chronological fragmentation both as structure and theme, a plain description of the plot is difficult, since Erdrich deliberately confuses history and legend, individual self and ancestral lineage, present and past. The narrative opens in the middle nineteenth century in the midst of a nasty skirmish between a cavalry detachment and a band of Ojibwe. During the raid on the Indian camp, a mother, Blue Prairie Woman, is separated from her infant daughter, who is carried from the fighting lashed to the back of a dog. Cavalryman Scranton Roy deserts his troop and pursues the child across the prairie, where he raises her to atone for the atrocities he has committed in the village. In time he renames the girl Matilda and marries a white schoolteacher with whom he has a son, Augustus. Meanwhile, Matilda's Indian mother, renamed Other Side of the Earth for her heart that wanders in search of her lost daughter, conceives twin daughters, Mary and Josephette (Zosie), with her Ojibwe husband, Shawano. Unable to forget her lost child, however, she leaves her newborn twins with her mother and sets out in search of Matilda, finding her just in time to nurse her from a severe fever but sacrificing her own life in return. Motherless, Matilda chases a herd of antelope across the prairie, hypnotized by their grace, and never, it seems, to return.

From these partly historical, partly legendary origins, the Roy and Shawano families are bound together by trauma and magic. The remainder of the novel traces their intermingling over the succeeding six generations, eventually supplying a third strand for the genealogical braid of the Whiteheart Beads family, linked to the others by marriage. Only two characters, the twin sisters Cally and Deanna Whiteheart Beads, can trace their roots through all three of these strands. When Deanna dies in a childhood accident from carbon monoxide poisoning during her father's suicide attempt, Cally, who adopts the surname Roy after her father's eventually successful suicide, is left alone to untangle the truth of her origin in present-day Minneapolis, a city, like Alexie's Seattle, that seems to efface tribal tradition and identity. She reflects:

> I am a Roy, a Whiteheart Beads, a Shawano...all in all, we make a huge old family like a can of those mixed party nuts....Some bloods they go together like water—the French and Ojibwas: You mix those

up and it is all one person. Like me. Others are a little less predictable. You make a person from a German and an Indian, for instance, and you're creating a two-souled warrior always fighting with themselves. . . . Swedish and Norwegian Indians abound in this region, too, and now, Hmong-Ojibwas, those last so beautiful you want to follow them around and see if they are real. Take an Indian who shows her Irish, like Cecille [her cousin], however, and you're playing with hot dynamite.[18]

Although she considers herself nondescript, she recognizes also that she occupies a unique place among these comically varied mixed party nuts both as sole heir to the three intertwined families and, more significantly, as the one "sent here to understand and report" on the long process, where Indians, whites, and all those in between "are scattered like beads off a necklace and put back together again in new patterns, new strings" (*AW*, 220). At this moment, the narrative voice who introduces herself on the first page as one who relates the fading memory of Scranton Roy "in order that it not be lost," emerges as Cally's (*AW*, 3). Like Other Side of the Earth, or Blue Prairie Woman, from whom Cally takes her traditional spirit name, Cally, with her simultaneous consciousness, exists in "both places at once" (*AW*, 14), in the forgotten past of the burning Ojibwe village and in the present of a Christmas gathering where her grandmother reveals the story of the blue beads that represent Cally's physical link to this past. Cally stands apart from the vacillating, internally conflicted mixed-bloods in previous fictions, occupying "both places at once," not divided in half but rather doubled in two wholes, expanded rather than diminished by her hybridity. Her ties to all three families enable her, as "reporter" on the final page of the novel, to bridge the temporal disjunctions that confound the novel's reader: "All that followed, all that happened, all is as I have told. Did these occurrences have a paradigm in the settlement of the old scores and pains and betrayals that went back in time? . . . Who is beading us? Who is setting flower upon flower and cut-glass vine? Who are you and who am I, the beader or the bit of colored glass sewn onto the fabric of this earth?" (*AW*, 240). Like Rowson and Apess almost two centuries

18. Louise Erdrich, *The Antelope Wife*, 110–11. Further citations will be made parenthetically with the abbreviation *AW*.

earlier, like Mathews two generations earlier, Erdrich casts the mixed-blood not as a ghost lurking on the margins of American society but, more intimately, as a spirit that defines "you," directly addressing a reader who, regardless of ethnicity, bears the weight of a collective, interwoven past, who exists as both the beader of her own destiny and the bead in a larger, only partly comprehensible pattern. For Erdrich, hybridity is not a condition that divides, delimits, or silences; it does not represent a corruption or a compromise of a more authentic Native consciousness. Rather, it increases; it illuminates the past and the language to report such insight; it binds old wounds, reunites far-flung forgotten kin, and binds all that seemed *daashkikaa*, or "cracked apart."

Erdrich introduces the peculiar Ojibwe word *daashkikaa* in the opening pages of the novel, as an old woman, her gut impaled by Scranton Roy's bayonet and her family scattered and dying, cries in her death throes, "Daashkikaa. Daashkikaa" (*AW*, 4). In one of the novel's many genealogical ironies, Cally Roy claims as her ancestors both participants in this fatal encounter. The great-great-great-great granddaughter of the old Indian woman and the great-great granddaughter of Scranton Roy, Cally seems to remember this ancient murder in her blood. With a slip on the ice and a bump on the head, the fearful word itself inexplicably returns to her, six generations later. When she asks her grandmother its meaning, the older woman marvels at Cally's vision and wonders whether her granddaughter is "the Namer," who communicates through dreams with the dead and receives from them the spirit names of those in the present who share both a name and an identity with a particular ancestor (*AW*, 213). These perplexing metaphysical correspondences, which tend to necessitate the charts provided by Beidler and Barton, render a novel that frequently assigns multiple names to a single character or a single name to multiple characters. Erdrich consciously blurs identities within the novel in order to collapse the sense of separation of past and present, self and ancestor. As the Namer, Cally is the medium of this correspondence, the crucial bead that marks the confluence of the distinct but interwoven strands of the grand design.

As Kathleen Brogan argues in *Cultural Haunting*, "American national presence can be seen as predicated upon a native absence. The potential confusion of mixed ancestry is heightened when one feels . . . a member of two distinct nations, one of which founded its identity on the erasure or 'ghosting' of the other." Ghosts in Erdrich's fiction, which Brogan reads as a symbol for the paradoxes of mixed ancestry, represent both "the destruction of traditional native cultures" and "continuity with the past . . . [a] reconstructive agent."[19] As the descendant of both Scranton Roy and the old Ojibwe woman, of both the killer and the victim, Cally strikingly represents the paradox observed by Brogan, as well as the oxymoron that Cheryl Walker has sensed in hybrid texts, embodying the paradigm of simultaneity rather than alternation. She does not feel herself a member of two distinct nations, as the mixed-blood protagonists in *The Surrounded* and *House Made of Dawn* do. She expresses none of their anxiety of divided self, none of the acute alienation that characterizes the early writing of the Native American renaissance. Cally's consciousness of her traumatic origin does not occasion self-destructive urges as it does in the half-breed renegades of the dime novel or in Momaday's Abel. She does not have to be erased or ghosted in order to become Brogan's reconstructive agent. Rather, like Mourning Dove, who textures her narrative with Salish words and stories, with translations intended to make white and Indian cultures mutually intelligible, Erdrich reconstructs the lost links between past and present through acts of translation. Throughout the novel Erdrich uses Native words and names more extensively and more consciously than Mourning Dove or perhaps any other Native American writer does. Titles marking major divisions of the narrative, seasons, place names, and names of people, animals, or significant objects are alternately given in English, Ojibwe, or even German. Minneapolis is also *Gakahbekong;* Other Side of the Earth is also *Ozhawashkwamashkodeykway.* Perhaps most importantly, Cally's consciousness of herself as "one sent to understand and report," to name the "new patterns, new strings," immediately arises from the act of translating the lost word that returns to her in a concussive daze—*daashkikaa*—a consciousness of things "cracked apart" that, through her, may be woven together again. Erdrich represents these new patterns in all her works, constructing, in her own words, an elaborate "drama of identity" that produces the contemporary urban mixed-blood and resurrects Susanna Rowson's vision of an alternative American genealogy (*AW,* 112).

19. Brogan, *Cultural Haunting,* 30–31.

Erdrich's representation of hybridity conceives of possibilities beyond those offered by McNickle's choice to be different, which recalls Spivak's definition of hybridity as circumscription; or by Momaday's syncretism, which recalls Bhabha's definition of hybridity as vacillation; Erdrich's view of hybridity gestures to a consciousness that neither of these theoretical positions considers. While both of these positions assume a dialectical opposition of discourses that coexist either in willful separation or in unstable mixture, Erdrich's characters most closely represent what Louis Riel described a century earlier, when he declared: "We are *Métis*." The "mixed party nuts" in *The Antelope Wife* are not separate from whites like McNickle's Archilde, nor are they separate from themselves like Momaday's Abel. Liberated from the dialectical Indian-white paradigm, they are unitary beings who clearly stake out that independent space between races only tentatively explored by Apess, Ridge, and Mathews, and they present the most compelling revision of the model of racial difference that has, for almost two centuries, formed the basis of our national idea.

Reconsidering Race

Perhaps because she has evolved this idea of hybridity as simultaneity, Erdrich—like Momaday, Mathews, Mourning Dove, Vizenor, and other Native writers who have adopted hybridity as a narrative or theoretical paradigm—has been criticized for her inauthenticity, for her hesitancy or insincerity in depicting the reality of contemporary Native life. Most notoriously, Leslie Silko accused her of spinning "fairy tales" in a review of Erdrich's second novel, *The Beet Queen* (1986). While Silko's comments primarily address a novel only peripherally concerned with Native characters, Silko more generally criticizes Erdrich's "academic, postmodern...influences" that evade racial and political controversies in favor of overly complex and ultimately inconsequential linguistic "experimentation."[20]

Claudia Egerer notes a more common tendency among Erdrich's critics to "situate the novels within the framework of Native American

20. Leslie Marmon Silko, "Here's an Odd Artifact for the Fairy-Tale Shelf," 178–79.

literature" by insisting upon the "ethnic elements . . . such as myths of the Chippewa people and Native American tradition." This "separatist" approach to Erdrich's work, Egerer argues, isolates Erdrich as an Indian writer and also ignores the significant ways "her texts question notions of purity by focusing on characters of mixed heritage who grapple with the challenge of hybridity." Egerer further suggests that critics experience "uncertainty and uneasiness" with this aspect of Erdrich's writing because it challenges "the old and perhaps useless label of 'marginality'" that has defined postcolonial theory and Native American studies.[21] Lucy Maddox writes:

> The full story of Indian-white relations in North America . . . is already taking two different forms. One version is being produced through the collaboration of a variety of traditionally white academic disciplines. . . . The same matter is simultaneously being treated from an Indian perspective, through academic programs in Native American Studies and, especially, through the recent proliferation of works by Indian writers that mark what has already been called the Native American Renaissance. Thus far, however, the two versions of the story remain separated by fundamental differences in the very nature of their structure and their discourse.[22]

Robert Young similarly observes that contemporary cultural theory threatens to replicate the polarizing racial doctrines of the nineteenth century: "Today the dominant models often stress separateness, passing by altogether the process of acculturation whereby groups are modified through intellectual exchange and socialization with other groups. . . . Postcolonial criticism has constructed two antithetical groups, the colonizer and colonized, self and Other, with the second only knowable through a necessarily false representation, a Manichean division that threatens to reproduce the static, essentialist categories it seeks to undo."[23]

Perhaps this process of Manichean division has already begun to change, even within the work of Silko herself, who offers the sternest criticism of Erdrich. In *Ceremony*, for example, Silko portrays a traumatized mixed-blood World War II veteran, Tayo, who returns to the

21. Claudia Egerer, *Fictions of (In)Betweenness*, 62–63, 66.
22. Maddox, *Removals*, 3.
23. Young, *Colonial Desire*, 4–5.

Pueblo reservation in a state of sickness and confusion. Plagued by guilt over the deaths of his cousin, Rocky, whom he had watched Japanese soldiers execute on the Bataan Death March, and his uncle, Josiah, left alone to work the family ranch during the war, Tayo believes that he has caused the drought that now ravages the reservation. His aunt compounds his feeling of alienation, constantly reminding him that he is a bastard born to a woman who disgraced herself by whoring with white men and who eventually killed herself with drink. Other men on the reservation similarly deride Tayo, viewing his hazel eyes and pale skin as signs of collusion with the dispossessors. For Silko, however, as for Momaday and Erdrich, hybridity underlies both the sickness and the cure. Tayo begins to appreciate his hybrid status when meets Night Swan, a Mexican prostitute, who tells him, "They are afraid, Tayo. They feel something happening, they can see something happening around them, and it scares them. . . . They think that if their children have the same color of skin, the same color of eyes, that nothing is changing. . . . They are fools. They blame us, the ones who look different. That way they don't have to think about what has happened inside themselves."[24]

The mixed-blood medicine man Betonie, in whom Tayo recognizes the same hazel eyes as his own, also represents such change, using talismans from both the white and Indian worlds in his healing ceremonies and interweaving past and present like Cally Roy. When Tayo questions his nontraditional methods, Betonie tells him, "At one time, the ceremonies as they had been performed were enough for the way the world was then. But after the white people came, elements in the world began to shift; and it became necessary to create new ceremonies. I have made changes in the rituals. The people mistrust this greatly, but only this growth keeps the ceremonies strong." Echoing the complaints of literary critics who argue that translation somehow compromises Native authenticity, more traditional Indians fear such changes. But, like the feast of Santiago depicted in *House Made of Dawn*, performed by Indians who have blended old and new beliefs as a means of survival and resistance, Betonie's hybrid ceremonies represent the strength and future of a people who exist in a necessarily changing world, a world in flux,

24. Leslie Marmon Silko, *Ceremony*, 99–100.

Silko suggests, even since long before the white man came. Like Josiah's hybrid cattle, bred from the lanky desert breed and the meaty white Herefords, that adapt and thrive in the parched conditions of the drought, Tayo, Betonie, and Night Swan are similarly equipped to survive in a world mortally threatened by "the Destroyers," evil spirits in Silko's novel that take the forms of both whites and Indians. Tayo claims, "I'm a half-breed.... I'll speak for both sides," representing the unique simultaneous position of writers, like Silko and Erdrich, who refuse to regard their hybridity as the brand of a pariah or a curse of invisibility, who rather draw from it that "word of creation" lost to the profane world, both white and Indian.[25]

Like Momaday, Erdrich herself, since the beginning of her career, has resisted these oppositional categories and denied any political positions that would limit the ways readers receive her works. In a 1988 interview with Kay Bonetti, Erdrich and Michael Dorris, then her husband and cowriter, discussed their conception of mixed-blood characters "outside their ethnic background" not as political symbols of "contact between Indians and non-Indians" but instead as "people in a small community," as expressions of locality rather than racial universality, a position inevitably bound to historical stereotypes. When asked, "Do you see yourselves as Native American writers?" Erdrich replied, "I don't think it's right to put everything off in a separate category. All of the ethnic writing done in the United States is American writing, and should be called American writing."[26]

Erdrich's comments recall Momaday's enigmatic remark, "I don't know what an Indian is," and leads us to the more fundamental question: Has race—traditionally conceived as a function of biological, social, or cultural difference—become irrelevant in literary critical studies? In this book, I have approached the question of racial and cultural hybridity in relation to the parallel construction of American national identity over the last two centuries, demonstrating the disturbances provoked by the mixed-blood, who undermines the notions of difference at the heart of our national idea. Within the scope of this book, the rele-

25. Ibid., 126, 42.
26. Bonetti, "An Interview with Louise Erdrich and Michael Dorris," 87, 95.

vance of race therefore depends in part on the relevance of nationalism. Observing the proliferation of scholarship on nationalism over the past three decades, Benedict Anderson has posed this same question: Does the ascendance of nationalism as a primary subject of academic discourse mean that it has ceased to have any relevance in the real world? Does the visibility that nationalism has gained signal that it has ceased to be a naturalized part our consciousness? In response to these questions, Bhabha argues that nationalistic ideals have not been superceded by "those new realities of internationalism or even 'late capitalism,' once we acknowledge that the rhetoric of these global terms is most often underwritten in that grim prose of power that each nation can wield within its own sphere of influence."[27] In the same way, Michaels reminds us of the social relevance of race, even though it has ceased to have a scientific meaning. I do not dispute these claims of the continuing though perhaps changing relevance of race and nationalism in this era of globalism. But the evolution of the mixed-blood figure in popular American fiction and the expression and experimentation of mixed-blood writers with regard to their hybrid positions over the last two centuries suggest that American literature and literary studies will witness fundamental revisions in the conception of race that have already begun. These revisions, moreover, will bear a direct relationship to the continuing evolution of our national idea. As nationalism ebbs and flows against the growing current of internationalism, racialism will similarly fluctuate in response to the increasingly sustained voices of interracialism that this book has traced. At the beginning of the twentieth century, La Farge, Mourning Dove, Mathews, and McNickle liberated the fictional mixed-blood from the chains of biology and from nineteenth-century stereotypes as a grotesque or an outlaw. Yet none of these writers could escape the pervasive sense of difference that usually manifested itself in their narratives as the alienation of the mixed-blood from the white world and his white self. While their narrative and linguistic experiments illustrated a revolution in the way American culture represented racial blending, their difference, as Michaels's essay suggests, was still socially apparent and therefore acutely felt. Although they

27. Bhabha, introduction to *Nation and Narration*, 1.

no longer saw themselves as Indians exiled by their blood, they remained exiled by their culture and traditions, by their poverty, dumbness, or paralysis.

Writers of the later twentieth century, creating a synthetic rather than dialectical consciousness of hybridity, have begun to lose this sense of alienation, and in doing so they have suggested that the tendency among critics of their work to insist upon their authentic Indianness reduces and isolates them and their writing in the same way that the more obviously racialist discourse of earlier eras did. If Native writing of the last twenty years has begun a revolution similar to that sparked during the Indian New Deal, it will likely result in a new understanding of race and the literary canon that recognizes the unsupportability of classification and division of writers, readers, and literatures as ethnically distinct, a canon without clearly defined margins or recognizable dominant or subaltern voices. Since the early twentieth century, writers have consistently challenged these distinctions, and even as they have been continually reasserted in the work of such nostalgic writers as Edmonds and McMurtry, they have appeared increasingly obsolete in comparison to the narratives that have replaced them. In 1829, when Apess published *A Son of the Forest,* the wild voice of the half-mad half-Indian decrying the Massachusetts antimiscegenation law shrank beside the monumental historical romances, which drew from the grand narratives of history and science in order to suppress the possibility of racial blending in the new nation. Now the nation's counternarratives have become its master narratives. Its performative texts have become pedagogical. The subaltern has not only spoken, but it has usurped the dominant discourse and shattered the idols—the vanishing Indian, the uncrossed hero, the undefiled white maiden—that were once unassailable. Krupat's "voice in the margin" has moved out of the margin into the forefront of our cultural consciousness. We might, of course, owe this to many historical or social changes over the past two centuries: the removal of the Indian as a military or sexual threat, the closing of the frontier, the gradual establishment of economic and political stability in the United States and the consequent waning of a nationalist impulse. I have focused here on changes less generalized. I have attempted to illustrate that the figure of the mixed-blood in our fiction, largely overlooked by scholars, provides a mirror in which we might observe and interpret changes in the way we view ourselves as a nation, a kind of fun-house mirror that is not quite right, that might jar us when we see the image looking back, uncanny not in its strangeness but in its familiarity. For in this grotesque image we see, simply and impossibly, the image of ourselves.

Bibliography

Alexie, Sherman. *Indian Killer.* New York: Warner Books, 1996.

Anderson, Benedict. *Imagined Communities: Reflections on the Origin and Spread of Nationalism.* New York: Verso, 1991.

Apess, William. *On Our Own Ground: The Complete Writings of William Apess, a Pequot.* Ed. Barry O'Connell. Amherst: University of Massachusetts Press, 1992.

Aquila, Richard, ed. *Wanted Dead or Alive: The American West in Popular Culture.* Urbana: University of Illinois Press, 1996.

Ashcroft, Bill, Gareth Griffiths, and Helen Tiffin, eds. *The Post-Colonial Studies Reader.* New York: Routledge, 1995.

Austin, F. Britten. "Toward the Millennium: The Railroad Builders." *Saturday Evening Post* 202, no. 24 (December 14, 1929): 37, 39, 92, 94, 96, 101, 104.

Austin, Mary. *One-Smoke Stories.* Boston: Houghton Mifflin, 1934.

Axtell, James. "The Ethnohistory of Early America: A Review Essay." *William and Mary Quarterly* 35 (1978): 140–41.

Badger, Joseph E., Jr. *Redlaw, the Half-Breed; or, The Tangled Trail.* New York: Beadle and Adams, 1870.

Baker, Frank. "The Ascent of Man." *American Anthropologist* 3, no. 4 (1890): 297–320.

Balmer, Edwin. "A Wild-Goose Chase." *Saturday Evening Post* 187, no. 9 (August 29, 1914): 3–5, 45–46; 187, no. 10 (September 5, 1914): 23–25, 69–70; 187, no. 11 (September 12, 1914): 21–23, 49, 51; 187, no. 12 (September 19, 1914): 21–23, 41–42, 45–46; 187, no. 13 (September 26, 1914): 21–23, 57–58, 61–62.

Barnett, Louise K. *The Ignoble Savage: American Literary Racism, 1790–1890.* Westport, Conn.: Greenwood, 1975.

Baym, Nina. "How Men and Women Wrote Indian Stories." In *New Essays on the Last of the Mohicans,* ed. H. Daniel Peck, 67–86. New York: Cambridge University Press, 1992.

Beidler, Peter G. "The Indian Half-Breed in Turn-of-the-Century Short Fiction." *American Indian Culture and Research Journal* 9, no. 1 (1985): 1–12.

———. "Literary Criticism in *Cogewea:* Mourning Dove's Protagonist Reads *The Brand.*" *American Indian Culture and Research Journal* 19, no. 2 (1995): 45–65.

Beidler, Peter G., and Gay Barton. *A Reader's Guide to the Novels of Louise Erdrich.* Columbia: University of Missouri Press, 1999.

Beidler, Peter G., Harry J. Brown, and Marion F. Egge. *The Native American in Short Fiction in the* Saturday Evening Post: *An Annotated Bibliography.* Lanham, Md.: Scarecrow, 2001.

Beirne, Piers. *Inventing Criminology: Essays on the Rise of "Homo Criminalis."* Albany: State University of New York Press, 1993.

Berkhofer, Robert F., Jr. *The White Man's Indian: Images of the American Indian from Columbus to the Present.* New York: Vintage Books, 1978.

Bhabha, Homi K. *The Location of Culture.* New York: Routledge, 1994.

Bhabha, Homi K., ed. *Nation and Narration.* New York: Routledge, 1990.

Bloom, Harold, ed. *Native American Writers: Modern Critical Views.* Philadelphia: Chelsea House, 1998.

Boas, Franz. "The Anthropology of the North American Indian." In *The Shaping of American Anthropology, 1883–1911: A Franz Boas Reader,* ed. George W. Stocking, 191–201. New York: Basic Books, 1974.

———. "Human Faculty as Determined by Race." In *The Shaping of American Anthropology, 1883–1911: A Franz Boas Reader,* ed. George W. Stocking, 221–42. New York: Basic Books, 1974.

———. "The Instability of Human Types." In *The Shaping of American Anthropology, 1883–1911: A Franz Boas Reader,* ed. George W. Stocking, 214–18. New York: Basic Books, 1974.

———. "Physical Characteristics of the Indians of the North Pacific Coast." *American Anthropologist* 4, no. 1 (1891) 25–32.

———. "Race Problems in America." In *The Shaping of American Anthropology, 1883–1911: A Franz Boas Reader,* ed. George W. Stocking, 331–34. New York: Basic Books, 1974.

———. "Remarks on the Theory of Anthropometry." In *The Shaping of American Anthropology, 1883–1911: A Franz Boas Reader,* ed. George W. Stocking, 77–82. New York: Basic Books, 1974.

Bold, Christine. "Malaeska's Revenge; or, The Dime Novel Tradition in Popular Fiction." In *Wanted Dead or Alive: The American West in Popular Culture,* ed. Richard Aquila, 21–42. Urbana: University of Illinois Press, 1996.

———. *Selling the Wild West: Popular Western Fiction, 1860–1960.* Bloomington: Indiana University Press, 1987.

Bonetti, Kay. "An Interview with Louise Erdrich and Michael Dorris." *Missouri Review* 11, no. 2 (1988): 79–99. Reprinted in *Conversations with American Novelists: The Best Interviews from the* Missouri Review *and the American Audio Prose Library,* ed. Kay Bonetti, Greg Michalson, Speer Morgan, Jo Sapp, and Sam Stowers. Columbia: University of Missouri Press, 1997.

Brogan, Kathleen. *Cultural Haunting: Ghosts and Ethnicity in Recent American Literature.* Charlottesville: University Press of Virginia, 1998.

Brown, Alanna K. "The Choice to Write: Mourning Dove's Search for Survival." In *Old West–New West: Centennial Essays,* ed. Barbara H. Meldrum, 261–71. Moscow: University of Idaho Press, 1993.

———. "The Evolution of Mourning Dove's *Coyote Stories." Studies in American Indian Literatures* 4, nos. 2–3 (1992): 161–80.

———. "Looking through the Glass Darkly: The Editorialized Mourning Dove." In *New Voices in Native American Literary Criticism,* ed. Arnold Krupat, 274–90. Washington, D.C.: Smithsonian Institution Press, 1993.

Brown, Bill, ed. *Reading the West: An Anthology of Dime Westerns.* New York: Bedford, 1997.

Brown, Charles Brockden. *Edgar Huntly; or, Memoirs of a Sleep-Walker.* 1799. Reprint, ed. Norman S. Grabo. New York: Penguin Books, 1988.

Burdick, Debra. "Louise Erdrich's *Love Medicine, The Beet Queen,* and *Tracks:* An Annotated Survey of Criticism through 1994." *American Indian Culture and Research Journal* 20, no. 3 (1996): 137–66.

Burley, David, and Michael Gates. "The Dawson Film Discovery: An

Outline of Parks Canada's Involvement." *Research Bulletin* [Parks Canada] 140 (1980): 1–5.

Carr, Helen. *Inventing the American Primitive: Politics, Gender, and the Representation of Native American Literary Traditions, 1789–1936.* New York: New York University Press, 1996.

Carroll, Noel. *The Philosophy of Horror.* New York: Routledge, Chapman, and Hall, 1990.

Carver, Mary Alden. "The Indian Who Was a White Man." *Overland Monthly* 52 (1908): 462–65.

Cassuto, Leonard. *The Inhuman Race: The Racial Grotesque in American Literature and Culture.* New York: Columbia University Press, 1997.

Child, Lydia Maria. *Hobomok and Other Writings on Indians.* Ed. Carolyn L. Karcher. American Women Writers Series. New Brunswick, N.J.: Rutgers University Press, 1995.

———. *Letters of Lydia Maria Child.* Ed. John G. Whittier. Boston: Houghton Mifflin, 1883.

Churchill, Ward. Review of *Manifest Manners,* by Gerald Vizenor. *American Indian Culture and Research Journal* 18, no. 3 (1994): 313–18.

Cohn, Jan. *Covers of the* Saturday Evening Post. New York: Smithmark, 1998.

Colden, Cadwallader. *The History of the Five Indian Nations; Depending on the Province of New York in America.* 1727. Reprint, Ithaca: Cornell University Press, 1980.

Collier, John. *From Every Zenith: A Memoir and Some Essays on Life and Thought.* Denver: Sage Books, 1963.

Columbus, Christopher. "Letter of Columbus to Various Persons Describing the Results of His First Voyage and Written on the Return Journey." In *The Four Voyages,* ed. and trans. J. M. Cohen, 115–23. New York: Penguin, 1969.

Cooper, James Fenimore. *The Last of the Mohicans.* 1826. Reprint, ed. Richard Slotkin. New York: Penguin Books, 1986.

Cox, J. Randolph. *The Dime Novel Companion: A Source Book.* Westport: Greenwood Press, 2000.

Dekker, George, and John P. McWilliams, eds. *Fenimore Cooper: The Critical Heritage.* Critical Heritage Series. London: Routledge and Kegan Paul, 1973.

Del Olmo, Rosa. "The Development of Criminology in Latin America." *Social Justice* 26, no. 2 (1999): 19–45.

Deloria, Philip. *Playing Indian*. New Haven, Conn.: Yale University Press, 1998.

Deloria, Vine, Jr. *Custer Died for Your Sins: An Indian Manifesto*. New York: Avon Books, 1969.

Denning, Michael. *Mechanic Accents: Dime Novels and Working-Class Culture in America*. New York: Verso, 1987.

Dinan, John A. *The Pulp Western: A Popular History of the Western Fiction Magazine in America*. San Bernardino, Calif.: Borgo, 1983.

Dorris, Michael. Introduction to *Ramona*, by Helen Hunt Jackson, v–xviii. New York: Signet Classic, 1988.

Douglas, Mary. *Purity and Danger*. New York: Praeger, 1966.

Drinnon, Richard. *Facing West: The Metaphysics of Indian Hating and Empire Building*. Norman: University of Oklahoma Press, 1980.

Eagleton, Terry, Frederic Jameson, and Edward W. Said. *Nationalism, Colonialism, and Literature*. Minneapolis: University of Minnesota Press, 1988.

Edmonds, Walter D. "The Captives." *Saturday Evening Post* 209, no. 32 (February 13, 1937): 10–11, 35, 37–38, 40.

———. "Delia Borst." *Saturday Evening Post* 209, no. 40 (April 3, 1937): 14–15, 42, 45–46, 48, 50.

———. *Drums along the Mohawk*. 1936. Reprint, New York: Bantam, 1988.

———. "Dygartsbush." *Saturday Evening Post* 209, no. 46 (May 15, 1937): 24–25, 76, 78, 81–84, 86–88.

Egerer, Claudia. *Fictions of (In)Betweenness*. Göteborg, Sweden: Acta Universitatis Gothoburgensis, 1997.

Ellis, Edward S. *The Half-Blood; or, The Panther of the Plains*. New York: Beadle and Adams, 1882.

———. *Seth Jones; or, The Captives of the Frontier*. In *Reading the West: An Anthology of Dime Westerns*, ed. Bill Brown, 169–268. New York: Bedford, 1997.

Erdrich, Louise. *The Antelope Wife*. New York: HarperCollins, 1998.

Evers, Lawrence J. "Words and Place: A Reading of *House Made of Dawn*." In *Native American Writers: Modern Critical Views*, ed. Harold Bloom, 5–23. Philadelphia: Chelsea House, 1998.

Fetterly, Judith. "'My Sister! My Sister!': The Rhetoric of Catherine Sedgwick's *Hope Leslie.*" *American Literature* 70, no. 3 (1998): 491–516.

Fiedler, Leslie A. *Love and Death in the American Novel.* New York: Dell, 1960.

———. *The Return of the Vanishing American.* London: J. Cape, 1968.

Fisher, Dexter. Introduction to *Cogewea, the Half-Blood: A Depiction of the Great Montana Cattle Range,* by Mourning Dove. 1927. Reprint, Lincoln: University of Nebraska Press, 1981.

Fletcher, Robert. "The New School of Criminal Anthropology." *The American Anthropologist* 4, no. 3 (1891): 201–36.

Ford, Douglas. "Inscribing the 'Impartial Observer' in Sedgwick's *Hope Leslie.*" *Legacy* 14, no. 2 (1997): 81–92.

Friedman, Lawrence M. *Crime and Punishment in American History.* New York: Basic Books, 1993.

Gardner, Jared. *Master Plots: Race and the Founding of an American Literature.* Baltimore: Johns Hopkins University Press, 1998.

Goddu, Teresa A. *Gothic America: Narrative, History, and Nation.* New York: Columbia University Press, 1997.

Gould, Philip B. *Covenant and Republic: Historical Romance and the Politics of Puritanism.* New York: Cambridge University Press, 1996.

Hager, Hal. "About N. Scott Momaday." In *House Made of Dawn,* by N. Scott Momaday. New York: Perennial Classics, 1999.

Haller, John S. *Outcasts from Evolution: Scientific Attitudes of Racial Inferiority, 1859–1900.* Urbana: University of Illinois Press, 1971.

Harte, Bret. "The Mermaid of Lighthouse Point." *Saturday Evening Post* 173, no. 12 (September 22, 1900): 3–6.

Hays, Robert G., ed. *A Race at Bay: New York Times Editorials on "the Indian Problem," 1860–1900.* Carbondale: Southern Illinois University Press, 1997.

Henshaw, Henry Weatherbee. "Who Are the American Indians?" *American Anthropologist* 2, no. 3 (1889): 193–214.

Hergesheimer, Joseph. "Scarlet Ibis." *Saturday Evening Post* 193, no. 20 (November 13, 1920): 5–7, 61–62, 65–66, 68.

Highwater, Jamake. *Shadow Show: An Autobiographical Insinuation.* New York: Alfred Van Der Marck Editions, 1986.

Hoffman, Frederick L. *Race Traits and the American Negro*. New York, 1896.

Horsman, Reginald. *Race and Manifest Destiny: The Origins of American Anglo-Saxonism*. Cambridge: Harvard University Press, 1981.

Hough, Emerson. "My Lady's Furs—What They Cost." *Saturday Evening Post* 180, no. 24 (December 14, 1907): 6–7, 28.

Howard, Joseph Kinsey. *Strange Empire: A Narrative of the Northwest*. Minneapolis: Minnesota Historical Society Press, 1994.

Huffman, Bert. "Ah-lo-ma." *Overland Monthly* 45 (1905): 491–93.

Ignatiev, Noel. *How the Irish Became White*. New York: Routledge, 1995.

Institute for Government Research [Lewis Meriam]. *The Problem of Indian Administration*. Baltimore: Johns Hopkins University Press, 1928.

Irving, Washington. *The Adventures of Captain Bonneville, U.S.A., in the Rocky Mountains and the Far West*. New York, 1869.

———. *Astoria*. New York, 1868.

———. *A Tour on the Prairies*. New York, 1835.

Jackson, Helen Hunt. *A Century of Dishonor: The Early Crusade for Indian Reform*. 1881. Reprint, ed. Andrew F. Rolle. New York: Harper and Row, 1965.

———. *Ramona*. 1884. Reprint, ed. Michael Dorris. New York: Signet Classic, 1988.

Jackson, Joseph Henry. Introduction to *The Life and Adventures of Joaquín Murieta, the Celebrated California Bandit*, by John Rollin Ridge, xi–l. Norman: University of Oklahoma Press, 1955.

Jefferson, Thomas. *Notes on the State of Virginia*. 1787. Reprint, ed. William Peden. New York: Norton, 1982.

———. *The Writings of Thomas Jefferson*. Vol. 8. Ed. H. A. Washington. Washington, D.C.: Taylor and Murray, 1854.

Johannsen, Albert. *The House of Beadle and Adams and Its Dime and Nickel Novels: The Story of a Vanished Literature*. 3 vols. Norman: University Oklahoma Press, 1950–1962.

Jones, Daryl. *The Dime Novel Western*. Bowling Green, Ohio: Bowling Green University Popular Press, 1981.

Jones, David A. *History of Criminology: A Philosophical Perspective*. Westport, Conn.: Greenwood Press, 1986.

Jones, Kathy. "Rare Silent Film Filled Dawson Pool: Film Mystery Solved." *Whitehorse Star* (October 13, 1978): 14.

Karafilis, Maria. "Catherine Maria Sedgwick's *Hope Leslie:* The Crisis between Ethical Political Action and U.S. Literary Nationalism in the New Republic." *American Transcendental Quarterly* 12, no. 4 (1998): 327–44.

Karcher, Carolyn L. Introduction to *Hobomok and Other Writings on Indians,* by Lydia Maria Child, ix–xxxviii. American Women Writers Series. New Brunswick, N.J.: Rutgers University Press, 1995.

———. Introduction to *Hope Leslie; or, Early Times in the Massachusetts,* by Catherine Maria Sedgwick, ix–xxxviii. New York: Penguin Books, 1998.

Kenny, Kevin. *The American Irish: A History.* New York: Longman, 2000.

Knox, Robert. *The Races of Men.* London, 1850.

Kolodny, Annette. *The Land before Her: Fantasy and Experience of the American Frontiers, 1630–1860.* Chapel Hill: University of North Carolina Press, 1984.

Kroeber, Karl, et al. "Louise Erdrich's *Love Medicine.*" In *Critical Perspectives on Native American Fiction,* ed. Richard F. Fleck, 263–75. Washington, D.C.: Three Continents, 1993.

Krupat, Arnold. *For Those Who Come After: A Study of Native American Autobiography.* Berkeley: University of California Press, 1985.

———. Introduction to *Native American Autobiography: An Anthology,* 3–17. Madison: University of Wisconsin Press, 1994.

———. *The Voice in the Margin: Native American Literature and the Canon.* Berkeley: University of California Press, 1989.

Kula, Sam. "Rescued from the Permafrost: The Dawson Collection of Motion Pictures." *Archivaria* 8 (1979): 141–48.

———. "There's Film in Them Thar Hills!" *American Film Magazine* 8 (1979): 14–18.

La Farge, Oliver. "Hard Winter." *Saturday Evening Post* 206, no. 27 (December 30, 1933): 5–7, 45–47.

———. "Higher Education." *Saturday Evening Post* 206, no. 40 (March 31, 1934): 8–9, 66–67, 69–71.

———. "Horse Tamer." *Saturday Evening Post* 210, no. 29 (January 15, 1938): 10–11, 69–70, 72.

———. *Laughing Boy*. 1929. Reprint, New York: Signet Classic, 1971.

Larson, Charles R. *American Indian Fiction*. Albuquerque: University of New Mexico Press, 1978.

Leps, Marie-Christine. *Apprehending the Criminal: The Production of Deviance in Nineteenth-Century Discourse*. Durham: Duke University Press, 1992.

Loughead, Flora Haines. "In the Shadow of the Live-Oak." *Overland Monthly* 34 (1899): 14–19.

Maddox, Lucy. *Removals: Nineteenth-Century American Literature and the Politics of Indian Affairs*. New York: Oxford University Press, 1991.

Marshall, Emma Seckle. "An Infusion of Savagery." *Out West* 28, no. 4 (1908): 321–25.

Mathes, Valerie Sherer. *Helen Hunt Jackson and Her Indian Reform Legacy*. Austin: University of Texas Press, 1990.

———. "Helen Hunt Jackson as Power Broker." In *Between Indian and White Worlds: The Cultural Broker*, ed. Margaret Connell Szasz, 141–57. Norman: University of Oklahoma Press, 1994.

Mathews, John Joseph. *Sundown*. 1934. Reprint, ed. Virginia H. Mathews. Norman: University of Oklahoma Press, 1988.

Mathews, Virginia H. Introduction to *Sundown,* by John Joseph Mathews, v–xiv. Norman: University of Oklahoma Press, 1988.

McNickle, D'Arcy. *Native American Tribalism: Indian Survivals and Renewals*. New York: Oxford University Press: 1973.

———. *The Surrounded*. 1936. Reprint, Albuquerque: University of New Mexico Press, 1994.

Michaels, Walter Benn. "Autobiographies of the Ex-White Men: Why Race Is Not a Social Construction." In *The Futures of American Studies,* ed. Donald E. Pease and Robyn Weigman, 231–47. Durham: Duke University Press, 2002.

Miller, Perry. *Errand into the Wilderness*. Cambridge: Harvard University Press, 1964.

Mills, Bruce. *Cultural Reformations: Lydia Maria Child and the Literature of Reform*. Athens: University of Georgia Press, 1994.

Mirsalis, Jon C. "The Place beyond the Winds." 1996. The Lon Chaney Home Page, http://members.aol.com/ChaneyFan/84.htm (accessed May 2, 2002).

Momaday, N. Scott. *House Made of Dawn*. 1968. Reprint, New York: Perennial Classics, 1999.

Mourning Dove. *Cogewea, the Half-Blood: A Depiction of the Great Montana Cattle Range*. Ed. Lucullus Virgil McWhorter. 1927. Reprint, Lincoln: University of Nebraska Press, 1981.

Namias, June. Introduction to *A Narrative of the Life of Mrs. Mary Jemison*, by James E. Seaver, 3–45. Norman: University of Oklahoma Press, 1992.

———. *White Captives: Gender and Ethnicity on the American Frontier*. Chapel Hill: University of North Carolina Press, 1993.

Neal, Della R. "A Strife in the Blood." *Overland Monthly* 46 (1905): 195–203.

Neihardt, John. "The Alien." In *Indian Tales and Others*, 116–35. New York: Macmillan, 1926.

Nielson, Parker M. *The Dispossessed: The Cultural Genocide of the Mixed-Blood Utes*. Norman: University of Oklahoma Press, 1982.

O'Connell, Barry. Introduction to *On Our Own Ground: The Complete Writings of William Apess, a Pequot*, xiii–lxxvii. Amherst: University of Massachusetts Press, 1992.

Odell, Ruth. *Helen Hunt Jackson*. New York: D. Appleton-Century, 1939.

Parker, Dorothy R. "D'Arcy McNickle: Living a Broker's Life." In *Between Indian and White Worlds: The Cultural Broker*, ed. Margaret Connell Szasz, 239–60. Norman: University of Oklahoma Press, 1994.

Parkman, Francis, Jr. *The Oregon Trail*. 1849. Reprint, ed. David Levin. New York: Penguin, 1985.

Pearce, Roy Harvey. *Savagism and Civilization: A Study of the Indian and the American Mind*. Rev. ed. Berkeley: University of California Press, 1988.

Pearson, Edmund. *Dime Novels; or, Following an Old Trail in Popular Literature*. Boston: Little, Brown, 1929.

Peck, H. Daniel, ed. *New Essays on* The Last of the Mohicans. New York: Cambridge University Press, 1992.

Perez-Castillo, Susan. "Postmodernism, Native American Literature, and the Real: The Silko-Erdrich Controversy." *Massachusetts Re-*

view: A Quarterly of Literature, the Arts, and Public Affairs 32 (1991): 285–94.

Poe, Edgar Allan. *The Narrative of Arthur Gordon Pym of Nantucket.* 1839. Reprint, ed. Richard Kopley. New York: Penguin, 1999.

Powell, J. W. "From Barbarism to Civilization." *American Anthropologist* 1, no. 2 (1888): 97–123.

Prats, Armando José. *Invisible Natives: Myth and Identity in the American Western.* Ithaca: Cornell University Press, 2002.

Reid, Mayne. *The White Squaw.* New York: Beadle and Adams, 1876.

Remington, Frederic. "Sun-down's Higher Self." *Harper's* 97 (1898): 846–51.

Renan, Ernst. "What Is a Nation?" In *Nation and Narration,* ed. Homi K. Bhabha, 8–22. New York: Routledge, 1990.

Ridge, John Rollin. *The Life and Adventures of Joaquín Murieta, the Celebrated California Bandit.* 1854. Reprint, ed. Joseph Henry Jackson. Norman: University of Oklahoma Press, 1955.

———. "The Stolen White Girl." 1868. In *The Heath Anthology of American Literature,* 3d ed., vol. 1., ed. Paul Lauter, et al., 1896–97. New York: Houghton Mifflin, 1998.

Rohner, Ronald P., ed., trans. Hedy Parker. *The Ethnography of Franz Boas.* Chicago: University of Chicago Press, 1969.

Ross, Alexander. *The Fur Hunters of the Far West.* 1855. Reprint, ed. Kenneth A. Spaulding. Norman: University of Oklahoma Press, 1956.

———. *The Red River Settlement.* London, 1856.

Rowson, Mrs. [Susanna]. *Reuben and Rachel; or, Tales of Early Times.* Boston, 1798.

Ruoff, A. LaVonne Brown. "William Apess (Pequot)." In *The Heath Anthology of American Literature,* ed. Paul Lauter et al., 1:1398. Boston: Houghton Mifflin, 2002.

Said, Edward. "Reflections on Exile." In *Legacies,* ed. Carley Rees Bogarad and Jan Zlotrik Schmidt, 1113–24. New York: Harcourt Brace, 1995.

Samuels, Shirley. "Generation through Violence: Cooper and the Making of Americans." In *New Essays on* The Last of the Mohicans, ed. H. Daniel Peck, 87–114. New York: Cambridge University Press, 1992.

Scheckel, Susan. *The Insistence of the Indian: Race and Nationalism in Nineteenth-Century American Culture*. Princeton: Princeton University Press, 1998.

Scheick, William J. *The Half-Blood: A Cultural Symbol in Nineteenth-Century American Fiction*. Lexington: University Press of Kentucky, 1979.

Schueller, Malini Johar. *U.S. Orientalisms: Race, Nation, and Gender in Literature, 1790–1890*. Ann Arbor: University of Michigan Press, 1998.

Seaver, James E. *A Narrative of the Life of Mrs. Mary Jemison*. 1824. Reprint, ed. June Namias. Norman: University of Oklahoma Press, 1992.

Sedgwick, Catherine Maria. *Hope Leslie; or, Early Times in the Massachusetts*. 1827. Reprint, ed. Carolyn L. Karcher. New York: Penguin, 1998.

Silko, Leslie Marmon. *Ceremony*. New York: Penguin, 1977.

———. "Here's an Odd Artifact for the Fairy-Tale Shelf." *Studies in American Indian Literature* 10 (1986): 177–84.

Slotkin, Richard. *Gunfighter Nation*. Norman: University of Oklahoma Press, 1998.

———. "Introduction to the 1831 Edition." In *The Last of the Mohicans*, by James Fenimore Cooper, ix–xxviii. New York: Penguin, 1986.

Smith, Henry Nash. *Virgin Land: The American West as Symbol and Myth*. Cambridge: Harvard University Press, 1950.

Sollors, Werner. *Beyond Ethnicity: Consent and Descent in American Culture*. New York: Oxford University Press, 1986.

Spivak, Gayatri Chakravorty. "Can the Subaltern Speak?" In *Marxism and the Interpretation of Culture*, ed. Cary Nelson and Larry Grossberg, 271–313. Urbana: University of Illinois Press, 1988.

———. *In Other Worlds: Essays in Cultural Politics*. New York: Routledge, 1987.

Spurr, David. *The Rhetoric of Empire: Colonial Discourse in Journalism, Travel Writing, and Imperial Administration*. Durham: Duke University Press, 1993.

Stanton, William. *The Leopard's Spots: Scientific Attitudes towards Race in America*. Chicago: University of Chicago Press, 1960.

St. Clair, Janet. "Fighting for Her Life: The Mixed-Blood Woman's Insistence upon Selfhood." In *Native American Writers: Modern Critical Views,* ed. Harold Bloom, 151–59. Philadelphia: Chelsea House, 1998.

Stedman, Robert. *Shadows of the Indian.* Norman: University of Oklahoma Press, 1982.

Steele, Rufus. "Scar Neck." *Saturday Evening Post* 185, no. 26 (December 28, 1912): 10–11, 30–31.

Stephens, Ann S. *Malaeska; The Indian Wife of the White Hunter.* In *Reading the West: An Anthology of Dime Westerns,* ed. Bill Brown, 56–164. New York: Bedford, 1997.

Stocking, George W., Jr., ed. *The Shaping of American Anthropology, 1883–1911: A Franz Boas Reader.* New York: Basic Books, 1974.

———. *Victorian Anthropology.* New York: Free Press, 1987.

Tompkins, Jane. *West of Everything: The Inner Life of Westerns.* New York: Oxford University Press, 1992.

Towner, Lawrence W. Afterword to *The Surrounded,* by D'Arcy McNickle. Albuquerque: University of New Mexico Press, 1994.

Train, Arthur. *Mr. Tutt Comes Home.* New York: Scribners, 1941.

Turner, Frederick Jackson. "The Significance of the Frontier in American History." In *A Documentary History of the United States,* ed. Richard D. Heffner, 183–91. New York: Mentor, 1991.

Twain, Mark. *The Adventures of Tom Sawyer.* 1876. Reprint, Mahwah, N.J.: Watermill, 1980.

Unrau, William E. *Mixed-Bloods and Tribal Dissolution: Charles Curtis and the Quest for Indian Identity.* Lawrence: University Press of Kansas, 1989.

Vanderbeets, Richard. "The Indian Captivity Narrative as Ritual." *American Literature* 43 (1972): 548–62.

Velie, Alan. "Magical Realism and Ethnicity: The Fantastic in the Fiction of Louise Erdrich." In *Native American Women in Literature and Culture,* ed. Susan Castillo and Victor M. P. Da Rosa, 57–67. Porto, Portugal: Fernando Pessoa University Press, 1997.

Vickers, Scott B. *Native American Identities: From Stereotype to Archetype in Art and Literature.* Albuquerque: University of New Mexico Press, 1998.

Vizenor, Gerald. *Crossbloods: Bone Courts, Bingo, and Other Reports.* Minneapolis: University of Minnesota Press, 1990.

———. *Earthdivers: Tribal Narratives on Mixed Descent.* Minneapolis: University of Minnesota Press, 1981.

———. *Manifest Manners: Postindian Warriors of Survivance* [excerpt]. In *The Norton Anthology of Theory and Criticism*, ed. Vincent B. Leitch, et al., 1977–86. New York: Norton, 2001.

Wald, Priscilla. *Constituting Americans: Cultural Anxiety and Narrative Form.* Durham: Duke University Press, 1995.

Walker, Cheryl. *Indian Nation: Native American Literature and Nineteenth-Century Nationalisms.* Durham: Duke University Press: 1997.

Walsh, Susan. " 'With Them Was My Home': Native American Autobiography and *A Narrative of the Life of Mrs. Mary Jemison.*" *American Literature* 64 (1992): 49–70.

Warman, Cy. *Frontier Stories.* New York: Scribner's, 1898.

Welch, James. *The Death of Jim Loney.* 1979. Reprint, New York: Penguin, 1987.

White, Stewart Edward. "The Long Rifle—The Statesman." *Saturday Evening Post* 203, no. 33 (February 14, 1931): 20–21, 75, 78, 83.

[Whitman, Walt.] *The Half-Breed: A Tale of the Western Frontier.* 1846. Reprint, in *The Collected Writings of Walt Whitman: The Early Poems and Fiction*, ed. Gay Wilson Allen and Sculley Bradley, 257–91. New York: New York University Press, 1963.

Wiener, Martin J. *Reconstructing the Criminal: Culture, Law, and Policy in England, 1830–1914.* New York: Cambridge University Press, 1990.

Wister, Owen. "A Kinsman of Red Cloud." In *The Jimmyjohn Boss*, 67–99. New York: Harper, 1900.

Wong, Hertha Dawn. *Sending My Heart Back across the Years: Tradition and Innovation in Native American Autobiography.* New York: Oxford University Press, 1992.

Young, Robert J. C. *Colonial Desire: Hybridity in Theory, Culture, and Race.* New York: Routledge, 1995.

Ziff, Larzer. *Writing in the New Nation: Prose, Print, and Politics in the Early United States.* New Haven: Yale University Press, 1991.

Index

Adams, James Fenimore Cooper
(pseud. Edward Ellis), 117
Adams, Robert, 85, 87, 88, 92, 117
Adventures of Captain Bonneville
(Irving), 101
Adventures of Huckleberry Finn
(Twain), 15
Adventures of Tom Sawyer, The
(Twain), 11, 13–16, 29, 169
"Ah-lo-ma" (Huffman), 169
Alcatraz Island, occupation of, 231
Alcohol abuse, 70, 75
Aldrich, Thomas Bailey, 137
Alexie, Sherman, 16, 21, 26, 221–23,
224, 236
Algonquian tribes, 35, 55
"Alien, The" (Neihardt), 169
Allen, Ebenezer, 67–68
Allotment. *See* General Allotment Act
(1887)
Amalgamation, 2, 34, 77–78, 81, 83–
84; definition of, 34*n*7
American Anthropologist, 109
American Indian Movement, 231
American writing, 33, 243. *See also*
Native American literature
Anderson, Benedict, 20–21, 30–31, 244
Anderson, Jack, 223
"And Lesser Breeds without the Law"
(Train), 184–85
Anglo-Saxonism, 61, 160, 165, 168,
170, 172, 176, 177–78, 181
Antelope Wife, The (Erdrich), 17, 21,
26, 235–40
Anthropology, definition of, 175
"Anthropology of the North American
Indian, The" (Boas), 176
Anthropometry, 174, 176
Apess, Mary Wood, 80*n*45
Apess, William: authenticity of, 64;
autobiographical writing of, 1–3, 73,

74, 80; conversion of, 79; double
consciousness of, 73, 75–76, 84,
99, 128, 136; on hybridity, 73–81,
240; on Indian degradation, 70, 75,
76–77, 99, 132, 136; on Indian
origins, 78–80, 91; on Indian
redemption, 116; on Mashpee
autonomy, 3, 10, 80–81, 82, 143;
on mixed-bloods, 24, 88, 237;
obituary of, 3; on racial blending,
144; on simultaneity, 136; use of
conventions of mass fiction, 21,
30, 245
Aristidean, The, 101
Arrow-Tip (Whitman), 101
"Ascent of Man, The" (Baker), 109
Assimilation: desirability of, 37, 129,
130–31; and disappearance of racial
and geographic frontiers, 20; exploited by mixed-bloods, 179; failure
of, 173, 179, 188–90; fear of, 97–
98, 110, 116, 127, 141, 152; governmental encouragement of, 25,
89, 134, 142, 145–49, 153, 154;
impossibility of, 37, 145; as means
of survival, 178; as natural course of
civilization, 89, 91; political barriers
to, 122, 148, 149; and protection of
disappearing cultures, 156–57; and
social anarchy, 90, 91; sympathy for,
134, 141. *See also* General Allotment
Act (1887)
Astoria (Irving), 101
Atlantic Monthly, 183
Austin, F. Britten, 159
Austin, Mary, 178, 181, 183–84, 185,
215
Authenticity, of hybrid texts, 8, 64, 72,
180, 190
Autobiographies, 21, 64. *See also*
Indian autobiography